TEACHING WESTERN LITERATURE IN A WORLD CONTEXT

Volume One
The Ancient World through the Renaissance

AND

Volume Two
The Enlightenment through the Present

Paul Davis
Gary Harrison
David M. Johnson
Patricia Clark Smith
John F. Crawford
THE UNIVERSITY OF NEW MEXICO

ST. MARTIN'S PRESS
NEW YORK

Manufactured in the United States of America.
9 8 7 6 5
f e d c b a

For information, write:
St. Martin's Press, Inc.
175 Fifth Avenue
New York, NY 10010

ISBN: 0-312-08123-5

PREFACE

The anthology *Western Literature in a World Context* grew out of a course that was team-taught at the University of New Mexico by several of the editors. The course was an attempt to revive the sort of world literature course that had died out of this and many other universities during the late 1960s and early 1970s. Rather than reviving a 1950s great books course based on formalist principles, we decided to take an approach that would place great works in their historical and cultural contexts. We also wanted to broaden the list of Western classics to include works that truly represented world literature. The globalization of culture in the postcolonial world calls for students who are well-versed in the fundamental ideas and literature of the West, as well as in the cultural achievements of places such as Africa, Asia, Latin America, and the Middle East. In addition, the flourishing in the last quarter century of diverse literatures and cultures within the West encourages us to broaden the dimensions of what we consider to be our cultural heritage.

In order to highlight the continuities and changes in the Western tradition, we organized *Western Literature in a World Context* according to major themes found in the six historical periods covered. The Representative Texts develop central themes of each period. Following these texts are selected Western works that address and explore the major ideas of the period. Major works of literature from around the world, included in The World Context section, invite cross-cultural comparisons between literary works and cultures. The major themes of the Western tradition provide a basis for investigating the literature and thought of non-Western cultures; in fact, the juxtaposition of texts allows for a dialogue between traditions.

This instructor's manual allows us to extend this discussion even further. In addition to the information provided in the section introductions and author headnotes in the anthology itself, the author introductions in the instructor's manual include expanded coverage of important themes in the works and suggestions for comparing various works in lectures and classroom discussions. Because the Ancient and Medieval periods cover large periods of time and multiple cultural traditions, we have also included overviews (General Introductions) of these periods.

The instructor's manual contains two tables of contents. The first lists selections in order of their appearance in the anthology and manual. The second lists selections by genre—fiction, poetry, drama, autobiography, and nonfiction/scriptural prose—for each volume.

The section called Questions for Discussion and Writing is largely drawn from our own experiences in the classroom. Because classes differ, we have provided a broad range of topics and questions to accommodate a variety of teaching approaches for different kinds of classes. The writing assignments ask students to analyze particular arguments, compare positions or points of view, discuss stylistic and structural features, and relate works or themes to contemporary concerns. We have raised issues rather than provided answers because in the world of literature there are no ultimate answers, only an ongoing dialogue by people from various parts of the world about what it means to be human. In the Projects sections, we provide extended assignments that encourage research and student creativity and stimulate thoughtful comparisons with other works.

For the reader's convenience, we have supplied titles to untitled parts of works in the main text and in the instructor's manual. These titles appear in brackets to indicate that they are neither original to the selection nor provided by the translator. Whereas we have retained the older Wade-Giles system of transliteration for classical Chinese literature in Volume One, we have adopted the newer Pinyin system for the modern work of Lu Xun.

This instructor's manual is intended to assist the teacher who might be dealing with a particular work or literary period for the first time, but we also hope that we have uncovered fresh insights or perspectives suitable for the specialist or expert. Whenever we team-taught these works we were amazed at how much we learned from each other—regardless of our specialties—and from students. Our experience shows that it is particularly important to include both men and women in a team-teaching situation because the reevaluation of the canon and the reinterpretation of the major texts involve many gender issues. Team-teaching enabled us to more effectively discover the issues involved in the current debate about the meaning, value, and importance of "great books" in our society and the need to open the canon to other works. This manual is an extension of this cooperative venture in learning and instruction. As a way of continuing this dialogue, we invite you to send us your ideas and suggestions.

—The Editors

CONTENTS

VOLUME ONE
The Ancient World through the Renaissance

VOLUME TWO
The Enlightenment through the Present

Readings by Genre

§Ψ

Volume One
The Ancient World through the Renaissance

(References are to the main text pages.)

Volume Two
The Enlightenment through the Present

NONFICTION/SCRIPTURAL PROSE

TEACHING WESTERN LITERATURE IN A WORLD CONTEXT

Volume One
The Ancient World
through the Renaissance

THE
ANCIENT
WORLD

꽃

The Heroic Ideal
and the Rise of Patriarchy

GENERAL INTRODUCTION

Greek myths and legends tend to cluster around the major city-states of the Mycenaean Period (c. 1500–1100 B.C.E.). The stories about Cadmus, Pentheus, Oedipus, Creon, and Antigone were connected to Thebes, the central city of Boeotia, a region northwest of Athens. Besides the Theban saga, the most popular cycle of stories involved the House of Atreus and the city of Mycenae. Intertwined with the family of Atreus were the stories arising out of Troy and the exploits of the Trojan War.

These cycles of stories became the thematic materials for Greek and Roman poets, dramatists, and artists. Patterns of family conflict, violence, and revenge were repeated in one generation after another, reflecting the warrior heritage of the Indo-Europeans, who had migrated from the north into the Mediterranean region in the second millennium B.C.E. The stories in Hesiod's *Theogony* about the succession of early deities reflect the generational conflict being played out in society, where sons rebel against their fathers and then fear the rebellion of their own sons.

Greek writers used stories from the Trojan War to explore a wide range of themes and issues: the nature of war and the character of the hero; the obligations of friendship; the role of gods in human affairs; and the importance of the *polis*, citizenship, and patriotism. The Greeks supported the idea that individuals were free to find out who they were and what their destinies were, while they were conscious of the dangers of excess and *hubris*. Despite the importance of war and the warrior ethic in Greek culture, they also recognized the roles of parents and family in human affairs.

3

The story of the House of Atreus that intersects with the Trojan War is particularly bloody.

THE HOUSE OF ATREUS

Pelops' father was the notorious Tantalus, whose scandalous offense against the gods brought him perpetual punishment in Hades. In order to win Hippodamia's hand through a race with her father, Pelops bribed the king's charioteer, Myrtilus, to sabotage Oenomaus' chariot; when Pelops reneged on his promise of land and sex and, instead, pushed him over a cliff into the sea, Myrtilus cursed Pelops, providing the basic curse on his lineage.

Pelops' sons were Atreus and Thyestes. Atreus became the king of Mycenae and Thyestes seduced his wife, Aethra. Thyestes was banished, then recalled to a banquet in which his own sons were butchered and served to him. Fleeing in horror, Thyestes reiterated the curse on the house of Atreus. By his own daughter Pelopia, Thyestes had a son, Aegisthus, who carried on the feud. Following the pattern of other heroes such as Oedipus, Aegisthus was left to die as a child, but shepherds brought him up and Atreus, the father of Agamemnon and Menelaus, adopted him. Atreus sent Aegisthus to murder Thyestes, but because of a lost sword, Thyestes recognized in time his own son. Together they planned how Aegisthus would kill Atreus at the seashore.

Thyestes thus became king of Mycenae until he was driven away by Agamemnon, who ruled until he led the Greek expedition to Troy, leaving the throne to his wife, Clytemnestra. She took Aegisthus as a lover and together they plotted Agamemnon's murder when he returned from the Trojan War. Agamemnon's son, Orestes, with assistance from his sister, Electra, killed both Aegisthus and Clytemnestra. In Aeschylus' trilogy *The Oresteia*, the cycle of blood revenge was ended with a public trial in which Orestes was acquitted.

LEGENDS OF THE TROJAN WAR

The Judgment of Paris

Zeus decided to thin the growing population of the earth with a great war. Zeus blessed the marriage of the nymph Thetis to the mortal Peleus, but Eris, the goddess of discord, was not invited to the wedding. Eris came anyway and rolled a golden apple across the floor, inscribed with the words "For the Fairest." The goddesses Hera, Athena, and Aphrodite argued about who should receive the apple and called upon Zeus to settle the quarrel. Shrewdly, Zeus chose Paris, a prince of Troy, to judge the beauty contest.

Because of a prophecy that Paris would cause the fall of Troy, he had been exposed in the countryside, but a shepherd found him and raised him on a mountain. The goddesses went to his foster home and bribed him: Hera offered him political power, Athena offered him wisdom, and Aphrodite promised him the most beautiful woman in the world. Paris chose Aphrodite and the two losers became hostile toward Troy.

Paris wandered to Troy, where he was welcomed and sent on an embassy to Sparta, where he visited King Menelaus, son of Atreus, and Menelaus' beautiful wife, Helen, the daughter of Zeus and Leda and sister to Clytemnestra. When Menelaus left for a political visit to Crete, Paris and Helen fell in love; they took a large part of the Spartan treasury and fled to Troy. In one version, Paris and Helen were then married; in another version, Hera provided Paris with a phantom Helen while the real one resided in Egypt during the Trojan War. (See Euripides' *Helen*.)

Angered by the betrayal, Menelaus called on his brother, King Agamemnon of Mycenae, to put together an army to take revenge on Troy. The Atreidae (sons of Atreus) were joined by Helen's former suitors and their armies. Peleus and Thetis' son Achilles and his Myrmidons (inhabitants of Phthia) also joined them.

The Achaean ships congregated at Aulis on the east coast of Greece, but were unable to continue. Agamemnon had killed an animal sacred to Artemis and she quieted the winds. The seer Chalchas, who had already prophesied that the Greeks would fight Troy for nine years and win in the tenth, advised that the sacrifice of a virgin was necessary, so Agamemnon lured his youngest daughter, Iphigenia, to Aulis with the promise of marriage to Achilles. Father sacrificed daughter, the winds were restored, and the boats sailed for Troy, a fortress city in the northwest corner of Asia Minor. (See Aeschylus' *Agamemnon* and Euripides' *Iphigenia at Aulis*.) En route, Philoctetes directed the fleet to an island shrine of Chryse for a sacrifice. Philoctetes, who had inherited Heracles' bow and arrow, was bitten by a snake. (See Sophocles' *Philoctetes*.) He moaned so much from the pain that the Greeks left him on the island of Lemnos and sailed on.

Arriving in the vicinity of Troy, the Greeks, led by Achilles, drove the Trojans back from the shore and into the stronghold of the city. The Trojans rebuffed an embassy from the Greeks requesting Helen and the Spartan treasury. After nine years of stalemate, the greatest of the Achaean warriors, Achilles, quarreled with Agamemnon, leader of the combined armies. (See Homer's *Iliad*.) Forced to give up Chryseis, daughter of a priest of Apollo, Agamemnon insulted Achilles by taking away his war-prize, the lady Briseis. Achilles withdrew from the fighting, retreated to his tents with his powerful army of Myrmidons, and refused to fight.

The Trojans took advantage of Achilles' absence to drive the Greeks back to their ships. Hard pressed, Agamemnon offered restitution if Achilles would rejoin the battle, but the proud Achilles rejected his overtures. When the Trojans broke through into the Greek camp and burned some of the Greek ships, Achilles relented. Instead of rejoining the battle himself, however, he sent his best friend Patroclus, who led the Myrmidons into battle dressed in Achilles' armor.

For a time, Patroclus was successful in battle; he killed Sarpedon, and with the Myrmidons, drove the Trojans back to the city, attacking the walls of Troy itself. But Patroclus finally exceeded his ability, fought Hector, was killed, and lost Achilles' armor. Enraged, and perhaps shamed, by the death of his friend, Achilles finally reentered the war. Arrayed in new armor crafted by Hephaestis (god of metallurgy), Achilles sought revenge by chasing Hector three times around the walls of Troy and finally killing him in full sight of the city. Achilles then defiled Hector's body by dragging it around the city walls and around the grave of Patroclus. Aided by Hermes, the bereaved King Priam came to Achilles' tent to ransom his son's body. In the old man's presence, Achilles remembered his own father and relented, turning over Hector's body to Priam for burial. (Homer's *Iliad* ends with the burning and burial of Hector.)

The Trojans were reinforced by Penthesilea and her army of Amazons and by King Memnon of Ethiopia, but Achilles killed both Penthesilea and Memnon and once again the war settled into a stalemate. Guided by Apollo, Paris shot a poisoned arrow from atop the Trojan wall and wounded Achilles in the heel, killing him. (Achilles' mother had held him by the heel when she had dipped him in the river Styx to make him invincible.) After Achilles' death, Odysseus and Ajax quarreled over his armor. When Ajax failed to win the prize, he committed suicide. (See Sophocles' *Ajax*.)

When seer Helenus, son of Priam, was captured by the Greeks, he told them that Troy would fall only when Philoctetes reentered the war with Achilles' son, Neoptolemus. Using trickery, Odysseus and Neoptolemus lured Philoctetes from Lemnon to Troy, where

5

the bowman killed Paris with Heracles' bow. When the war still did not end, Odysseus and Diomedes sneaked into the city of Troy by night and stole the sacred statue of Athena, the Palladium, believed to be the source of Trojan strength. But even with its heroes dead and the Palladium stolen, Troy did not fall.

Finally, guided by Odysseus, the Greeks resorted to deception. Epeius built a large wooden horse and the strongest warriors hid in its belly. When the rest of the Greeks sailed away, leaving the horse behind them, the curious Trojans came out of the city and found Sinon, a lone Greek soldier, on the beach. Lying to the Trojans, he said that he had been abandoned and that the horse was an atonement for the theft of the Palladium, but it had been built too large to be pulled through the gates into Troy. Falling for the trick, the Trojans dragged the horse inside the walls. In the middle of the night, the Greek soldiers emerged from the horse, called their compatriots back from a nearby island, and sacked and burned Troy.

The Aftermath

By the next morning, the Greeks had pillaged the city and divided the spoils. Menelaus retrieved Helen, Agamemnon claimed Priam's daughter Cassandra, and Odysseus received Hecuba. Hector's wife, Andromache, was the prize of Neoptolemus. Amid the toppling towers of the burning city, Hecuba saw the body of her daughter, Polyxena, slaughtered on the tomb of Achilles and the body of her grandson, Astyanax, prepared for burial. (See Euripides' *Trojan Women, Hecuba*, and *Andromache*; Seneca's *Trojan Women*.)

The Greeks set sail for home. Some, like Nestor, Diomedes, Idomeneus, Philoctetes, and Neoptolemus, reached their homes quickly and safely. Agamemnon arrived home with Cassandra only to be assassinated by his wife, Clytemnestra, and her lover Aegisthus. This regicide and patricide was avenged by Agamemnon's son Orestes. (See Aeschylus' *Oresteia* and Euripides' *Electra*.) Others took many years to return. Menelaus and Helen went to Egypt, where they spent seven years before returning to Sparta. The most famous of the Greek wanderers, Odysseus, spent ten years filled with love and adventure making his way back to his wife, Penelope, and son, Telemachus, on the island of Ithaca.

The most famous Trojan survivor was Aeneas, son of Aphrodite and Anchises, who set out from the ruins of Troy with his wife, Creusa, son, Iulus (also Ascanius), and his father to fulfill his destiny by founding a new Troy in a distant land. After losing his wife and wandering the seas—much like Odysseus—he gained the Italian coast and founded a colony that would later become Rome. (See Virgil's *Aeneid*.)

Questions for Discussion and Writing

1. In the Greek creation stories and hero stories, a major theme is warfare and combat. Explain how conflict can be a world view and how a personal ethic can be derived from the principle of conflict.

2. What is a hero? How does a hero affect society? How does one become a hero? What characterizes the hero journey or quest? Do we have heroes today?

3. In addition to the warrior hero or the hero of adventure, there are moral or spiritual heroes who commit their lives to improving society, to the idea of citizenship, of reforming or changing society and its values. Who are these heroes and where do they get their ideas? What characterizes their lives? What would ancient writers say about modern morality or value systems?

4. Citing two or three of the works we have read, explain how the concept of heroism changes, if it does, over the classical period. Are there constants or similarities? What are the major differences?

5. Consider the moral conflict between public duty (or destiny) and private desire. Is it possible to balance the demands of both the outside and the inside worlds, the public world of commerce and politics and the private world of family and friends? Citing *The Iliad, The Eumenides, The Aeneid,* or the *Bhagavad Gita,* consider whether you see a change in the separation of public and private life.

6. Does the suppression of women in ancient society represent a dangerous neglect of half of the population and also a neglect of the inner, "feminine" world? Are there two sides to human nature? What significant roles do women play in the literature of the ancient world? Does our society appreciate women and the powers of the feminine today?

7. Taking your examples from three works, discuss the place of women's power in the ancient world. How do the writers represent such power? What purposes does it serve? What is its relation to men's power?

8. Compare and contrast the relationship between Thetis and Achilles with that between Venus and Aeneas.

9. Discuss the roles of underground or underworld places in classical literature: Plato's cave, Inanna's underworld, the cave where Dido and Aeneas take shelter, and the cave for the Eumenides beneath the Acropolis.

Project

The myths, legends, and deities of ancient Greece were originally connected to various cities or places. Hand out a blank outline of Greece and western Turkey and have your students locate the following places: Troy, Mycenae, Argos, Sparta, Lesbos, Ionia, Delos, Ithaca, Thera, Crete, Knossos, Athens, Thebes, Eleusis, Corinth, Epidaurus, Mt. Olympus, Olympia, Marathon, Attica, Hellas, the Aegean Sea, and Delphi.

HOMER
The Iliad

Nothing is known for certain about the person called Homer except that the dialect of *The Iliad* and *The Odyssey* was from Ionia. The question of the authorship of these epics, however, leads to important matters such as the oral tradition, the role of bards, the importance of epithets, the uses of stock situations and stock phrases in the poems, the use of a lyre for rhythm, and the occasions and audiences for epics. (See Albert Lord's *The Singer of Tales* and G. S. Kirk's *The Songs of Homer.*)

The stories and legends of the Trojan War became important themes in Greek history and culture. The war elevated heroism and celebrated honor, fame, and glory. *The Iliad* reveals several kinds of heroes in two different situations; heroes of the battlefield are different from heroes in the city who have wives and children. Although Achilles' heroism might be appropriate for warfare, Hector's sensitivity is also admirable. Nestor provides wisdom and Odysseus adds shrewdness and cleverness.

Homer uses his skillful visual, or cinematic, writing to depict the differences between life on the battlefield and life in the city. Although the poem seems to promote the values of warfare, Homer nevertheless makes his readers aware of the negative consequences of the warrior ethic, especially with his descriptions of Troy's women and children.

Questions for Discussion and Writing

1. At the beginning of *The Iliad*, why is Apollo angry?
2. Why does Achilles withdraw from the war?
3. To what extent does Achilles show proper respect for authority?
4. What different qualities are associated with various Achaean chieftains?
5. How would you describe the organizational structure of the various Greek leaders and armies participating in the Trojan War?
6. Who is the most heroic character in *The Iliad*? Why?
7. Does our estimation of Achilles change during the epic?
8. In Book 18, Homer focuses on the manufacture of Achilles' shield. What is so important about this shield? What role does the shield play in legends of the Trojan War? What is significant about the scenes on the shield?
9. Why is the story of Priam and Achilles an important part of the resolution of *The Iliad*? What does the encounter with Priam reveal about Achilles' character?
10. What makes Hector such a sympathetic hero to a modern audience? What does the scene between Hector and Andromache in Book 6 add to the reader's estimation of Hector's character? How does Hector's treatment of his son in Book 6 serve as an indirect comment on war?
11. Today, you can be honorable without becoming famous and you can be famous without being honorable. Discuss.
12. Define the following terms: epic, Ilium, tragedy, epithet, epic simile, *in medias res*, invocation to the Muses, allegory.

Projects

1. Historians suggest that one of the causes of the Trojan War was economic, involving trade with Black Sea settlements; storytellers blame the love affair between Paris and Helen. Analyze the different ways that people might use to describe the causes of war and apply this analysis to the Trojan War.
2. Heroes and heroines have played important roles in family and cultural histories; write the story of a flesh-and-blood hero or heroine. Be able to discuss this person's heroic traits.

HOMER
The Odyssey

It is possible to approach *The Odyssey* from a wide variety of perspectives: At one extreme, the epic is a series of adventures drawn from folk materials, loosely strung together around the idea of Odysseus' return from the Trojan War to his home in Ithaca.

At the other extreme, some critics interpret each of Odysseus' adventures as a necessary stage in his growth toward self-knowledge—the gathering together of pieces of himself—a prerequisite for repulsing the suitors, reuniting with Penelope, and once again assuming the throne of Ithaca. After an absence of twenty years, Odysseus must recreate his psychological and spiritual role as king in Ithaca.

For purposes of discussion, the epic easily divides into sections: I. Telemachus and the Suitors, II. Odysseus' Adventures on the Journey Home, III. Father and Son Defeat the Suitors, and IV. Reunion of Odysseus and Penelope.

Questions for Discussion and Writing

1. The epithets most often associated with Odysseus are *wily* and *clever*. List several examples of his cleverness. Are there any examples of his stupidity?
2. What role does Pallas Athena play in the lives of Telemachus and Odysseus?
3. What are the basic ingredients of the "code of hospitality" involving visits by dignitaries? Discuss the uses of sacrifices (hecatombs) in this epic.
4. In Book 9, Polyphémus admits in his pain that it was prophesied that a man called Odysseus would rob him of his sight; in Book 10, Circe also speaks about Odysseus' arrival on her island being predestined. What is the role of destiny or fate in Odysseus' adventures?
5. What is the origin of the Cyclops? How does Odysseus escape from the Cyclops' cave?
6. Who is Teiresias and what does Odysseus learn about himself in Hades?
7. What is significant about the meaning of Odysseus' name? How does Odysseus' impetuousness get in his way?
8. Throughout *The Iliad* and *The Odyssey*, women are shown to be a major force in relationships between men and between countries. Helen, Clytemnestra, and Penelope are important figures. In Book 4, Helen is described with respect and honor; Menelaus listens to her words and follows her lead. But in Book 11, Odysseus exclaims:

> Long since, the bitter hate of thundering Zeus
> against the sons of Atreus has used
> conniving women as its instruments:
> how many of us died through Helen's fault;
> and Clytemnestra, while you were far off,
> devised her plot. (Book 2, lines 434–39)

What did Homer think about women's role in society?
9. Consider Odysseus' careful planning: He waited until the suitors were most vulnerable before revealing himself and destroying them. Do Odysseus' plans for vengeance in Book 22 demonstrate that he is a special kind of hero?
10. In the last section of *The Odyssey*, Homer builds suspense through the encounters between the main characters and the plans for dealing with the suitors. Penelope almost recognizes Odysseus several times; in one of the most famous scenes, the old nurse does recognize Odysseus, but is forced to keep her secret. Homer adds to the suspense by a long, drawn-out description of Odysseus stringing and shooting the bow in Book 21. What other scenes demonstrate this suspense-building technique?
11. How does Penelope's final test for Odysseus in Book 23 lead to a suitable climax for *The Odyssey*?
12. Compare Odysseus with Achilles; compare these Western heroes with Arjuna in the *Bhagavad Gita*.
13. There are interesting differences between *The Iliad*, which focuses on an argument between Achilles and Agamemnon and its consequences, and *The Odyssey*, which is a romance–adventure story that set the trend for later novelists. Why would Homer suddenly change styles? Is there serious evidence for the idea that the two epics were written by two or more authors?

1. In the ancient world, certain occupations were associated with men and women. What are the mythic origins of weaving, and why is weaving associated with Penelope, Helen, and Calypso? How is weaving used in *Lysistrata*?
2. Several women and goddesses are associated with the knowledge of herbs and drugs; Egypt was famous for cultivating this knowledge. Explore the connections between women, plants, and Egypt.

SAPPHO
Selected Poems

Sappho's characteristic themes of nature, the presence of the Goddess, the emotional turmoil in the lives of young women, and the overwhelming power of romantic and sexual love are naturally appealing to students, and yet no other selection in this anthology presents the problems that teaching Sappho does. Even in *Descent of Inanna*, we can trace a more or less coherent narrative line; Sappho's is the only text here made up almost totally of salvaged bits of separate poems. Students can be encouraged to talk about their reactions to the experience, unusual for many undergraduates, of reading a fragmented text, and their differing responses of frustration, anger, intrigue, or bewilderment. Students are often delighted by these tantalizing lines, and drawn to speculate about the lost poems that incorporated them.

Another natural discussion topic springing from a reading of Sappho is the issue of censorship. We don't have her complete works—but what made people so eager to repress her work, given the lines we do know? What's considered dangerous in a given time, a given place? Can your students think of groups who might wish to suppress Sappho's work now? What readings are currently under threat of being censored in schools locally and around the country? (As of March 1994, two short stories by Alice Walker have been deleted as "inappropriate" from the California Learning Assessment examinations administered to high school students in that state; children's books about Halloween are currently forbidden in public schools in many communities in the United States.)

Students reading Sappho often want to talk about whether they think there is a difference between male and female voices, subjects, and attitudes; they may be very emphatic on either side of that question, and they will certainly not always split along predictable lines.

Questions for Discussion and Writing

1. How does Sappho's vision of the deities, especially the female ones, differ from those of other classical authors you have read?
2. What insights into Greek social life and daily routine do you find in Sappho that you have not found in other classical authors?
3. What might church authorities have found in Sappho's work that made them fear it so deeply?
4. How does Sappho characterize the contradictory effects of romantic love?
5. How does the circumstance of possessing only fragments of Sappho's work both complicate and enhance your reading of her?

Invite students to choose one of the Sappho fragments and write a poem that incorporates it.

AESOP
Fables

Who Aesop was and where he came from have been much disputed. Some legends say that he was a slave from Thrace, Phrygia, or Egypt. Many modern scholars question whether there ever was a writer named Aesop; they see him instead as a convenient fiction to ascribe the tales to. Whatever the truth about the authorship, the fables might have been placed among the world texts rather than with Western literature, for the origins of many of them can be traced to the East, especially in India. One way to approach the question of authorship is to ask what sort of person emerges from the tales. We have included tales such as "Androcles" and "The Dog and the Wolf" that tend to support the characterization of Aesop as a slave.

We usually teach Aesop along with Chuang Tzu to present two contrasting modes of storytelling. The narrative strategy in Aesop usually begins by defining an opposition or conflict that builds to climax and resolution. The Taoist stories, on the other hand, might be called assimilationist stories rather than oppositional ones, for they seek to identify subject and object, self and other, and they are not resolved with an explicit moral.

Questions for Discussion and Writing

1. How does Aesop characterize each of the animals in his fables? Are these characterizations stereotypical? Do any of the animals surprise you?
2. Could Aesop have used a wolf or a bear in "Androcles" instead of a lion and made the same point?
3. Can you attach a moral to one of the fables other than the one Aesop draws? How would you revise the narrative to point the story to your moral?
4. Take one of the fables and identify the details in it that specifically point to the moral. Are there any details given that are not directly linked to the moral? If there are, what do they contribute to the tale?
5. How do these fables differ from a modern short story? How do they differ from the tales of Chaucer, Boccaccio, or Marguerite de Navarre?
6. Can you retell one of the episodes on Odysseus' journey as an Aesopian fable? Why or why not?
7. Compare "Androcles" to Jesus' parable of the Good Samaritan. How are they similar? How are they different?
8. Compare the fables of Aesop with the Taoist tales of Chuang Tzu.

Projects

1. Write a modern fable in the manner of Aesop.
2. Rewrite one of Jesus' parables in the form of an Aesopian fable.

AESCHYLUS
The Oresteia:
Agamemnon *and* The Eumenides

In these two plays, which make up two-thirds of *The Oresteia*, Aeschylus displays his talent as an innovator of the Greek stage, a mythical storyteller, and a supporter of Athenian democracy. He adapts to the theater one of the obsessive tales of Homeric epic, the death of Agamemnon at the hands of his wife, Clytemnestra, and her consort, Aegisthus. Aeschylus addresses a problem of huge proportions: how to stop the age-old cycle of violent retribution of which the murders of Agamemnon, Clytemnestra, and Aegisthus are only the most recent examples. He transforms the story into a parable of Athenian justice in which Athena, casting the determining vote, finds Orestes innocent on what we would call a technicality after the jury deadlocks. The play also attempts to reconcile the old form of justice, represented by the Eumenides, with the new ideal represented by Athena and the citizen jury. Each form of justice is provided with its area of influence as well as specific obligations and duties; inevitably, however, the old gives way to the new in cases of serious crime such as homicide.

Several teaching issues are raised by the plays. One concerns Clytemnestra. Is she a heroine, a bold and intelligent woman forced to take the law into her own hands to avenge the sacrifice of her daughter, Iphigenia? Or is she a cold-blooded villain with no respect for the gods or the legal process of her time? Her ominous, mocking speeches to the helpless chorus reveal her ruthlessness as well as her unflinching pride. Aegisthus is another character study: despite his strong motivation, he reveals through his speeches a cowardly, self-serving mentality that belies his justification for his murderous act. The chorus must also be interpreted: Its apparent terror of the future leads it to repress its memory of the past, an action that appears to the modern reader as psychological denial. Finally there is the treatment of women in the play: We find not only Clytemnestra, the "liberated" woman who is a cold-blooded murderer, but Athena, the true heroine, who confesses that she always takes the man's part, and the Eumenides, descendants of the classical Furies, pictured as loathsome old hags who will soon be stripped of their remaining powers. The plays have often been seen as the epitome of the ancient Greek patriarchal attitude.

These plays look back and forward to other great works of Greek literature. We should recall how obsessively *The Odyssey* returns to the idea of the unfaithful wife as Odysseus plots his return to Ithaca to avenge his house against the suitors. At the same time, the scene depicting the Athenian trial by jury leads us to consider the plight of Socrates in similar hands a little over a generation later. Aeschylus also connects in our minds to Shakespeare. Orestes in the *Choephori* anticipates Hamlet; Clytemnestra in *Agamemnon* reminds us of Lady Macbeth. Finally, the French existentialist playwright Jean-Paul Sartre offers a powerful revisioning of *The Eumenides* in his World War II drama *The Flies*.

Questions for Discussion and Writing

1. What use has Aeschylus made of the story of the return of Agamemnon from the Trojan War? Discuss how his concerns differ from those of Homer.

2. What do you think of the character of Clytemnestra? Is she admirable, understandable, disturbing, hypocritical, evil? If none of these terms apply, how would you describe her?

3. Is Pallas Athena a real character to you in *The Eumenides*? What does she do that renders her realistic or unrealistic in your eyes?

4. Describe the changing Greek concept of justice in Aeschylus' time. How faithfully do you think the play mirrors this concept?
5. What do you make of the depiction of women in positions of authority in these plays? How do they suggest the attitude of the time about the proper role of women in society?
6. What is the primary message of the plays? Are these plays principally entertainment, education, or political propaganda? How seriously does Aeschylus want us to take them?
7. Compare the characterization of Orestes in Aeschylus' and Sartre's versions of the story. Is he a hero in both plays? In only one?

Projects

1. The Eumenides have an ancient heritage; their elder sisters appear, for example, in the cave of Erishkegal in the Sumerian epic story of Inanna. Trace their development from the Furies of ancient times to their appearance in Aeschylus' play.
2. Stage a modern trial of Orestes for the murder of Clytemnestra and Aegisthus. Invent proper arguments for the prosecution and defense and come up with a verdict in the case.
3. Define the old and new concepts of law in *The Oresteia*. Compare them to the Old and New Covenants in the Bible.

SOPHOCLES
Antigone

Antigone is one of Sophocles' most familiar plays, and some students may have preconceived notions that the play boils down simply to a question of the individual against the state. One way to get started is to ask students to explore the range of possible conflicts that the opposition between Creon and Antigone may represent—religious law versus civic law, subject versus king, women versus men, the chthonic feminine versus the Uranian patriarchy. This discussion leads to one question we've been exploring in this unit: the nature of the hero or heroine and his or her personal and public responsibilities. Both Creon and Antigone believe they are acting in accordance with the law, yet both rigidly interpret their respective laws beyond the possibility of compromise. Such unyielding adherence to principle turns out to be one of the main themes of the play, most notably expressed in Haimon's images of the trees that do not bend in the flood and the sail that does not slacken in the gale (Scene 3). Given their range of heroic action and their essential flaws, both Creon and Antigone can be compared to Achilles as a means to measure the refinements in the Greek idea of the hero in the fifth century.

Although the story of Oedipus is explained in the headnote to the play, students may have some trouble following the chorus's allusions to the curse on the house of Labdacus. A detailed presentation of the complexities of the Theban saga may do more to confound than to clarify here, but a brief discussion of the Oedipus cycle will help to establish the kinship relations that motivate the conflict in *Antigone* and that led to the fighting between Eteocles and Polyneices in the first place (see Headnote). Oedipus has, after all, cursed his two sons for refusing to protest against Creon, who exiles the blinded Oedipus from Thebes at the end of *Oedipus Rex*. Because Antigone stayed by her father, her antipathy toward Creon extends beyond his refusal to bury Polyneices and beyond her own sense of religious duty to her offended brother. The *Bhagavad Gita* similarly raises the question of kinship loyalty versus duty to a higher responsibility. Comparing Creon or Antigone to Arjuna may illuminate some of the similarities and differences between the Greek and the Hindu resolution of this issue.

Questions for Discussion and Writing

1. Creon and Antigone appear in the play as mighty opposites, yet they seem to share some common flaws of character, not the least of which is their lack of flexibility. Discuss whether you agree with this statement. You may, of course, find other ways in which they are alike.
2. Some critics claim that Creon is the tragic hero of the play. How would you defend or refute this view? That is, whose tragedy are we reading in *Antigone*? Explain your answer in terms of the classical definition of tragedy and be sure to anticipate possible counterarguments.
3. What role does Fate play in *Antigone*? How responsible do you think Antigone, Creon, and the other characters are for their destiny?
4. Consider *Antigone* as an example of Aristotle's theory of tragedy. Examine the classical concepts of *hamartia* (the essential or fatal flaw) and *hubris* (overweening pride) as they apply to the main characters, the unities of space and time in the setting, and the structure of the plot.
5. Discuss the sexual politics of the play. What does Creon appear to think the role of women in the state should be? Antigone? Ismene?
6. Compare Antigone, as a unique kind of heroine, to other female characters such as Clytemnestra or Medea.
7. How do the repeated observations of the Chorus and the pleas of Haimon affect our interpretation of the play?
8. Examine the relationships between Ismene and Antigone, Haimon and Antigone.

Projects

1. Create a courtroom situation in the classroom, with one group of students (the defense team) representing Antigone, another (the prosecutors) representing Creon, and a third serving as the jury. After a mock trial in which either Antigone or Creon is the defendant, discuss or have students write an essay about the issues raised during the trial.
2. Have students act out parts of the play and discuss how it might be staged.

EURIPIDES
Medea

Many readers contend that in *Medea* Euripides raises questions about women's status and rights in Athenian society. Others deny that this is his intent, given that Medea is explicitly depicted as a non-Greek, a "barbarian" from an island off the coast of Asia Minor. Xenophobia is certainly a note strongly sounded throughout the play, but it is also true that Medea makes a strong case for the plight of women who have no legal recourse if their husbands decide to put them aside. (Historically, both foreigners and women had very little legal status in Euripides' Athens, although most male aliens had more rights than Athenian women.)

As with most Greek plays, students will be better able to appreciate the imagery and a good many of the allusions if they know something about the characters' history. It is especially important to understand the crucial role Medea has played in Jason's youthful adventures (see Headnote). In aiding her beloved on his quest, she has gone all out in her loyalty to him and alienated herself forever from her own family and homeland by betraying her father and slaughtering her baby brother, acts that Jason apparently accepted as normal love-offerings at the time. In the course of the play, he belatedly begins to wonder what sort of woman he has espoused.

This play has provided in its infanticidal heroine one of the classic images for misogynist literature, although here again some readers claim that Euripides means Medea's savage actions to be laid more to her ethnicity than to her gender. Jason does say that no Greek woman could ever bring herself to do what his wife has done in killing their sons. History has largely ignored that distinction and concentrated on the image of Medea's cool plotting and of her triumphal exit aloft, shrieking with laughter at the utterly devastated Jason. Students may need help in seeing Medea as anything but monstrous, even if it is only to acknowledge that she is very good at what she does, plotting rings around the slower male characters who surround her. Bringing up contemporary cases of crimes of passion and child abuse may help students to understand that this play does not deal only with the realms of the mythological and the marvelous, but with the all-too-grimly human one as well.

Questions for Discussion and Writing

1. How important is it to the action of the play that Medea is from Colchis, a kingdom in Asia Minor?
2. Medea unquestionably has magical powers, but how much does she depend on them during the action of the play?
3. How do the minor characters of the Nurse and the Tutor contribute to the action of the play?
4. In what sense is Medea a hero like Achilles, Antigone, or Odysseus? What qualities has she that might command our admiration?
5. Trace the steps through which Medea's plan of action gradually solidifies.
6. Compare Medea with Aeschylus' Clytemnestra, another wife and mother out for revenge. How are their situations and their responses alike? Not alike?
7. Compare Jason with Virgil's Aeneas, another man who denies the legitimacy of his alliance to a foreign woman. Are either man's actions defensible?
8. In an alternate version of the story of Jason and Medea, Medea does not kill the children, but instead escapes with them safely tucked beside her in her dragon chariot. If Euripides' play followed this version, how would your response to it differ?

Project

Try writing the final scene for *Medea* using the alternate ending described in Question 8.

ARISTOPHANES
Lysistrata

The frank and bawdy sexuality of Aristophanic comedy has traditionally led to a discussion of the origins of Old Comedy in Dionysian fertility rites. Students today think of themselves as more sophisticated about sex than the protected youth of generations past, but R-rated movies and TV sitcoms have not really prepared them for either the outlandish phallic tomfoolery or the metaphoric seriousness of Aristophanes. The mounting horniness in the play is more than an extravagant set of variations suggested by the priapic costuming of the Dionysian rites; it acts metaphorically to undermine unrestrained male power and forces the reconciliation of Athens and Sparta in the reconciliation of the sexes. Tracing the stages in this conflict from the ineffectual confrontation between the choruses of old men and women to the climactic frustration of Cinesias and the final reconciliation, one can see the ways in which the sexual conflict acts as a metaphor for politics and war.

Questions for Discussion and Writing

1. List the reasons that motivate Lysistrata and the other women to take up their scheme. Do the different women have different reasons? How does Lysistrata convince them to go along with her plan?
2. Why might Aristophanes have chosen to make the choruses groups of old men and old women? How do the conflicts between the men and women mirror the conflicts between Lysistrata's group and their warrior husbands?
3. How does the play tell us what roles men and women were expected to play at the time? Which characters express these conventional expectations? How are gender roles reversed in the course of the play? How different are the men and women by the end of the play?
4. In the Greek theater, all the parts would have been played by men. What would this have added to the comedy in the play?
5. Trace the spinning and weaving metaphor through the play. How is it used metaphorically to articulate larger issues?
6. How does the scene between Myrrine and Cinesias set up the ending of the play?
7. How does Lysistrata finally reconcile the Spartans and Athenians?
8. *Lysistrata* is often called an antiwar play. In the Vietnam era, for example, it was often updated as a commentary on the war. Supporting your case by citing the text, argue either that the play condemns war generally or condemns only the Peloponnesian War.
9. Compare *Lysistrata, Antigone,* and *Agamemnon.* Do these plays suggest that men and women have different values? In what ways might the issues that lead to the women's strike in *Lysistrata* be said to contribute to the tragedies in the other two plays?

Projects

1. Discuss *Lysistrata* as a critique of the ideal of heroism in a warrior culture. Read up on the immediate historical context of the play and consider how exhaustion brought about by the long Peloponnesian War and changing attitudes toward military heroes may have helped to shape the play.
2. Write a treatment for a contemporary film adaptation of *Lysistrata*. In your proposal, indicate how you would update the play to turn it into a commentary on issues and events in our time.

PLATO
Apology, Phaedo, *and* The Republic

Our selections from Plato address two different topics. The *Apology* and the excerpt from the *Phaedo* are about Socrates' trial and execution. "The Parable of the Cave" from

The Republic is a metaphoric expression of Plato's doctrine of forms, but it can also be taught as a work that presents several central ideas of the Western tradition.

Socrates is often seen as the symbolic representative of Hellenism. His account of his search for truth and his testing of the Delphic Oracle's assertion that there was no man wiser than he illustrate his commitment to skepticism, analysis, and questioning—to the Socratic method. Although the question-and-answer format of the Socratic method is used only briefly in the *Apology*—in Socrates' questioning of Meletus—this passage can be used to illustrate the method.

The *Apology* as a whole presents the values in which Socrates believed and the principles that guided his life. Students should be asked to identify these principles as they are stated in the essay and to discuss their meaning and application—especially his commitment to the Delphic Oracle's injunction to "know thyself" (restated in Socrates' assertion that the unexamined life is not worth living), his realization that the wise man knows how little he knows, his valuing of virtue over knowledge, and his characterization of the philosopher's mission as that of a gadfly who stings others out of intellectual complacency. Socrates' life, as recounted in the *Apology* and *Phaedo*, can be read as an embodiment of these principles.

Socrates' story resembles a heroic legend or saint's life and Socrates can be compared with other heroes and saints. How, for example, does he represent a new ideal from that of the Homeric heroes, Achilles and Odysseus? He can also be considered a tragic hero in the light of Aristotle's discussion. Identifying his flaw or flaws can provide heated discussion. (I. F. Stone's discussion of Socrates as arrogant and dictatorial in *The Trial of Socrates* can be useful in this regard.) Socrates can also be fruitfully compared to Christian heroes and martyrs such as Jesus and Paul, as we suggest in our Headnote. When making this comparison, spell out some of the differences between Socrates' ideals and those of the Christian and Greek heroes.

"The Parable of the Cave" presents an initial challenge of simply understanding what the relationships are between the shadows and the various figures in the cave. Drawing or diagramming these relationships can be a useful exercise before trying to figure out their allegorical significance. We have sometimes taught the Parable as a literary ascent myth along with *Descent of Inanna* in order to contrast descent myths of death, rebirth, and growth with ascent myths in which truth or enlightenment comes down from above, as in the story of Moses receiving the Ten Commandments.

Questions for Discussion and Writing

1. What is an apology? Is there any sense in which the word *apology* as used in the title of this dialogue is similar to the sense in which we use it now? Could the gospels in the New Testament be called apologies?
2. Debate one of the following propositions:
   a. The Socratic method is the way to arrive at the truth.
   b. The Socratic method forces false conclusions by constructing the search for knowledge as a conflict between truth and error.
   c. The Socratic method leads to conclusions only when one of the two participants plays the stooge for Socrates, who knows the answer beforehand.
3. Compare Socrates' conviction to Orestes' acquittal in *The Eumenides*. What did you think of the defense in each case? Is the result of either of these trials just? If you find one or the other an unjust decision, what seems to you to be the cause for this injustice? Is there a flaw in the jury system?
4. Compare Socrates' philosophy and his way of reaching conclusions to the philosophies and methods of Lao Tzu and Chuang Tzu.

1. Write a legal brief for the prosecution or for Socrates, listing the charges against him and outlining the prosecution's arguments for or the defense's arguments against each of the charges.
2. Write a Socratic dialogue, considering one of the following questions:
   a. What is philosophy?
   b. What principles are worth dying for?
   c. Are material objects real?
3. Compare and contrast Plato's "Parable of the Cave" with one of Jesus' parables. In which is the message clearer, less ambiguous, more explicit?
4. Draw a picture or diagram of Plato's cave.
5. Read up on the history of Athens at the time of Socrates' death. How might the political and social pressures of the time have contributed to his conviction?
6. Write a dialogue between Socrates and Chuang Tzu.

ARISTOTLE
Metaphysics,
The Nicomachean Ethics,
and Poetics

Aristotle was one of the great philosophers of the ancient world; having discovered the power of reason and logic, he set the goal of systematizing all knowledge. The complexities of his method and his concepts, however, make the understanding and application of his ideas a real challenge.

Aristotle was the father of taxonomy; he believed that classification was an essential step toward knowledge. Today taxonomy is particularly important in biology, but, in fact, is critical in the social sciences and humanities as well. Although students often find Aristotle difficult to read, the principles of taxonomy provide an excellent basis for appreciating Aristotle's methodology. We have included excerpts from his writings that exemplify his strategy for arriving at basic classifications, which then can be applied to life and literature.

In "On Philosophical Wisdom," Aristotle establishes several hierarchies involving knowledge and wisdom: a hierarchy from utility to first principles and a hierarchy from sense-experience to contemplation. From these hierarchies he proceeds to his idea of wisdom. In "The Philosophy of Happiness," he establishes criteria for determining the virtue or excellence of any particular thing, a necessary step for discussing the virtue of man. Then he provides a strategy for arriving at the "mean" and its application to moral virtue and the principle of moderation.

Aristotle's *Poetics* deals with several classification schemes: how to distinguish plays from other forms of literature; how to classify kinds of plays; how to label the basic ingredients of a single play; how to analyze the various kinds of these ingredients. This procedure results in definitions that can be discussed and then applied to the plays in this anthology. It is important to question whether the results of Aristotle's procedure actually provide us with important knowledge of a particular play.

Questions for Discussion and Writing

1. How is wisdom different from knowledge that is useful?
2. According to Aristotle, how did philosophy evolve?

3. What are the two criteria for determining the virtue of a thing?

4. How does one arrive at the mean or moral virtue of a particular feeling or action?

5. Are there certain actions that are simply bad and therefore lie outside of the principle of moderation?

6. Our translation uses the word *purification* for the effect involving pity and fear; other translations use *catharsis* or *purging*; discuss what Aristotle means by the purification of these emotions. Are there forms of entertainment today that achieve similar effects? (See Sections 6 and 14.)

7. Aristotle stresses the idea that "tragedy is the imitation of an action." What does he mean by this statement and why is this an important concept?

8. Although Aristotle's division of a plot into a beginning, middle, and end seems overly simplistic, it is nevertheless a useful tool for discussing the movement of a plot. Choose one or more of the plays in this section and discuss how the division of the play into three segments provides a means for discussing the plot structure.

9. Aristotle's distinction between poetry and history is used by teachers to celebrate the universal themes of poetry. How might Aristotle's distinction be applied to the poetic and historical writings in this section? Do you disagree with this distinction and find it overly rigid? (See Section 9.)

10. Aristotle maintains that there are four guidelines for characters in a play: goodness, appropriateness, trueness to life, and consistency. Discuss how these four things are applicable or not applicable to the plays in this section.

11. Aristotle maintains that "manliness in a women, or unscrupulous cleverness" is inappropriate. Discuss strong women such as Clytemnestra or Antigone in light of Aristotle's criteria.

12. Students are often attracted to the idea of a tragic flaw and its usefulness in explaining the actions of a tragedy. From where does this idea of tragic flaw come?

Projects

1. In Section 15 of the *Poetics*, Aristotle says that the poet must observe the rules he has discussed. Other artists and critics have maintained that great art results from breaking or extending the rules obeyed by previous generations. Discuss these two points of view in relation to Sophocles' *Antigone* and Euripides' *Medea*; are these plays effective because they comply with Aristotle's rules or because they break them?

2. The idea of a play's catharsis brings the audience into consideration. Does the chorus in Greek dramas stand in for the audience? What important roles did drama play in Greek society? Could it be said that the theater in some ways replaced the church or temple in Greek culture?

CATULLUS
Selected Poems

After the high solemnity and public nature of classical epic and tragedy, students are likely to find a welcome change in the intimate voice of Catullus, who is by turns passionate, snarling, tender, hilarious, and grave. One usual assignment is to compare him to Sappho, the Greek writer of lyrics whom he revered and imitated, and to Renaissance poets, especially Petrarch and Donne, who remind us of Catullus in the lithe vigor of their lines and in the astonishing shifts of tone they display even within a single poem. The outright bawdiness of poems 25 and 37 may trouble some members of the class, and it may be useful to talk a little about the relatively tolerant attitudes Greeks and Romans held toward bisexuality and homosexuality, and toward sex and scatology in general (Eva C. Kuel's *The Reign of the Phallus: Sexual Politics in Ancient Athens*, 1986, is an excellent study of those issues).

Because Catullus often seems more familiar to students than other classical writers, they may want to compare him not only to other poets, but also to popular song lyricists who both celebrate and debunk romantic love and who savagely critique their own times. The bitter and loving eulogy one of my students just wrote for Kurt Cobain reminded me how the passionate, scurrilous, and elegiac spirit of Catullus is present for every generation.

Questions for Discussion and Writing

1. Compare Catullus' treatment of death in the mock-elegy of Poem 3 to the lament of Poem 101. Is Poem 3 only a mock elegy? Where and how does the poem's tone darken?
2. In Poems 2 and 3, how does the poet use his description of the pet sparrow to express his own desires?
3. In Poem 101, what difference does it make that Catullus' brother has died in the Middle Eastern land of Bithynia, far from home?
4. Compare Catullus and Sappho's views of love. How are they similar? Does their gender make a difference in how they speak of love?
5. What contemporary popular music lyricists echo Catullus' themes?
6. Compare Catullus' work to *The Tale of Genji* and the attitudes toward love demonstrated there.
7. Compare Catullus' Poems 3 and 101 with the elegiac drinking songs of Li Po.

Projects

1. If you have studied Latin, get a Latin text of Catullus and try your hand at translating one of his shorter lyrics.
2. Imagine that Aeneas in the underworld is shown not only Augustus' Rome, but Catullus' as well. Write the speech in which he tells Anchises his reaction to that scene.

VIRGIL
The Aeneid

By including most of the first half of *The Aeneid*, we are making several strategic choices. Because students will be able to refer back to the story of the Trojan War as told in *The Iliad* and *The Odyssey*, they will see that this is a continuation of the story of Troy. Beyond this, most of the early action of Virgil's epic focuses on the testing of Aeneas and his men at sea and the episode at Carthage, including the love story of Dido and Aeneas. At the same time, by leaving out the second half of *The Aeneid*, including the conquest of Italy and the final victory of Aeneas over his enemy Turnus, we are dramatically altering the intention of the work. We are rendering inaccessible to the reader the parallelism between Aeneas in love (Books 1–6) and Aeneas at war (Books 7–12), with his terrible twin "victories" over the helpless Dido and the defeated Turnus. But in the story of Dido alone we have the fundamental crisis of the work, portrayed in its more personal aspect: the conflict between Aeneas the leader, sworn to do his duty to the Roman race and to history, and Aeneas the human being, seeking the love of a lady strangely and sympathetically his equal but destined to become only his victim.

The headnote to this work stresses the development of Aeneas' character, his observance of *pietas*, and the claim it will make on his actions. Although it alludes to the conniving of the goddesses Juno and Venus in first bringing Aeneas and Dido together, it also interprets their love affair as a matter of free choice between them—up to a point. When Aeneas obeys the command to depart for Italy, it is a death sentence for Dido. Her mad conniving leading to her own suicide, and her shade's subsequent snubbing of Aeneas when he spies her in Hades, establish both her personal tragedy and her singular defiance. Given enough of the historical context not to succumb to outright romanticism, the student must still ask, Is Aeneas really justified in leaving Dido? What *is* the price of public virtue? Aren't these still questions that we face today?

Any translation of such a great work of literature must emphasize some virtues at the expense of others. The Copley version opts for a realistic, colloquial tone at the expense of the magisterial verse quality of the original. We can see this even when the verse is supposed to emphasize the gravity of Virgil's theme, expressed by Anchises' admonition in Hades:

> You, Roman, remember: Govern! Rule the world!
> These are your arts! Make peace man's way of life;
> spare the humble but strike the braggart down.

Aeneas should be compared not only to these earlier heroes of the Greeks, Achilles and Odysseus, but also to the Moses of Exodus and the Jesus of the Gospels. Because of the nearness in time of the composition of *The Aeneid* to the life of Jesus, one should also compare Virgil's ideas on the topic of humility to the Christian conception. At the same time, Aeneas is a warrior, and he may be compared in that capacity with later heroic figures such as Beowulf and Roland in the Middle Ages. Aeneas' behavior as a lover might be compared (cautiously) to that of Don Juan in Tirso de Molina's *The Love Rogue of Seville*. Finally, one might also compare the author of this poem (through what we can know of his ideas) to the character Virgil who serves as Dante's guide in *The Divine Comedy*.

Because of the importance of *The Aeneid* in forming the Western conception of character in the ruling elite, it remains a crucial canonical work today. Therefore, the reading of even part of this epic poem might be a good starting point to discuss the nature of the canon with your students. Is it important for us to learn what Virgil thought the ruler of the world should know about heroism and the virtues appropriate to a leader? Do the ethical implications of assuming leadership as Virgil understands it still affect us? Should or should not this work remain part of the canon? And—inevitably—should a canon exist, in the sense that it teaches us things we should know as descendants of Western Europe or subjects of the European sphere of influence? These are questions your students might try to answer from their own personal perspectives.

Questions for Discussion and Writing

1. If Virgil really wrote *The Aeneid* as a work of instruction for Augustus Caesar, what do you think he hoped his powerful friend would learn from this work?
2. What do you think Virgil means by the adjective *pious*?
3. Give your interpretation of the love story of Dido and Aeneas. Concentrate on (1) the degree of free will the lovers had when choosing to be together, (2) what actually happened in their coming together and how much of a bond this amounted to for Aeneas, and (3) the conflicting claims of love and duty as they appeared to Aeneas. Do you feel Dido was wronged by Aeneas? What, if anything, should he have done differently?

4. Compare Aeneas to another epic hero of similar importance and comment on their similarities and differences. What do you think the two different poets might have tried to convey to their respective audiences concerning their heroes?
5. Do you think *The Aeneid* is important to a modern understanding of how leadership works? Would your opinion differ depending on whether you saw yourself as a leader or one governed by others?
6. Compare the formulation of the conflict between love and duty in *The Aeneid* to that in *The Princess of Clèves*.

Projects

1. Imagine a situation in which Dido and Aeneas come before a jury to state their cases in their love dispute. Assume that even the gods and goddesses can be called as witnesses. Determine who is responsible for Dido's death.
2. Discuss whether you think Aeneas' ethical values would make him suitable as a modern world leader or the CEO of a major corporation.

OVID
Metamorphoses

Ovid's *Metamorphoses*, a poem that tells "of bodies changed / To different forms" and the "gods who made the changes," marks a radical departure from the Greek treatment of the gods. Indeed, one way to approach the text is to discuss the further secularization of Greek mythology, begun in Virgil and carried to an extreme in this work. The playful, literary quality of the tales in *Metamorphoses*, fortunately, make reading the stories of Apollo and Daphne, Jove and Io, Orpheus and Eurydice, Apollo and Hyacinthus, and Pygmalion and Adonis a delight in themselves, and many students will recognize some of these characters from encounters with them in other works. It's important to emphasize that Ovid took great liberties with the original Greek material, that his treatment of the original myths is far more literary and detached than that of Hesiod, for example, and that his work became a kind of sourcebook on which many later writers based their versions of these stories.

In our sample, the creation story and the myth of the Golden Age receive the most serious treatment. In the separation of Heaven from Earth, the creation of human beings in God's image, and the privileged place of human creation, students will hear echoes of the creation story in Genesis; it is a useful exercise to compare the stories of creation here with those in Genesis, in the selections from Hesiod, and in the Aztec materials. Another parallel between Book I of *Metamorphoses* and Genesis is the story of the flood, which Jove visits upon the earth after a period of decline from the Golden Age to the Iron Age. Here Deucalion takes the part of Noah. In comparing the Genesis version to that in the *Metamorphoses*, students should see that Ovid's version takes a more disinterested perspective on these events than the Hebrew text. Moreover, the flood story also appears in *The Epic of Gilgamesh*, which contains the oldest literary version of the flood.

Questions for Discussion and Writing

1. Compare the creation story or the flood story in Book I of *Metamorphoses* with those in Genesis, *Gilgamesh*, or the Aztec materials. What do the similarities and differences

suggest about the uniqueness of each culture? What aspects of these stories does Ovid seem to emphasize?

2. Ovid and Virgil emphasize the literary potentials of the original myths. Compare Ovid's account of creation with Hesiod's. How does Ovid's version suggest a different approach to mythology?

3. Compare the Jove in *Metamorphoses* to the Zeus in Homer. How are they different? Why?

4. One important function of myths was to instruct people in certain principles or codes of conduct. Does Ovid's treatment of myth here suggest such a didactic purpose? (The stories of Adonis and of Atlanta and Hippomenes serve as good test cases here.)

5. Why is metamorphosis or change such a compelling theme?

Project

Many of Ovid's tales have been converted into dramas, operas, and even films. The story of Orpheus and Eurydice (which we include here), in particular lends itself to musical treatment. It inspired Gluck, Haydn, Offenbach, Claudel, and others to compose operatic versions of the story. Some students might enjoy listening to one of these operas and exploring the way post-Enlightenment composers have treated the theme.

THE OLD TESTAMENT

Although the Bible has been a central document in Western history with enormous influence, many college students have not actually read the Bible—or have not read it critically. Indeed, a surprising number of students are largely ignorant about what might be called the Judeo-Christian heritage. One of the first and most important challenges of reading selections from the Bible is discovering what the Bible says and what actually happens in its stories.

Because the Bible might be a religious text for some students, it is helpful to provide guidelines for reading and discussing biblical stories. It is possible to respect Judaism, Christianity, and Islam while maintaining the importance of open, honest, and sincere discussion. Students sometimes assume that they are more familiar with the Bible than they actually are; the preparation of study questions assists students in the close reading of the stories. In addition to creating questions about major characters and events, an instructor might emphasize the following themes: nomadic versus village life, monotheism versus polytheism, obedience versus idolatry, patriarchy versus matriarchy or goddess culture, and separateness versus assimilation. These themes are expressed in several kinds of literature, including myth, legend, drama, lyric, and oratory.

The fact that students are reading a translation raises issues about the nature of the text and the inevitability of interpretation, cultural bias, and multiple meanings. A comparison of the various translations of a particular passage exemplifies the complexity of deriving meaning from translations. However, it has been said that the English of the sixteenth century used in the King James Bible was a good match for the original Hebrew of the Old Testament—at least in terms of syntax and rhythm.

By locating the biblical texts in a historical context, it is possible to show how Hebrew poets and prophets were influenced by their powerful neighbors on both sides. The Babylonian version of the flood in *The Epic of Gilgamesh* is very similar to the flood story in Genesis, but about one thousand years earlier. It is instructive to compare the Egyptian "Hymn to Aton" to Psalm 104.

Genesis

1. The two different accounts of creation in Genesis 1 and 2, with the different names for God and the different orders of creation, provide an opportunity for discussing the Old Testament's documentary structure as discussed in the headnote. How was it composed and how can we account for the differences between the two creation accounts?
2. What particular qualities of the Hebrew God are shown in the book of Genesis?
3. The first chapter of Genesis says that humans have dominion over the earth and its creatures; discuss how the idea of dominion might have shaped attitudes toward nature.
4. How are women portrayed in the book of Genesis?
5. Discuss how the conflict between Cain and Abel might represent the antagonism between the differing life-styles of nomadic and agricultural peoples.
6. Treat the story of Joseph and his brothers as a short novel or novelette. What is the basic plot of this story and who are the main characters? What role do dreams play in the story? How is suspense created? What is the climax of the story? What happens to Joseph's body when he dies?

Exodus and Joshua

7. What characteristics of Moses' life make him a hero?
8. What is the basic pattern of the exodus? What are the psychological meanings of Egypt, the wilderness, the Red Sea, Mt. Sinai, the golden calf, the Jordan River, and the Promised Land?
9. How do their experiences in the wilderness prepare the Hebrews for the invasion of Canaan?
10. Discuss the role of Mt. Sinai in the negotiations between Moses and God. How have the Ten Commandments influenced Western society? What religion is represented by the golden calf?

Job

The book of Job may be divided into the following parts: Prologue (Chapters 1–2); Dialogues (3–31); Elihu's speeches (32–37); Theophany (38–42:6); and Epilogue (42:7–17).

11. The Hebrew word for *Satan* in the Prologue means "the adversary" or "the accuser" and is apparently a legal term, not the evil being later associated with the name. Discuss the role of Satan in Job. Does Job deserve the punishment he receives?
12. How do Job's companions explain why Job suffers?
13. Do you think that God gives an adequate answer to Job for his suffering?

Psalms

14. Psalms 6 and 137 are laments; discuss the reasons for a lament. Are there situations today that might call for a lament?
15. Psalm 19 is a hymn or song of praise. How does the psalmist use imagery to effectively express his feelings?
16. What reasons might account for the popularity of Psalm 23?

Projects

1. One of the most influential stories in all of Western literature is the short story of Adam and Eve in the Garden of Eden. Separate the class by gender into women and men and

have them discuss separately how this story has influenced them. Reunite the class and compare notes. Often this is a good time for men to listen because we have found that women tend to be more conscious of Adam and Eve's influence on relationships and attitudes toward sexuality and the human body.

2. It has been suggested that the Hebrew God in the Bible reveals himself through speech and that humans relate to him through hearing; on the other hand, Homer is a visual poet and the Greek deities are fit subjects for art. Select passages from the Bible and from Homer that illustrate the different ways in which deities are perceived. How do our senses influence our concepts of God?

3. Compare the flood stories in *The Epic of Gilgamesh* and in Genesis with the flood stories in other mythic traditions. Investigate the expeditions to Mt. Ararat in Turkey that have led some modern explorers to believe in the historical truth of the flood story.

4. Victor Hugo said: "The Book of Job is perhaps the greatest masterpiece of the human mind." One reason for this praise involves the perennial questions about the existence of suffering, evil, and free will in this world. One way to frame a complicated philosophical question about the existence of evil is this: If God created the world and continues to run it, why do innocent people suffer? Investigate the various ways in which religions have attempted to answer this question.

5. The Old Testament psalmists were famous for expressing the profound and various feelings of the Jewish people. Are there any poets or songsters today who express the important feelings of a people or group in the United States?

6. A longstanding tradition of Jewish discussion and debate about religious and ethical issues lies behind the writing of the book of Job. Two famous Jewish educators were Hillel the Elder (73–4 B.C.E.) and Shammai (50 B.C.E.–30 C.E.). Investigate the influence of rabbis such as Hillel and Shammai on the educational practices of early Judaism.

7. Compare the pact between God and Satan in Job to the similar pact in Goethe's *Faust*. In what ways does Goethe use Job?

THE NEW TESTAMENT

The selections from the New Testament can be read as examples of different literary genres: the gospel materials as spiritual biography or heroic narrative containing sermons and parables; Corinthians as letters of moral advice, theological discussion, and poetry (ch. 13); and Revelations as apocalyptic narrative. Among the biblical classics included within our selections are the Christmas story from Luke, the Sermon on the Mount, the Beatitudes, the parables of the Prodigal Son, the Good Samaritan, and the Talents, and Paul's sermon on faith, hope, and charity. Any of these passages may be treated separately or as background to other works of literature.

Our selections can also be read as parts in a larger narrative, parts of what Northrop Frye calls the "great code." We have found that an approach that treats the Bible as a single work, tracing the story of humankind from Genesis to the Last Judgment, enables students to make connections between the biblical narratives and to see the repetitions in them. It is especially useful to draw the parallels between Old and New Testament stories, particularly between the exodus and the life of Jesus. These connections do not have to be as exhaustively spelled out as they would have been by a medieval typologist to enable students to see how the biblical patterns repeat themselves and how the New Testament can be read as a repetition and fulfillment of the Old. Among such repetitions are the omens relating to the births of Moses and Jesus, the orders to kill first-born sons, the bondage of the Hebrews in Egypt and Jesus' exile in Egypt, the forty years and forty days in the wilderness, and the deaths of Moses and Jesus before the fulfillment of their missions.

As a hero story, the life of Jesus models values very different from the warrior ethic of the Homeric heroes, the moral and civic virtues affirmed by Socrates, and the stern judgmental ideals of the Old Testament patriarchs. One can use the Sermon on the Mount and the parables to identify many of Jesus' key ideas.

The biblical materials are especially important in providing background for other literature. The King James translation is the version of the Bible that has most influenced English and American writers, so we have made our selection from the King James Bible even though it is sometimes more difficult and more ambiguous than modern translations. In this anthology, the life of Jesus as a journey narrative sets up many of the pilgrimage narratives in medieval and later works. The selections from St. Paul are particularly relevant to St. Augustine and to the Wife of Bath's Prologue.

Questions for Discussion and Writing

1. What omens surrounding Jesus' birth indicate that it is unusual or special? What indications are there in Jesus' infancy and childhood of his special mission?
2. What events in the life of Jesus are similar to events in the life of Moses or to events in the exodus of the Hebrew people?
3. In the Sermon on the Mount, especially in Matthew 5, Jesus says that he has come to preach a new law to extend and supersede the old law. What old laws does Jesus revise and what new laws does he offer in their place? *The Oresteia* could also be said to be about replacing an old law and an old ideal of justice with a new law. Compare Jesus' new law with that in *The Oresteia*.
4. What does Jesus mean when he says, "Ye cannot serve God and mammon" (Mat. 6:24)? Does this contradict his teaching in Mark 12:17 to "Render to Caesar the things that are Caesar's, and to God the things that are God's"?
5. Notice the metaphors that Jesus uses in the Sermon on the Mount. List the most important of them. How would you characterize the kinds of metaphors he chooses?
6. Take one of the parables and discuss it as a short story. What is its conflict? Who are the main characters and how are they characterized? What is the stated theme or teaching? What other themes might the story also be said to teach?
7. Compare the trial and death of Jesus to the trial and death of Socrates. What similarities do you find in their situations, in the advice they receive from their friends, in their courage facing death?
8. On the basis of the passages from Corinthians I, how would you characterize Paul? What does he see as his mission as an apostle?
9. In the vision of the Last Judgment from Revelations, Babylon symbolically stands for Rome. Why would the writer have used this symbolism? What sins is Rome/Babylon guilty of?
10. How does the view of the relationship between Jesus and the disciples in the Gospel of Mary differ from that in the New Testament?

Projects

1. Write a parable that teaches a value you believe in.
2. Find two modern translations of one of the passages or parables in the New Testament and compare the differences between the King James version and the modern versions.
3. Write the same story in the manner of Aesop, Jesus, and Chuang Tzu.

DESCENT OF INANNA

In Greek and Roman literature, students will have encountered female deities. However, in most classical works, Athena, Hera, and Aphrodite are mainly depicted as intervening in mortal affairs, and as subordinate divinities who are ultimately subject to the rule of a patriarchal male Zeus or Jove. Students are less likely to have dealt with goddess-heroes such as Inanna, who has adventures and performs mighty deeds in her own right, or with a ritual, oral text that was very likely used in ceremonies honoring the goddess and celebrating the seasonal cycles of growth, death, and renewal. Because of its ceremonial and dramatic nature, and because students may initially find this oldest of all goddess texts somewhat forbidding, we like to begin by showing the class storyteller-performer Diane Wolkstein's wonderful videotape of *Inanna*, available from Cloudstone Productions.

Both *Descent of Inanna* and the Gospel of Mary are fruitful texts to compare with the overwhelmingly patriarchal Old and New Testaments. In these two texts, also of Middle Eastern origin, women play strong roles as major heroes and villains—if, indeed, Erishkegal can properly be called a villain. Probably it is more accurate to view these two powerful female figures as two halves of a whole. Inanna is the Queen of Heaven, the ruler of light and love, fertility and life; Erishkegal, Queen of the Nether World, controls darkness and sorrow and death. The provinces of both deities taken together make up our earthly existence; although we do not welcome her, we need Erishkegal as much as we need Inanna. She, too, is part of us.

Inanna's story is one of ultimate testing; no worldly power, no wealth or beauty or protection, no human concept of what is just or fair can make us immune to physical death. Similarly, most of us must go through life-changing experiences in which we suffer some sort of death of a part of our self. The inexorable way in which Inanna is stripped, one by one, of all her adornments and tokens of rank is dramatic and devastating. With luck, like Inanna, we will at least have friends to stand by us. One of the most moving aspects of this spare story is her helper Ninshubar's unwavering loyalty even in the face of death; he will not rest until Inanna is restored.

Students may be interested in comparing this story to other versions of underworlds and the various means of entering and escaping from them; this volume contains underworlds in *The Odyssey, The Aeneid,* Dante's *Inferno,* in Ovid's account of Orpheus and Euridyce, in *Paradise Lost,* in *Dr. Faustus,* and—in a manner of speaking—in the parable of Plato's cave.

Questions for Discussion and Writing

1. Why does Inanna wish to venture into the Nether World? Does the motivation for her descent seem different from the motives of Odysseus or Aeneas for their underworld journeys?

2. In later versions of this story from other Middle Eastern cultures, an Inanna figure called Ishtar or Isis makes her descent because she wants to free a male lover from the bonds of death. Would such a change in the plot alter the effect of the story for you?

3. How does Inanna prepare for her descent? Do any of these preparations hold her in good stead?

4. What do you think are the main characteristics of Erishkegal? "Pure" is one of the adjectives applied to both her and Inanna. In what way might both be thought of as pure?

5. Scholars often remark that in confronting her sister Erishkegal, Inanna is symbolically coming to terms with the most negative and frightening parts of herself. Does this ring true for you? Why or why not?

6. The narrative of Inanna's descent contains a number of catalogues such as the lists of Inanna's domains, her allies, and the adornments and objects that symbolize her personal power. The narrative also relies heavily on repetition, as when Inanna is told time and again not to question the rites of the Nether World. Lists and repetitions are devices we often love when we are children, but don't encounter much in contemporary literature. How do these lists and repetitions add to or detract from the story for you?

7. When Dante and Virgil enter the Inferno, they see engraved over the gate the words *Abandon Hope, All Ye Who Enter Here*. Is Inanna's Nether World hopeless? Which of the underworlds you have encountered in literature seems the most truly hopeless? How does one enter and emerge from other underworlds in literature?

8. Does it make a difference to this story that the heroic divinity is a woman?

Projects

1. Have you ever gone through a testing experience similar to Inanna's descent into the Nether World? Write an account of your personal ordeal. You can write either a poetic account modeled on the Inanna story, or you can simply describe your experience in your normal voice and compare it to Inanna's journey.

2. Since you were a child, has popular culture (comics, novels, cartoons, movies, video games) provided more and better female heroes? Have you identified with any of them? Who are the heroic women, real or fictional, you'd like to see children emulate?

THE EPIC OF GILGAMESH

The Epic of Gilgamesh is the oldest hero story in Western literature. In mythology and legend, a hero is usually a man with mixed parentage—one mortal and one divine parent—who, because of his great courage and strength, performs extraordinary feats, is favored by the gods, and is celebrated in art and literature. *Gilgamesh* perhaps set a standard for subsequent hero stories; it contains the basic ingredients we have come to associate with the hero journeys of Odysseus, Theseus, and Aeneas: a special birth, early tests of heroism, an extended journey, the struggle for a special treasure or reward, and a celebrated return to ordinary reality.

Otto Rank's *The Myth of the Birth of the Hero* (1914) describes the hero's early connection with water, a virgin mother, animals, and danger. These elements are found in the birth narratives of great Western heroes such as Moses, Sargon, Oedipus, Hercules, Jesus, and Romulus. Lord Raglan's *The Hero* (1936) extends the pattern of the generic hero by positing twenty-two basic hero characteristics by which he measures the famous heroes of world literature. By incorporating Otto Rank, Lord Raglan, and Carl Jung, Joseph Campbell's *The Hero with a Thousand Faces* (1949) provides yet another universal pattern for the hero by delineating the stages of the journey: the call to adventure, the aid of mentors, the crossing of the threshold, the road of trials, the supreme ordeal and the battle for the elixir of life, the road back, returning across the threshold, and bene-fiting the community with the elixir or boon. Furthermore, Campbell's book relates the hero journey to dreams and to each individual's personal quest for meaning. Today the hero quest is not simply the narrative of extraordinary individuals who, in various ages, sought adventure and killed the monsters of their particular cultures, but it has become the model for individuals living in a secular society, who must search for the meaning of life's journey themselves.

The Epic of Gilgamesh is truly remarkable; despite its antiquity, all parts of the narrative are accessible to a modern audience. By treating the episodes metaphorically, students can relate Gilgamesh's adventures to their own lives and to contemporary life. For the sake of discussion, it is convenient to divide this epic into several parts. The first half of Gilgamesh's story involves his birth, youth, friendship with Enkidu, the killing of Humbaba, the rejection of Ishtar, and the death of Enkidu. This first section provides a series of tests whereby Gilgamesh gains the strength and courage to undertake his legendary journey to the end of the world, which constitutes the second half of the poem. All of his adventures are a preparation for kingship and legendary greatness.

Questions for Discussion and Writing

1. Why is it significant that the hero Gilgamesh has one divine parent and one mortal parent?
2. What are Enkidu's characteristics? As Gilgamesh's soul mate, how does Enkidu represent an undiscovered side of Gilgamesh?
3. How does Humbaba represent the monsters that exist on the frontiers of civilization?
4. The repeated use of the number seven in Gilgamesh indicates that it is a sacred number; it has been suggested that seven gets its importance from the seven heavenly bodies visible to the naked eye: sun, moon, and five planets. Are there other possible theories for the importance of seven in ancient cultures? What role does seven play in The Epic of Gilgamesh?
5. Discuss how the rejection of Ishtar's advances represents a significant change of consciousness and a new role for the hero as an individual quester.
6. How does Enkidu's death raise questions about the meaning of life and provide motivation for Gilgamesh's journey?
7. What does Gilgamesh desire to learn from his journey?
8. The scorpion guardians on Mt. Mashu guard the threshold to the next world; why do they discourage Gilgamesh from continuing on his journey?
9. What does Gilgamesh learn from his conversations with Siduri and Utnapistim?
10. What is the symbolic meaning of crossing the waters on Urshanabi's boat?
11. How does Utnapistim answer Gilgamesh's questions about the meaning of death?
12. What is the connection between snakes and immortality?
13. What roles do women play in Gilgamesh?
14. Discuss the similarities and differences between Gilgamesh, Odysseus, and Moses.

Projects

1. Gardens provide important settings in the origin myths of Mesopotamia, Persia, and Israel. What are the basic ingredients of these paradisal gardens? How do the gardens differ in the different cultures?
2. In Gilgamesh, we have one of the earliest portraits of life after death. Investigate the early descriptions of afterlife in Mesopotamia, Egypt, Greece, and Rome. What are the connections between these different ideas about life after death and the roles of heroes?
3. Compare the flood story in Gilgamesh with the flood story in Genesis. What might account for the similarities and differences in the two accounts? Are there other flood stories in world mythology?

THE TAOISTS

The Taoists provide a real contrast to the literature of Mesopotamia, Greece, Rome, and Israel. The philosophy of Taoism reveals a way of living in harmony with the *Tao,* which is pronounced "dow" in Beijing and "daw" in Tokyo, and means the natural flow or way of the universe. Because of the difficulty of stating exactly what Taoism means, we suggest that students contrast the writings of Lao Tzu and Chuang Tzu to other writings; in fact, that is the method used by Taoists themselves. The philosophy of Taoism, which stresses simplicity, effortlessness, flexibility, and spontaneity, is often contrasted with the teachings of K'ung Fu-tse or Confucius, whose concerns with authority, rules, hierarchy, and propriety suggest affinities with authoritarian, legalistic movements in the West. Whereas Confucianism values hierarchical order, Taoism recommends the process of harmonizing with the flow of things.

China gave birth to the two founders of Taoism, Lao Tzu and Chuang Tzu, but Taoism's appeal reaches far beyond Asia. The Taoist texts offer a contrasting philosophy to the ethic of war, hierarchy, authority, and dominance found in a number of Western texts of the ancient world. In the latter part of the twentieth century, Taoism has become very popular in the West; its principles are applied to sports, art, diet, health, healing, business, and even physics.

Teaching these materials is a challenge; it is in the spirit of Taoism that there is no right or wrong interpretation of a particular poem or story. Lao Tzu's poems value imagination, intuition, and creativity more than reason and memory. Chuang Tzu's stories rely on contradiction and ambiguity to illuminate alternate views of particular events. In fact, the goal of a Taoist poem or story is *not* the accumulation of truths, but a change of consciousness, which might change the way one lives.

To some students, the lessons of Taoism are overly simple and unrealistic; how can one compete in a capitalistic society and subscribe to Taoism at the same time? A similar question has been raised about actually living according to Jesus' teachings in the Sermon on the Mount. Insights are gained from contrasting philosophies and religions. Two very popular books, *The Tao of Pooh* and *The Te of Piglet,* use children's characters as models of Taoism; obviously, they are diametrically different from either Rambo or Superman, the successors to the renowned Achilles.

Questions for Discussion and Writing

1. Discuss Lao Tzu's use of flowing water to suggest the Tao.
2. What does the word *tao* mean? Why isn't there a simple English equivalent for *tao?*
3. In poems 19, 20, and 81, Lao Tzu questions the value of formal education. From a Taoist perspective, what are the potential dangers of learning?
4. Why does Lao Tzu criticize domination by force or willpower?
5. Discuss the meaning of the phrase, "The way to do is to be" in poem 47. Is it possible to differentiate between being and doing?
6. Why does Chuang Tzu refuse to take public office?
7. Why does Chuang Tzu think it is wrong to grieve at his wife's death? To what natural process does Chuang Tzu compare his wife's death?
8. How does the swimmer respond when Confucius asks him how he learned to swim? What does it mean to be a good swimmer?
9. Why is a child more likely to be in harmony with the Tao than an adult?
10. How does the ideal of living in harmony with the Tao differ from the warrior hero ideal of the Greeks and Romans?

11. What advice would a Taoist sage such as Lao Tzu or Chuang Tzu give to Aeneas visiting Carthage?

12. In the West, the goals of flexibility, "going with the flow," and inaction might be condemned as being spineless, passive, and unprincipled. Discuss how a Taoist might respond to these charges.

Projects

1. How is Confucianism different from Taoism? How did these two philosophies serve different functions in China? Which of these patterns of action seems to be the more popular in the United States? Are we more concerned with rules and work or spontaneity and play?

2. Investigate the uses of aphorisms and parables in the wisdom literature of Asia, the Middle East, and Europe. What are the similarities and differences between a parable by Chuang Tzu and a parable by Jesus?

3. Describe how you would change your life if you were a Taoist.

4. Write a story in the manner of Chuang Tzu.

5. Alan Watts, a student of comparative religion and the author of *The Way of Zen* and *The Two Hands of God*, writes: "Everything flows, and therefore the understanding of water is the understanding of life." How does this statement apply to your life?

BHAGAVAD GITA

The *Bhagavad Gita* addresses directly the question of what it means to be a warrior-hero and what the warrior owes to society. Rather than advocating asceticism and withdrawal from the world, the *Gita* teaches that it is the warrior's duty to simultaneously act in the world and renounce the rewards that may come from that action. Its central conflict is similar to that of the great Greek tragedies: Arjuna, the hero, is divided between two conflicting duties. Facing an opposing army made up of many relatives, he must choose whether to honor his kinship ties or to fulfill his obligation as a warrior. Krishna, the incarnation of the divine spirit, serves as Arjuna's spiritual counselor and urges him to follow his highest duty as a warrior, keeping in mind that the corporeal world and its demands are transitory and illusory.

The entire dialogue between Krishna and Arjuna takes place at a moment poised before battle; it is a philosophical hiatus in the midst of the great epic of battle, the *Mahabharata*. Thus, the *Gita* represents a different genre—a metaphysical meditation in the form of a spiritual dialogue—from the other epic materials students have read in this unit. The circumstance leading to the dialogue is similar to the interludes of *The Iliad* in Book 6, where Hector explains his reasons for returning to battle, and in Book 9, where the Achaeans plead with Achilles to rejoin the fight. Indeed, the code of honor to which Hector and the Greek emissaries to Achilles appeal may be compared to Krishna's teaching about the warrior's duty to act in accordance with his nature in Books 2 and 3 of the *Gita*. Unlike the ascetic or saint, according to Krishna, the warrior must not abandon action, only the fruits of action; only by means of action can he or she fulfill the dictates of the warrior's nature and so reach a higher state of being. Thus, although the worldly appeal to the warrior's sense of honor and desire for fame praised in *The Iliad* at first may seem quite different from the metaphysical speculations about the nature of right action in the *Gita*, both texts underscore the importance of following the warrior's nature and living up to what is expected of him—fearlessness, discipline, action, knowledge, and duty.

Students may find similarities between the teachings of Book 4 of the *Gita* and the teachings of the New Testament because both advocate detachment from possessions in this world, self-sacrifice, and mastery over desire, and both promise a mystical union with an infinite spirit. However, they will be hard-pressed to find similar meditations in the heroic literature of Greece. Possibilities for comparison here extend to Plato and the teachings of Socrates, whose advocacy of detachment from the world of appearances and seeking after enlightenment bear some resemblance to the quest for self-knowledge and spiritual perfection in Books 4, 5, and 18 of the *Gita*.

Questions for Discussion and Writing

1. What are the major reasons Krishna presents for Arjuna to go to war?
2. How does Krishna reconcile his counsel for action with that of renunciation? That is, how can Krishna ask Arjuna to go to war, on one hand, and ask him to practice renunciation on the other?
3. Compare Arjuna to Achilles. How would Krishna advise Achilles in his dispute with Agamemnon, or in his decision to avenge the death of Patroclus?
4. How would you describe the difference between the spiritual entities such as Krishna in the *Gita* to the gods in the Old Testament or in the Greek materials? In general, compare the way the *Gita,* the Old and New Testaments, and the Greek epic materials depict the gods and spirituality.
5. Mahatma Gandhi called the *Gita* "an infallible guide of conduct" that helped to lead him through his daily life. Discuss how following Krishna's counsel might change the way you act in your everyday life.
6. Gandhi said that he could see no difference between the Sermon on the Mount and the *Bhagavad Gita*. Compare the two. Do you think Gandhi was right? Why?
7. What does Krishna mean by philosophy? How does his definition compare to Plato's or to Lao Tzu's?
8. How would you describe the genre of the *Gita?* Is it comparable to the Socratic dialogue or to the parables of Chuang Tzu or the New Testament?

Project

Write a dialogue between Krishna and Socrates, Krishna and Christ, or Krishna and Lao Tzu concerning the place of the soul and right action in the world, or write a dialogue between Arjuna and Achilles, or Arjuna and Odysseus, concerning the duty of the warrior-hero.

THE
MIDDLE
AGES

❧

The Pilgrimage
of Life

GENERAL INTRODUCTION

The terms *Middle Ages, medieval, Dark Ages,* and other attempts to name the vast historical period between the Fall of Rome and the Italian Renaissance are loaded with dangers of interpretation. First, they evoke in our minds a popular stereotype about a uniformly dark and primitive time in which no significant civilization or culture existed, a view as old as Tacitus' description of the barbarian tribes in *Germania* (98 C.E.). Second, there are no agreed-on beginning and end dates for the period. Finally, the terminology itself is biased toward Western Europe and against the Byzantine state and Islam, not to mention China and Japan, some of which were more advanced societies than Europe throughout much of the period. For a standard history of the Middle Ages that gives some account of Byzantium and Islam in their relations with Europe, see C. Warren Hollister's *Medieval Europe: A Short History* (fifth edition, 1982). For a brief treatment of the world picture in the same time period, see Kevin Reilly's *The West and the World: A History of Civilization* (second edition, 1989), especially "The Traditional World: 500–1500," pp. 215–233. For the general concept of the European Middle Ages as treated by modern scholars, see Norman F. Cantor's *Inventing the Middle Ages: The Lives, Works, and Ideas of the Great Medievalists of the Twentieth Century* (1991).

The trend of the future in medieval history tends to be comparative studies of the relations among civilizations on one hand and microhistorical studies of such topics as European feudalism on the other. An impressive new work in the latter area is Robert Bartlett's *The Making of Europe: Conquest, Colonization and Cultural Change 950–1350*

(1993). It is hoped that such efforts will expand our knowledge of medieval culture as a whole, especially of the cultural contacts between civilizations in the feudal period throughout Europe.

In recent years, certain medieval texts have become available in accessible modern translations. One emphasis we have taken in this section concerns the impact of the Christian conversion missions from Europe on the indigenous cultures of the British Isles. The story can be traced from the writings of Bede on the English missionary movement through Welsh, Irish, and English bardic poetry to the epic poem *Beowulf*. The chronicles of Bede, some of the Welsh poetry of antiquity, and the story of Derdriu from the Irish Ulster cycle have all recently appeared in readable modern editions. Together with existing translations of the Old English poems, including *Beowulf*, these new translations facilitate our study of an interesting era in European cultural history. There also has been a revival of interest in Romanesque lyric, with new efforts to translate Provençal poetry as well. Although the new translations may not equal in literary quality the efforts of major poets of nearly a century ago, they are more accurate and the originals are easily available for reference. The same holds for the Breton *lais* of Marie de France, which have gained new attention and are available in a brisk modern translation.

For many years we in the West have suffered from a lack of available Islamic texts in English translation and a parallel lack of up-to-date scholarship in this area. Gradually, both the texts and the scholarship are becoming available. The time of concern for us in this volume is that of the spread of Islamic culture from Baghdad to the West, with the disintegration of the Abbasid Empire in the tenth century, all the way to Cordova, on the Iberian peninsula. Along with the influence of the Koran, the vitality of Islamic culture may be seen in works as diverse as manuals on the art of love, travel accounts, and reflections on cultural history. For a convenient sampler of this literature, consult James Kritzeck, ed., *Anthology of Islamic Literature* (1964).

If the idea of The Middle Ages causes problems for us, marking the transition to the Renaissance is equally problematic. The Renaissance was self-consciously proclaimed in Italy in the early fourteenth century, but rather dimly understood in the rest of Europe over the next two hundred years. We tend to group the early Italian writers according to their influence on later work in the rest of Europe. Thus, we place Dante and Boccaccio (two major influences on the English "medieval" poet Chaucer) in the Middle Ages, but Petrarch (a major influence on European poetry in the sixteenth and seventeenth centuries) in the Renaissance. At this point in the general introduction we introduce the idea of medieval European literature and culture as a text Europe wrote about itself, borrowing our notion of textuality from the rhetoric of postmodernist criticism. The ensuing description of European cultural texts is largely thematic, relating them to larger archetypes in the manner of Northrop Frye in *The Anatomy of Criticism* (1957). The evolution of medieval literature is thus viewed from a mixed perspective, taking in the development of certain kinds of stories, the evolution of genres, and social and historical factors as they influence thematic development.

The bibliography at the end of the general introduction is designed primarily for the student intending to dig deeper into medieval studies or the teacher with previous background in the field seeking to revisit the critical, historical, or cultural interpretations. The authors cited—Auerbach, Bloch, Curtius, Gilson, Haskins, Heer, Huizinga, Lewis, Pirenne, Power, Southern, and Vossler—were giants in their fields whose work must be appreciated even when it is superseded. For the teacher who has neither the time nor the inclination to dip into such a formidable list, standard histories and guides to the literature should do. Particularly useful from the literary standpoint are two volumes edited by Boris Ford, *Medieval Literature Part One: Chaucer and the Alliterative Tradition* (1982) and *Medieval Literature Part Two: The European Inheritance* (1984).

Two areas of general interest that are developing as we write are scholarship on medieval women and on private life in the Middle Ages. Earlier scholarship on medieval women, collected and summarized in Eileen Power's *Medieval Women* (1975), has been powerfully extended in Peter Dronke's *Women Writers of the Middle Ages* (1984); Christiane Klapisch-Zuber, ed., *Silences of the Middle Ages* (1992); and vol. II of Georges Duby and Michelle Perrot, eds., *A History of Women in the West* (1992). For recent scholarship into ordinary lives, see Georges Duby, ed., *Revelations of the Medieval World* (1988); and vol. II of Philippe Aries and Georges Duby, eds., *A History of Private Life* (1988).

ST. AUGUSTINE
The Confessions

St. Augustine's *Confessions* is a work likely to both frustrate and attract the new reader. It will frustrate because it is not a "confession" in the modern sense—a personal tale of sensational, possibly lurid events in one's life to divert the listener—but in the traditional Catholic sense—a formal acknowledgment of sin, act of contrition, and affirmation of faith. (More is said about this in our headnote to the text.) Beyond this, however, the work will prove attractive, if for no other reason than that St. Augustine's life *was* sensational, no matter how formally he chose to treat it in his text. Covered in our selection are the following major incidents:

1. St. Augustine's childhood; his early "sins." (Book I)
2. Sins of the flesh. Theft of fruit. (Book II)
3. Studies at Carthage. Encounter with Manichaeism. (Book III)
4. Death of a friend and its effect on him. (Book IV)
5. Influence of St. Ambrose. (Books V, VI)
6. Conversion to Christianity in a garden. (Book VIII)
7. Death of his mother, St. Monica. (Book IX)

This is not simply effective didactic literature; this is great literature, written with passion and feeling. The stories of his youth provide an unparalleled insight into the life of a favored young man late in the life of the Roman Empire; his struggle to embrace Christianity is one of the great quest stories in the history of Europe; his conversion, the dramatic center of the book, is the model for such accounts in the future; and the story of his mother's death is remarkably honest and tender, although he must have been tempted to treat the matter formally and piously instead.

The first stumbling block for the student reading *The Confessions* is the matter of literary representation. Granted that this is an autobiography, in what sense is it a realistic one? What are we to make of this man who writes a letter to God in the second person, confessing his sins as if at confessional with a parish priest? What are we to make of him when he acknowledges and even diagnoses the "sins" of early childhood, or describes himself as burning with the fires of lust when he seems to be talking about getting married? Is he "for real"? If so, what kind of "real" is it?

It may help to describe the twofold or fourfold system of interpretation on which St. Augustine rests his reading of Scriptures, because it seems apparent that he "reads" himself in the same way. The levels are as follows:

Literal level: the story being told.

Allegorical level: significance in terms of Christian doctrine.

Moral level: allegorical level emphasizing moral conduct.

Anagogical level: allegorical level emphasizing the state of the soul in preparedness for salvation.

This method of biblical reading, or exegesis, was invented before St. Augustine's lifetime and used throughout the Middle Ages. The Italian poet Dante, in a letter dedicating his work *Paradiso* to his literary patron, explains a passage from the Bible, the departure of the children of Israel from Egypt, in this manner: On the allegorical level, it represents our redemption wrought by Christ; on the moral level, the conversion of the soul from the misery of sin to the state of grace; on the anagogical level, the departure of the soul from this corruption (Earth) to eternal glory (Heaven). All three allegorical levels can also, Dante suggests, be collapsed into one.

When St. Augustine tells us the story of his childhood, he does so on different levels. We know this because he stops and explains as he goes along many matters requiring Christian interpretation; for instance, whether an infant is guilty of sin. His own sins are personal, but they are also innate, part of the Original Sin of the descendants of Adam. The progress of his soul toward God is described in personal anecdotes, but it is also marked by steps of education and moral reawakening, and it has a clearly spiritual goal, as indicated in the scene in his garden when a voice tells him to "take up and read" his collection of the letters of St. Paul. So the story of St. Augustine's life is a realistic autobiography and more besides: an account of religious conversion, a pilgrimage toward freeing the soul from the state of sin, and a vision of the lifting of the soul to heaven in a state of salvation.

Another problem the student may encounter with St. Augustine is his polemical approach. He not only presents through allegorical interpretation an argument for his own salvation, he also argues *against* other philosophies and religions to the degree that they depart from Christianity. The modern student may feel unprepared for this kind of sustained attack, especially when it is based on faith, "the evidence of things not seen." To deal with this, the teacher might first of all discuss argument as a rhetorical strategy, and second discuss the rhetoric of Christian belief, possibly using one of the Gospels and selections from the letters of St. Paul as examples. (It is interesting that a polemical argument in the twentieth century is so often political; referring to a selection from the writings of Dr. Martin Luther King Jr., for example, might bring the student closer to St. Augustine's style of argument while still indicating its modern, political edge.)

Augustine introduces interesting possibilities for comparison of his work with that of other writers. His comments on the Dido episode of Virgil's *Aeneid* open up that text as a possibility. His praise of St. Paul's letters suggests a comparison with those works, both for style and for content. His use of allegorical interpretation brings up the uses that Dante and the author of *Everyman* make of both devices at the end of the Middle Ages. Also, his autobiography might be compared with later examples of the form, such as the story of Margery Kempe or Rousseau's *Confessions*.

Questions for Discussion and Writing

1. Explain the story of the conversion of St. Augustine on literal and allegorical levels.
2. What do you think of St. Augustine's ideas of Original Sin and its appearance in childhood? Pay attention to his use of examples in dealing with this subject.
3. Why does St. Augustine turn against Manichaeism? How does he regard neoplatonic philosophy? How does he come to place his belief in Christianity?
4. How does St. Augustine regard Virgil's story of Dido and Aeneas? What is its attraction? What is wrong with this kind of story in St. Augustine's view?
5. Read the selection from St. Paul's Corinthians in this anthology. Compare St. Augustine's work with St. Paul's. How is he indebted to St. Paul? How is he different?
6. How is *Everyman* similar to *The Confessions* with respect to the beliefs expressed in the two works?
7. Compare St. Augustine's account of his conversion with the story of Margery Kempe. Would St. Augustine understand Margery? Would he condone her practices?

Project

Imagine a conversation between St. Augustine and Dante. Would they agree or disagree on the role of literature in expressing, upholding, and supporting Christian doctrine?

DANTE ALIGHIERI
The Divine Comedy:
The Inferno, The Purgatorio, *and* The Paradiso

Dante's *Divine Comedy* consists of multiple layers of meaning that can be approached from several perspectives; Dante's range of learning and imagination confronts the reader with a variety of artistic and philosophical issues. Fortunately, the translator has provided a wealth of background information with excellent notes for each canto. In fact, the challenge for the teacher is what to include in discussions and what to leave out. A strategy for teaching this work might be envisaged as a series of concentric circles with the work itself in the center. The initial task for students is to read and enjoy selections of the work; then, depending on the time allotted for Dante in the course, students may explore the various circles involving politics, psychology, religion, aesthetics, science, and history.

Two literary terms are important tools for the student: allegory and symbol. The root meaning of *symbol* comes from the Greek *symballein*, meaning "to throw together." A symbol brings two worlds together by meaning itself and something else at the same time; when the cross is used symbolically, it means the instrument of torture, but it also evokes the religious meanings of the crucifixion. An *allegory* is an extended pattern of these dual meanings; it is an extended metaphor in which persons, objects, and events within a narrative are connected to meanings that lie outside the narrative itself. Typically, characters and objects in an allegory represent abstract qualities, and the narrative events represent relationships between these qualities. Thus an allegory has a dual focus: one on the narration itself, and another on the meanings represented by the story.

A single character in an allegory might have two or more allegorical meanings. In *The Divine Comedy*, for example, Dante the pilgrim may represent humankind, but also the individual soul. Virgil may be read as Reason or Philosophy, but also, at times, the Roman Empire. Beatrice is Revelation or the Church, but also Grace. The various punishments and, later, the rewards, are all symbolic, as are all the physical features of the three regions. A good place to begin the allegorical interpretation of this work is with the beasts in Canto 1. The symbol of Beatrice constitutes a different challenge. Dante's brief acquaintance with Beatrice Portinari produced a lifelong devotion that some students might find difficult to understand. The classical tradition of the feminine muse is helpful; Beatrice's similarity to the Virgin Mary provides insights into her religious role.

Dante's language is rich with metaphor and simile. By writing *The Divine Comedy* in Italian, rather than the more academic language of Latin, he promoted his vernacular tongue as a serious literary language. His use of the vernacular ranges from the sublime in *The Paradiso* to the scrofulous and filthy in the Malebolge. Dante invented a rhyme scheme, *terza rima* (triple rhyme), to carry the range of his melodies: *aba, bcb, cdc, ded*, etc.—some 1,500 triple rhymes in *The Inferno* alone. Whereas the sound structure of Italian makes this pattern possible, it is impossible to imitate in English. Fortunately, the translator of this version, John Ciardi, is also a poet, and he captures the range of diction and part of the rhyme scheme used by Dante.

Although Dante's artistry is likely to impress students, his judgmental moral vision and insistence on individual choice and responsibility might meet with student opposition.

In this modern age, many students are not familiar with the basic doctrines of Christianity concerning sin, judgment, penance, and redemption, and will need to be introduced to them. Dante had inherited a highly articulated hierarchy of vices and virtues. Most famous were the Seven Deadly Sins: pride, covetousness, lust, anger, gluttony, envy, and sloth. By the Middle Ages, scholasticism had created a philosophical method and system of thought that united the tenets of theology with the principles of a Christian society, and had described the basic, architectural features of the cosmos. From this body of knowledge, Dante could visually create the regions of Hell, Purgatory, and Heaven and construct the principles for populating them. For the epic scope of his poem, Dante was indebted to Virgil and *The Aeneid*.

Despite the inclusion of excerpts from *The Purgatorio* and *The Paradiso*, the main focus of our selection is on *The Inferno*, the most popular section of the poem. *The Inferno* is laden with politics: the intrigues and double-dealings of Florence and the civil wars in Italy. It is important to distinguish between the Guelphs and the Ghibellines, the Blacks and the Whites (see Headnote). The footnotes are invaluable in this area. In *The Inferno*, Dante presents the reader with several messages: From a religious point of view, the punishments of sinners are meant to deter readers from the kind of life that might result in the sufferings of damnation. But from the point of view of the writer or artist, the descent into Hell provides numerous aesthetic challenges and innumerable opportunities for creative excellence.

The descent into the Inferno is a passage from the least serious sin of the flesh to the most serious sin of betrayal; the principle of *contra passo* (see Headnote) provides a rationale for the various punishments; nevertheless the application of punishments is a complicated process. Dante himself seems torn at times in his assessments, particularly with several ministories or brief tragedies: Paolo and Francesca (Canto 5), Pier della Vigne (Canto 13), Jason (Canto 18), and Ulysses (Canto 26). In Canto 15, Dante is caught between his admiration for writer Ser Brunetto Latino and Latino's homosexuality. Morality and moral judgments have changed since Dante's day—especially regarding sexual conduct such as premarital relations and homosexuality; the nature of evil, however, remains a perennial question, which is characterized by urban violence in the United States and perpetual wars and revolutions around the globe.

Purgatory is the middle ground between Hell and Heaven, between eternal damnation and eternal bliss. Of the three regions, Purgatory most resembles the world we live in; it is filled with temptations, but it also contains the potential for reform. In *The Purgatorio*, suffering is temporary; penance is directed at correcting behavior. Dante's goal was to use penitential models for instructing and influencing his readers.

The ascent up the mountain of Purgatory reverses the arrangement used in the descent into the Inferno: Sins are arranged from the most to the least evil; the final seven terraces correspond to the Seven Deadly Sins. The summit symbolizes the Garden of Eden, the abode of Adam and Eve before the Fall. In our selection, Dante participates in his own penitential pilgrimage; Beatrice reminds him of his sins, whereby he confesses his shortcomings and grieves for his sins.

Dante drew on the scientific cosmology of the Middle Ages to create the structure of Heaven. Although modern physics tends to diminish one's interest in the details of this theological apparatus, the visual, poetic architecture in the poem remains impressive. In the end, there is the age-old anticipation of meeting God.

Questions for Discussion and Writing

1. What makes Virgil the ideal guide for the first stages of Dante's journey?
2. A discussion of the historical Beatrice and her role in *The Divine Comedy* provides an opportunity to discuss the possible allegorical meanings of Beatrice and Dante the

pilgrim. Why would it be inappropriate for Beatrice to be Dante's guide for the entire journey?

3. Do you agree with Dante's treatment of the great "pagans" of the classical world? Discuss the medieval world view that made such a treatment of "pagans" necessary.

4. What does the pilgrim Dante learn from his journey about human nature and the universe? How might you relate Dante's journey to analogous journeys today? Is there an analogy between the Inferno and the psyche or unconscious, between the descent into Hell and the Dark Night of the Soul? Are there other contemporary infernos?

5. Discuss the rationale for Dante's hierarchy of sins. Does our society subscribe to this hierarchy? Do you agree with Dante's treatment of suicides? How is his reluctance to condemn his friend Ser Brunetto Latino reflected in the poetry of Canto 15? Do you agree with his choices for the deepest circle of Hell? If not, who would you put there, and why?

6. Is Dante more successful at portraying Satan or God? What challenges did Dante face in depicting the nature of goodness in *The Purgatorio* and *The Paradiso*? How does Dante deal with the challenge of portraying God? Do believers and nonbelievers differ in their appreciation of Dante's descriptions of Heaven and Hell?

7. Does *The Divine Comedy* fit into the epic tradition established by Homer, Virgil, and *Beowulf*?

8. Discuss the similarities and differences between the last canto of *The Inferno* and the last canto of *The Paradiso*. How successful was Dante in his portrayal of a beatific vision?

9. Select a class or category of sinners and discuss how their punishments fit their crime.

Projects

1. Design your own Hell. You needn't do a full-dress version, but you should designate more than one group of sinners whom you wish to see punished. Are there new sins that need to be added to Dante's list? Be specific in your descriptions of your sinners, their sins, and the appropriate punishments you invent for them, using the principle of symbolic retribution. (We encourage you to designate real people, living or dead.) You may supplement your paper with drawings if you wish.

2. Dante's descent story invites comparisons with other famous descent or underworld accounts: Inanna, Odysseus, Aeneas, and Jesus (see Gospel of Nicodemus). How is Dante's journey into Hell different from the others? How do these journeys reveal different world views? Some students might be interested in researching and illustrating an evolutionary account of underworlds and hells.

3. Dante assumed that all individuals were capable of choice, that humans choose good or evil. Today our attitudes toward behaviors are complicated with theories about the influence of genetics and environment on peoples' actions. Have we swung too far in the opposite direction from individual responsibility? What are several modern theories that explain human evil? Use these theories to discuss Dante's judgments about premarital sex, homosexuality, suicide, and obesity.

4. As a method for investigating the differences between Italian and English, gather together several stanzas of *The Divine Comedy* in the original Italian and at least two different translations of these stanzas. Compare them, and then attempt a translation of your own.

5. Dante's poems written to Beatrice were influenced by the troubadour tradition. Who were the troubadours? Are there any women today who serve as Beatrices to artists? Are there men who serve as an inspiration to women artists? Write a troubadour poem to your love and inspiration.

BARDIC POETRY

The tangled history of the preservation of Irish, Welsh, and Anglo-Saxon literature is traced in the general headnote to this section. The student should be able to draw certain conclusions from this story: The cultural remains of a colonized people are frequently preserved by the colonizer; much may be lost in time through the accidents of textual transmission; and we are often only able to guess the grandeur of the original society as a result. Even so, the student should attempt to distinguish the unique qualities of the Irish, Welsh, and Anglo-Saxon cultures as far as possible.

One should note the common threads of the bardic tradition. Welsh scholar Gwyn Jones defines the bardic poet as a public figure with the business of recounting the life of the hero, the triumphs and disasters of society, the relationship of human life to that of the cosmos and nature, and the importance of certain virtues (valor, loyalty, service, and reward). This material and what might be called the bardic outlook are common to the Irish, Welsh, and Anglo-Saxon traditions.

The story of Derdriu, part of a much longer cycle in one of the great national epics of Ireland, is actually an explanation of certain desertions from the ranks of the Ulster heroes. But the character Derdriu (called Deidre in later versions) who emerges from this story absolutely overpowers it; her tragic rebellion is one of the great moments of epic literature.

The survival of the few authentic poems of Taliesin and Aneirin is extremely fortuitous. The work of these great bards of the North was undoubtedly collected and transcribed in their day, but the cruel wars their kinsmen fought and lost to the Anglo-Saxons must have led to the destruction of most Welsh bardic poetry, theirs included. What is left is fragmentary. Taliesin's poems of King Urien's court bear the stamp of the earliest bardic literature, lays sung or recited by a professional bard under a king's protection. Aneirin's more extended lament, *The Gododdin*, although available to us only in a poorly edited version, seems to express the Welsh tragic sensibility.

Anglo-Saxon culture was not buried under military defeat as was Welsh culture; it was slowly rendered obsolete by the native conversion to Latin Christianity and buried altogether by the subsequent arrival of the Norman culture and language after the Battle of Hastings in 1066. Although a large body of Anglo-Saxon literature survived, many of the great poems come down to us in single manuscripts. The major linguistic changes between the Old English of *Beowulf* and the Middle English of Chaucer have made the Anglo-Saxon poetic remains appear more marginal than they would otherwise seem.

It is tempting to read passages from Old English poetry in the original language in order to show students how different the language is from our own. But fairness demands an effort to show hidden similarities of vocabulary and syntax and the surprising energy of the Anglo-Saxon word stock in our language even today. (If you feel nervous about reading Old English aloud, excellent recordings are available, such as Jess Bessinger's rendition of lines from *Beowulf*.)

Questions for Discussion and Writing

1. Compare *The Exile of the Sons of Uisliu* to the opening of *The Iliad*, in which an argument among heroes weakens the Greek host on the battlefield. How is the Irish saga distinct from its Greek counterpart?

2. Compare the story of Derdriu with the tragedy of Dido in *The Aeneid*. Which woman do you believe is the stronger character?

3. The story of *The Gododdin* centers on the loss of an entire fighting force in a single battle. Compare the content, method of treatment, and poetic form of this story with *The Song of Roland*.

4. What do the *Cotton MS. Maxims* tell you about the culture of the Anglo-Saxon people?

5. Treat *The Wife's Lament* and *The Husband's Message* as part of the same story and describe what is "primitive" in this late Anglo-Saxon story.

Project

Jot down a number of ideas that you believe comprise the heroic ideal in epic literature; make a point-by-point comparison between one work from the British Isles and one from the ancient world (Mesopotamia, Greece, or Rome). You can include *Beowulf* in the answer to this question.

BEOWULF

Culturally speaking, *Beowulf* stands somewhere between *The Epic of Gilgamesh* and the works of Homer and Virgil. It is a heroic tale with some supernatural elements; it also reflects the warrior ethos of the Germanic tradition, as can be seen in the giving of treasure, the valuing of noble deeds, and the idea of the *comitatus,* or tribal society. The Christian overlay in the poem is more than a series of decorative additions; the entire last episode carries a strong Christian argument (the decline of paganism before the rise of a new society). There is also an antiquarian issue that is both challenging and frustrating to the would-be interpreter: How consciously does the composer of the poem date his characters?

The discursive structure of the poem may give students some difficulty. It is a good idea to start out with the genealogical charts of the major kingdoms: Geats, Danes, and Swedes (see illustration). The frequent digressions the poet makes should be explained in the light of Germanic history and culture. They provide a great storehouse of information about the proper attitudes a warrior should have, the deepest concerns of tribal society, and the relation of fairy tales about monsters to heroic narrative. At this point you might want to sketch out the linear plot of the narrative: the slaying of Grendel and Grendel's mother, the fifty-year interlude, and the slaying of the dragon.

The closest analogue to *Beowulf* among the surviving world epics is the Old Norse prose epic *Volsunga Saga*, which recalls the Germanic and Scandinavian traditions of the fifth to eighth centuries. The German *Nibelungenlied* contains much of the same epic material but was composed much later, at the beginning of the thirteenth century. Because there are no Scandinavian or Germanic epics in our anthology besides *Beowulf*, the teacher interested in pursuing themes of the Germanic heroic age might consult the operatic works of Richard Wagner. Scenes from the Nibelung Ring operas should sufficiently evoke Heroic Age symbolism, although an effort should be made to downplay Wagner's romanticism.

The serious themes of *Beowulf*—brotherhood in defense of the tribe or nation, valor in battle against the creatures of darkness, and the transience of the things of this world—are common enough that affinities with other literature will come to mind. A poem so socially and ethically rooted cries out for comparison to *The Iliad*, the story of Exodus, the Gospels of the New Testament, Virgil's *Aeneid*, and Milton's *Paradise Lost*. A theme that powerfully weaves its way through all these works is redemption or the quest for redemption. No classroom encounter with *Beowulf* should fail to bring in such abstractions.

For other useful discussion, see Jess Bessinger (ed.), *Approaches to Teaching Beowulf* (1984), a Modern Language Association book.

Genealogies

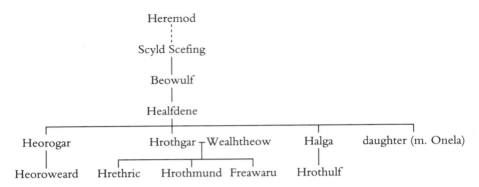

The Danes

Heremod

Scyld Scefing

Beowulf

Healfdene

Heorogar — Hrothgar ⊤ Wealhtheow — Halga — daughter (m. Onela)

Heoroweard — Hrethric — Hrothmund — Freawaru — Hrothulf

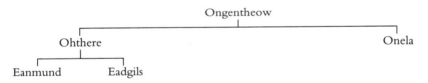

The Swedes

Ongentheow

Ohthere — Onela

Eanmund — Eadgils

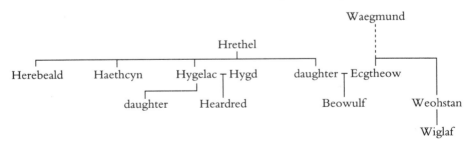

The Geats and the Waegmundings

Waegmund

Hrethel

Herebeald — Haethcyn — Hygelac ⊤ Hygd — daughter ⊤ Ecgtheow

daughter — Heardred — Beowulf — Weohstan

Wiglaf

GENEALOGY OF THE MAJOR KINGDOMS

1. Did the same poet or different poets compose the two parts of *Beowulf* (the fight with Grendel and his mother, and the dragon fight)? Could the poet of the youthful Beowulf also tell the story of the hero in old age?
2. Is this poem primarily a celebration of the days of monsters and dragons, a celebration of a community united under a hero, or a tragedy about the decline and fall of such societies? Or is it more than one of these things?
3. Compare the story of Wiglaf and the retainers to the story of Christ and the disciples at the time of the Crucifixion. Do you believe that the composer of *Beowulf* intended such a comparison? Why or why not?
4. What role do the historical digressions play in *Beowulf*? Why does the poet break in so often on the linear plot? Do you find this device effective? Why or why not?
5. Does *Beowulf*, in part or whole, remind you of a Western movie? What conventional elements of the Western do you find in the story? How do you account for this similarity?

Project

Locate the analogues for one or more of the creature stories in *Beowulf*. How does the poet go beyond the known material?

THE SONG OF ROLAND

Like *Beowulf*, the late-eleventh-century *Song of Roland* offers an ethical view of the hero as a battle leader and a symbol of moral purity to his followers. Roland is not a king but a feudal lord, a fierce fighter who has been given command of the rear guard of Charlemagne's forces. He exemplifies the virtue of *fortitudo* (strength) whereas his friend Oliver is known for his *sapientia* (wisdom). Roland can be said to have a tragic flaw: the stubborn pride that keeps him from blowing the horn Olifant when his forces are first attacked. The typical Christian knight at the time of the First Crusade, Roland is also another epic hero in the line of succession from Achilles to Aeneas to Beowulf. He is, of course, a hero in a context: in this case, the Church Militant, Christianity on the path of holy war.

The rigidity of Roland's position is even clearer in the verse that commemorates his activity. The system of *laisses*, grouped stanzas pursuing a common theme, emphasizes that Roland stands for certain virtues and follows a fixed course. Although the characters of this drama are highly conventional (the brave knight, the wise friend, the fighting priest, the great king), the realism is striking; if *The Song of Roland* were a movie, it would be rated "R" for violence. The final segment of the poem, omitted here, drives the point home that justice under the Christian Emperor is swift and unequivocal: The execution of Ganelon and his fellow conspirators is still difficult to read today.

Students may be put off somewhat by the formalized diction and repetitive stanzas of *The Song of Roland*. They should try to read some of the poem aloud, even in an edited, translated version. The incremental repetition lends a martial, rhythmical quality to the *chanson de geste* that must be heard to be appreciated. On a thematic level, the absence of other stories besides that of men at war means that love becomes the love of comrades facing death in battle, perhaps nowhere so evident in Western literature outside of *The*

Iliad. At the same time, the parallel descriptions of the Muslim and Christian forces suggest that all fighting men are essentially the same. Only the traitor is singled out for blame. The pursuit of war is given a status in this poem that may actually become a debating point for the class. What is ethical, one may ask, about a warrior ethic in the first place?

Roland should be compared to the other heroes of literature for his prowess, his virtues, and his faults. His specifically Christian stance may introduce questions of ideology, although it is hard to see this when the Muslims are carbon copies of the Crusader knights. The dynamics of Roland's betrayal by Ganelon are impressive enough to rate comparison with other famous betrayals in literature—Macduff by Macbeth, Caesar by Brutus and the conspirators. His friendship with his peers, especially Oliver and Turpin, calls up questions of other such male friendships from *The Epic of Gilgamesh* to *The Iliad* and on. The death of Roland invites comparison with that of Beowulf.

The Song of Roland should be read alongside the selection from *The Book of Reflections* by Usamah Ibn Munqidh and the "First Contact of Crusaders and Turks" from *History of the First Crusade*, also in this volume. The latter piece should be compared to *Roland* concerning its realism: Is it "more real" than the poem, or is realism a matter of wrestling with the conventions to give the *appearance* of reality?

Questions for Discussion and Writing

1. Compare *The Iliad* and *The Song of Roland* as war epics. In what way does the love of one's fighting companions take the place of love in civilized society? Can you say that the conduct of war may be ethical? Do you approve of the ethics you find in these two works?

2. Compare Roland with Achilles, Aeneas, or Beowulf. Indicate what type of society your two heroes come from, how they express the beliefs of their respective societies, what flaws each may have, and how well you think they represent the aspirations of their times.

3. In the scene where Oliver argues with Roland about the blowing of the horn, whom do you side with? Is Roland's stubbornness a boon or a burden to his men? Is he a good commander, or is he responsible for the bitter fate of his companions?

4. Explore the artistic dimensions of one major character in the work: Roland as hero, Oliver as friend, Turpin as fighter, Ganelon as villain, etc. How good is the poet's portrayal of character? Is it more or less satisfying because it is so conventional?

5. Compare *The Song of Roland* with the excerpts of the Welsh poem *The Gododdin*. The poems are written in a similar verse pattern. Do you see structural similarities in the two works? Thematic similarities? Similar poetic attitudes?

6. Compare *The Song of Roland* with the "First Contact of Crusaders and Turks" from the *History of the First Crusade*. Compare the two authors' views of the holy wars, their methods of treatment, and the success you feel each has attained.

LATIN LYRIC

The inclusion of a few medieval Latin poems, religious and secular, is a feature of most anthology collections going back many years. (See, for example, Charles W. Jones's *Medieval Literature in Translation*, 1950.) We have concentrated on Alcuin and his circle, a few later secular poems, and the Archpoet's *Confession*. Our selection shows the fusion of the religious and secular impulses leading up to the arrival of the European vernacular poetry of the twelfth and thirteenth centuries.

One exercise students might attempt—with caution—is trying to describe the nature of the affection expressed in the early lyrics—by Alcuin for the young monk, Fredugis for the dead Alcuin, and Walafrid Strabo for the cleric Liutger. Homosexual verse existed in the monasteries—Strabo's poem is probably an example—but the sublimation of affection is a literary device known to all time periods. One might find it in the later love poetry of the Provençal courts, the sonnets of Petrarch, Dante's praise of Beatrice, Renaissance lyric, and in other works.

The Latin lyrics "Come, sweetheart, come" and "Softly the west wind blows" actually anticipate Renaissance lyric, the first in its portrayal of a scene where the author hopes a seduction will occur, the second (declined in the feminine, making the speaker female) expressing sorrow over a lost love. The artistry of both pieces is evident in the excellent translations.

Walafrid Strabo, a versatile writer, is the author of one of the poems that gave rise to the notion of the *vagante* or wandering scholar. One suspects that this figure has always had a certain romantic appeal, from the early bardic poet to Jack Kerouac and the Dharma Bums. Certainly the motif is present in the Middle Ages from the eleventh to the thirteenth centuries in the secular Latin tradition. How easily this writing coexists with religious verse is shown in the two selections from Sedulius Scottus, an Easter song and an appeal to his bishop for money so the poet may go out drinking.

The Archpoet's *Confession* is difficult to translate; Helen Waddell has achieved some of the compression and even clumsiness of the fast-paced original. Satiric in intent, the poem invokes lust (the Archpoet is uncomplicatedly heterosexual), gambling, and drinking, placing us in a tavern that becomes a substitute church; a Mass is described in which the wine dispensed is far stronger than that given at Communion. He ends by invoking gluttony as a spur to his poetic gift. One strength of the poem is its pictorial quality; one sees the poet in his surroundings, daring anyone inclined to cast the first stone.

These poems teach well to any student willing to trouble over the poetry. Attention should be given to their humanity, as much as if one were reading Sappho, Catullus, or Li Po; to their contemporaneity, especially in the love poetry; and to their provocative quality. The Archpoet is a public figure, much like Boccaccio and Chaucer. His great daring is that he removes himself from past convention, letting the chips fall (so to speak) where they may.

Questions for Discussion and Writing

1. How conventional are the voices of "Lament for the Cuckoo," "Lament for Alcuin," and "To the Cleric Liutger?" Why does Alcuin disguise his young monk as a cuckoo? Why does Fredugis treat Alcuin's death as his sorrow over leaving his house? Is there a personal note in Strabo's memory of Liutger?

2. What do you make of the image of wandering or living off the land in Strabo's "The Wandering Scholar?" How much of this image seems conventional and how much of it fresh and original?

3. In the lyric "Come, sweetheart, come," why does the poet spend so much time describing the setting only to say that it matters nothing to him once his desires are satisfied? What does this suggest to you about the tone of the poem?

4. Comment on the fusion of nature imagery and romantic feeling in "Softly the west wind blows." Does a winter poem expressing grief over parting work the same as a spring poem expressing the delight of new love?

45

5. The Archpoet expresses his mood at the beginning of his *Confession* as "bitterness of soul" and "fierce indignation." Would you have gleaned this from the rest of the poem? What *would* you have thought was the dominant feeling? Can you reconcile these descriptions, if they differ?

6. At the end of his *Confession*, the Archpoet dares anyone who has not fallen prey to the same vices to cast the first stone. What company do you think he includes in this taunt and why does he make it?

Project

Compare the artistry and sincerity of one or more of these lyrics with works by one of the following: Catullus, Li Po, Petrarch, the Provençal poets, the Renaissance poets.

PROVENÇAL POETRY

The reader of Provençal lyric should also consult the treatise of Andreas Capellanus on *The Art of Courtly Love* and the Breton *lai* of Marie de France, *The Lay of Chevrefoil*, printed elsewhere in this section. The treatise of Andreas was composed at the height of Provençal troubadour poetry, in the last quarter of the twelfth century, in the court of Poitiers where some of the best poetry was being composed and recited. The *lai* of Marie de France brilliantly captures the *ethos* of courtly love, especially emphasizing the ideals of delicacy and concealment.

The origins of Provençal poetry from the more robust *pastourelle* are easy to trace; the first poem of Guillaume IX, Duke of Aquitaine (d. 1127), which begins mockingly, "My companions, I am going to make a *vers* that is refined," is a good example of the earlier, bawdy poetry that is about to be replaced by works in the courtly tradition. Guillaume's second, courtly poem, "Now when we see the meadows once again," along with Marcabru's "By the fountain in the orchard," show the masculine lover subdued and educated by the desires of the woman in question; the theme of surrender to a higher authority is both feudal in design (showing fealty to the lady) and psychologically sound, in that it is flattering to the recipient. Bernart de Ventadorn's "My heart is so full of joy," a flamboyant piece, still firmly places the power of adjudication of the lover's plea with the lady. Raimbaut d'Orange's "Listen, Lords ... but I don't know what" addresses a male audience but depends on the rules of courtly behavior; he simply says that his four-year pursuit of the lady is driving him mad. (There is an off-color metaphor in this poem reminiscent of the tone in Guillaume's *pastourelle*.) Clearly all of these poems, and poets, are steeped in the courtly love tradition.

The Countess of Dia provides us with a valuable reality check on the works of the above poets. A troubadour herself, rumored to have been a lover of Raimbaut, she writes openly in "I've lately been in great distress" of desiring to sleep with a knight if he will only follow her rule, and again in "Of things I'd rather keep in silence I must sing" of a knight's infidelity and haughty bearing, which she wishes him to curb for her sake. It may be that the dialogue she establishes with these knights is purely literary; whatever the case, her poems are a good example of the love debates Andreas Capellanus describes.

The later poets in our collection are concerned with other matters besides love. Bertran de Born in "I shall make a half *sirventes* about both kings" laments both the fortunes of war and its brutal outcome; his conclusion manages to be both ambivalent and moralistic at the same time. Peire Vidal's "With my breath I draw toward me the air" invokes both the land of Provence and the beautiful body of the lady he left there. Because it puts love in a context—even encloses it within a metaphor—it is broader in theme than the usual poem of courtly love.

Students should find some interest in the conventions of this poetry and how they come down through history. The poems of Petrarch and some of the writers of the Renaissance (Wyatt and Donne immediately come to mind) also revolve around sublimation on the one hand and masculine wit and passion on the other. Beyond just the poetry, students will be tempted to see in their own romantic relationships some lingering vestiges of the courtly *ethos*, as well as the problems it creates. How far the teacher is willing to go in encouraging personal revelation depends on bravery or foolhardiness. Be warned: The stuff still works.

For comments on the Provençal tradition, see Peter Dronke's *The Medieval Lyric* (1968), pp. 109–66. For a closer discussion, including treatment of several of the poems included in this collection, see Ingeborg Glier's "Troubadours and Minnesang," in Roris Ford (ed.), *Medieval Literature: The European Inheritance* (1984), vol. I, part 2, pp. 167–87.

Questions for Discussion and Writing

1. Show contrasting examples of the *pastourelle* and courtly love tradition. Do you think these are two sides of the same coin, or does the courtly love convention completely change the treatment of love expressed by the poets?
2. Why do you think humor enters so frequently into the poems of the troubadours? To whom is it directed? What is it intended to accomplish? Illustrate your view by analyzing one of the humorous poems included here.
3. Assume that Raimbaut d'Orange and the Countess of Dia are holding a love debate (whether or not they are actually lovers) in their poems. Discuss the attitudes about love the two take in light of your own understanding. Then ask yourself how much your understanding may depend on the ideal of love developed in the late Middle Ages.
4. Comment on the individuality of the troubadour poet compared with that of the medieval Latin poet or the Bardic singer. Is the new individual voice "pure," or is it, too, partly a poetic convention? How can you tell?

Project

Compare a troubadour poem with a poem by Petrarch, Donne, or Shakespeare. Itemize similarities and differences, mentioning the content of the material, the conventions of behavior implied by the work, the nature of the person addressed, and the poet's goal in writing the poem.

MARIE DE FRANCE
The Lay of Chevrefoil (The Honeysuckle)

The *lais* of Marie de France, at once mysterious and simple, are especially noteworthy for their deftness of touch and their condensation of poetic material. The reader should also notice the "signature" in this poem, the symbolic honeysuckle vine and hazel tree that, once grown together, require each other to survive. In the story of Tristan and

Isolt, rife with melodrama and the makings of tragedy, Marie economically uses this one reference to suggest the true nature of the lovers' mutual attraction.

The lovers' meeting takes place in a forest in Cornwall, in a context of mutual desire; as to the outcome the poet is discreet, saying the pair "took great joy in each other" but hastening to add, "He spoke to her as much as he desired, / she told him whatever she liked." Isolt promises Tristan she will plead for his right to return to King Mark's court, then leaves him. Tristan returns to Wales, where he writes down this *lai* "in order to remember the words" describing his adventure.

Superficially at least, the story follows the prescription of Andreas Capellanus in *The Art of Courtly Love* that the highest form of love is both secretive and adulterous. But of course that circumstance is already part of the matter of this famous story. Isolt's desire to negotiate Tristan's return to Cornwall also follows the material of the legend, this time without any particular relationship to the doctrine of courtly love. The refinement of the couple's love, however, again squares nicely with the theories of love being circulated around the courts of Marie of Champagne in the South of France at the time. Because Marie de France wrote many *lais*, some in conformity with the rules of courtly love and some not, the reader must decide whether there is a reference to those rules in this piece or not.

Questions for Discussion and Writing

1. This appears in the text to be a prearranged meeting. Why does it require good faith, intuition, and tact on the part of the two lovers? What about logistics?
2. Marie de France tells a complicated story in a short space. What part of the legend of Tristan and Isolt is important to her here? What is the essential story *she* wants to tell?
3. With so little being said, do you have any sense of the character of the two lovers? What do you see concerning their personalities?
4. What does the "signature" add to the poem? How would you say it is handled? Is the emphasis too much, just right, or too little?
5. Compare this story with the selection from *The Tale of Genji*, paying special attention to the use of gestures, the social conventions of the time, and the arrangement of meetings.

GIOVANNI BOCCACCIO
The Decameron

The Decameron might be included in either the Middle Ages or the Renaissance section of this anthology, for Boccaccio is contemporary with both Chaucer and Petrarch. We have placed *The Decameron* in the Middle Ages because its framed narrative connects it with the framed narratives in Chaucer and Dante and because its melding of flesh and spirit, comic and tragic, tavern and cathedral is characteristic of late medieval literature.

Boccaccio's tales are often read out of context—as one of *Playboy's* "ribald classics," for example. His tales of sexual exploits have a long literary ancestry, extending back to the satyr plays in classical Greece. In this anthology, some other examples of this tradition can be found in Catullus' writings, in Aristophanes' *Lysistrata*, and in Chaucer's Merchant's Tale. We have made a point of including the frame narrative and three quite different tales—from the bawdy story of Alibech and Rustico to the tragic story of Tancred and Ghismonda—to enable students to place the tales into the larger context that Boccaccio put them in and to suggest the range of his subject matter.

The frame narrative offers an interesting variation on the pilgrimage theme that unifies our medieval section. Escaping into the country would seem to be a way of running from the spiritual, life-and-death issues that inform such pilgrimages as Dante's. However, the apparent avoidance of such questions can also be read as a way of drawing attention to them by heightening the irony of the contrast between the Black Death and the diversions of storytelling.

Questions for Discussion and Writing

1. What does the frame situation do to contextualize the tales that are told? Would these tales work just as well without the frame?
2. What contemporary situations might provide a frame comparable to the one used by Boccaccio?
3. How does Filomena use a frame narrative in her tale of Melchisedech?
4. What does Filomena say is the theme of her tale of Melchisedech? What other themes does the tale develop?
5. In the tale of Alibech and Rustico, is it important that Rustico is a monk? Why or why not? What makes this tale funny? How might it be recast in contemporary terms to make the humor accessible to a contemporary reader?
6. Are Alibech and Rustico mere stereotypes or does Boccaccio individualize them? What does the marriage of Alibech and Neerbale contribute to the story?
7. The tale of Alibech and Rustico is one of a group of tales "of those who by their wits obtained something they greatly desired or regained something they lost." How does this category affect the way you read the story?
8. Is the story of Tancred and Ghismonda a tragedy? Why or why not?
9. What does the frame situation contribute to the impact of this story?

Projects

1. Compare Boccaccio's handling of the tale of Melchisedech with Lessing's version of it in *Nathan the Wise*.
2. Compare Boccaccio's tale of Tancred and Ghismonda with *Antigone*. How are the issues similar? How do they differ?
3. Take a joke and expand it into a tale like one of Boccaccio's. Notice the devices you use to elaborate the narrative.

JOHN MANDEVILLE
The Travels of Sir John Mandeville

Mandeville's Travels exists in the ill-defined space between literature that is popular in its own right and literature that is supplementary to some great work—in this case, *The Canterbury Tales* of Geoffrey Chaucer. Not so long ago, the *Travels* still commanded a broad readership through many successive printings. Its description of a pilgrimage to Jerusalem was also seen as a useful background to Chaucer's literary pilgrimage. Thus, its inclusion in this anthology should not be regarded as surprising.

In our excerpt, beginning at a "turn toward Jerusalem," we are plunged into a desert world of Bedouins and other nomadic tribes, depicted as strong and fierce warriors but also "right felonious and foul, and of cursed kind." We move on to Hebron, then as now one of the holy cities of the Middle East. So we are on our way, in the fluid, rolling prose we have come to associate with the author called Mandeville, whether he is a real English knight or a Dutch literary invention.

Mandeville's Travels is both a literary guide to pilgrimage and an ideological work that offers an opinion, balanced for its time, of the Muslim and Christian worlds of the fourteenth century. In its acerbity and inquisitiveness, the book is a lens probing into the Holy Land after hundreds of years of Christian invasions and bloody and fruitless conflict. At the same time, it presents a picture of the pilgrim himself, a moderate man, an Englishman, peering about, noting down, and remembering to judge not (at least, not *too* much) lest he be judged.

In this anthology, the book invites comparison not only with *The Canterbury Tales* but with an earlier account of a pilgrimage to Mecca, the *Travels* of Ibn Jubayr, composed in the tenth century. The differences are substantial; Jubayr's journey was real, the result of a desire for atonement, whereas Mandeville's is a composite account based on a number of other texts. Jubayr's religious piety is devout bordering on fanatical, whereas our author is always a little too curious about the world and its history to concentrate exclusively on the adoration of God. Jubayr's writing is purely descriptive, whereas this author's is also historical and more than a little gossipy.

Another possible comparison in our anthology is with the early fifteenth-century pilgrimage of Margery Kempe to Jerusalem, available in an excerpt. Here Kempe is the subjective one; it is fair to say that her real subject is always herself. But Mandeville's state of mind remains closer to that of his English counterpart of the fifteenth century than to the devout Muslim pilgrim from Cordova centuries before.

Mandeville's pilgrimage is, despite its professed religious yearnings, a human affair, pitched to human interests and human failings. The opinion, even the bias, that slips in is both diverting and entertaining: This is not, after all, a work of instruction. The political observations are designed for popular acceptance, and so are neither too zealous on one hand nor too timid on the other. The prose is serviceable almost to a fault. Make of it what you will, the *Travels* will hold the reader's attention until the main thread of the narrative is picked up again.

Questions for Discussion and Writing

1. Most of what the author of the *Travels* tells us seems to be derived from other sources. How does this affect the tone and style of his narrative?
2. What is the effect of describing the Church of the Holy Sepulchre and the surrounding area both physically and in the light of Old and New Testament tradition? Does it help or hurt the narrative to work from different perspectives?
3. At the time of writing, Jerusalem is in Muslim (Saracen) hands. The author says he has letters from the soldan (sultan) allowing him entry into the holy shrines. What is the effect on the reader of such information?
4. Compare the description of the *Templum domini* (Temple of the Lord) in Chapter 11 with the description of the Ka'bah in Mecca by Ibn Jubayr in his *Travels*. Comment on the narrative and descriptive strategies employed by each author.

Project

Compare Mandeville's description of the Muslims and his ideas concerning religious tolerance with the writings of other authorities in this collection: Usamah Ibn Munqidh on the Frankish Crusaders, the anonymous author on the Christian warriors in the First Crusade, and the author of *The Song of Roland* on the Muslims.

GEOFFREY CHAUCER
The Canterbury Tales

The Canterbury Tales is one of the centerpieces of the Western literature section of the Middle Ages unit. In form and content, it reinforces the theme of pilgrimage, even as it introduces a medley of other concerns important to the Middle Ages, including the place of chivalry in the social order, romantic and spiritual love, the proper duties of clergymen and friars, the petty rivalries between tradesmen and artisans, and the need for a jolly good sense of humor in a world where things were scarcely what they seemed and where accident, misfortune, and death tested the faith of even the most pious. As the Canterbury pilgrims engage in their lively merrymaking, their tales remind them (and us) that the medieval world, despite its spiritual and chivalric ideals, was full of falsehood, hypocrisy, greed, pride, gluttony, lust, despair, and finally death. Students catch on quickly to the excitement and irony of these tales and thoroughly enjoy seeing through the masks of their tellers.

We begin our approach to Chaucer by going through the descriptions of the major characters in the General Prologue, making sure the students sense the diverse social portrait that Chaucer has assembled here and underscoring the purpose of the journey to Canterbury. We examine the different ways Chaucer treats the characters, from the respectful portrayal of the Knight and Parson, to the gentle irony of the descriptions of the Prioress and the Wife of Bath, to the mocking depictions of the Friar and Summoner. Students may recognize certain stock character types among the pilgrims, and of course in the case of the Wife of Bath and the Pardoner, whose tales we include in our selection, we ask them to discuss the suitability of the tale to its teller. The framing story invites comparison with the tales within tales of *The Decameron* or the Arabic collection of tales the *1001 Nights*, which opens into further discussion about the role of stories—narratives—in society.

THE WIFE OF BATH'S PROLOGUE AND TALE

In contrasting the Wife's own story with the story she tells, many questions arise about the sexual politics during the medieval period, the role of women in the social order, the subordination of women by the church, and the place of marriage. It is useful to compare the Wife of Bath to Margery Kempe, and to discuss their very different relation to or use of church doctrine. The Wife's defense of women certainly invites comparison to that of Christine de Pizan. The Wife of Bath, of course, stands out as a powerful iconoclast, challenging the authority of the church fathers with her appeal to experience. It is useful to ask students about the strengths and limits of the Wife of Bath's apparent feminism.

THE PARDONER'S PROLOGUE AND TALE

As mentioned in the headnote, an essential question about the rakish, greedy Pardoner's tale is whether or not a man of his moral failings can tell a moral tale. His tale of the three greedy young men who kill each other in their lust for gold carries a powerful moral, despite the fact that the Pardoner himself ignores the moral implications of his tale and in fact brags about his success at extorting money. Indeed, he is so carried away with his story that he tries to collect offerings from his present audience, invoking the anger of the Host. Discussion here might center around the social or didactic function of narratives, the apparent moral blindness of the Pardoner, or the contempt for material wealth taught, if not practiced, by the medieval church.

1. Discuss how the pilgrimage in *The Canterbury Tales* compares to that in Dante's *Divine Comedy* or another pilgrimage narrative in this anthology. How do Chaucer's pilgrims differ from Dante's?

2. Discuss the various degrees of irony in Chaucer's presentation of the pilgrims in the General Prologue.

3. How are the Wife of Bath and the Pardoner suited to tell their tales? Are they right for their stories, intimately connected with them, detached, or engaged? How are these tales related to the frame story?

4. Discuss the Wife of Bath's views on marriage. How are her views different from those of the Church? Compare her reasons for going on pilgrimage to those of Margery Kempe, or her defense of women to that of Christine de Pizan.

5. Compare the structure of *The Canterbury Tales* to that of Boccaccio's *Decameron*. Discuss the effect and importance of the framing story. How do the individual tales and their prologues sustain the frame story?

Projects

1. Create a dialogue between Li Po and Chaucer on the relationship between drinking wine and spiritual enlightenment—that is, on the connection between the tavern and the cathedral.

2. How do Chaucer's *Canterbury Tales*, Dante's *Divine Comedy*, and the architecture of a Gothic cathedral characterize the Western Medieval world view? How is that view different from that we find in *The Tale of Genji*, the *1001 Nights*, or in Li Po's poetry?

CHRISTINE DE PIZAN
The Book of the City of Ladies

Like the Wife of Bath's prologue, *The Book of the City of Ladies* raises issues of misogyny and misogynist literature. It is a good strategy to make students aware of the long and powerful tradition behind such works as *The Romance of the Rose*, the text in a long line of woman-hating texts that finally drives de Pizan to despair. Ernst Robert Curtius' landmark study *European Literature and the Latin Middle Ages* (1953) sets forth that history in some detail in Chapter 6, "The Goddess Natura." Briefly, Curtius argues that the female deity Natura was thought of by classical writers from Ovid on as a personification of the power of nature, the cosmic force that did not procreate, like Zeus or Jove or the Judeo-Christian God, but that birthed and nurtured earthly life. Under Christianity, Natura increasingly became identified with human women, who, as the bearers and nurses of children, were thought to be closer than men to the cycles of nature. Woman is "the gate of hell" to Tertullian, and, according to Clement of Alexandria, "Every woman ought to be filled with shame that she is a woman." Woman is the temptress who lures man away from his goal of purity by her very being, and she is increasingly despised by male writers, especially after the clerical rules of celibacy were instituted in the eleventh century. By the time *The Romance of the Rose* was written, misogynist diatribe had a long smug tradition behind it.

In relation to this tradition, *The Book of the City of Ladies* is important in a number of ways. First, even though spiritual beings appear and wondrous events occur, de Pizan uses brilliant psychological realism to depict how an oppressed and despised person can come to believe her oppressor and proceed to oppress and despise herself and all her sex. That is exactly the despair Christine is in danger of succumbing to in the opening scene, as she finds herself overwhelmed by the chorus of misogynist voices, despite her own personal experience of the goodness of women.

Second, the text dramatically demonstrates the sheer relief from oppression that occurs the moment Christine inserts herself in what has been for centuries a wholly male dialogue, and begins simply to speak back to the massive body of misogynist literature, a hefty and many-storied city in its own right, a city built brick-by-brick of Wicked Women, of Eves and Jezebels, Helens and Medeas and Xantippes.

Christine is tutored and championed by the virtues of Reason, Rectitude, and Justice; although woman's sphere is said to be the heart and man's the head, the heart virtues of Faith, Hope, and Charity are too mild and gentle to prevail against misogyny. Christine chooses to fight with more tough-minded and more secular virtues: logic, firm concepts of morality, and legal principles.

Questions for Discussion and Writing

1. What precipitates de Pizan's despair and self-hatred? What sight breaks through the miasma of her depression, and how is that sight symbolically appropriate?
2. Although de Pizan remarks that they can be told apart only with difficulty, what are the particular attributes of Reason, Rectitude, and Justice? Why are these the qualities de Pizan chooses as her guides instead of Faith, Hope, and Charity, the virtues St. Paul lists as characteristic of Christianity?
3. What object does each lady carry, and what is its significance?
4. How does the central allegorical image of the city work? Does de Pizan's allegorical city bear any resemblance to the allegorical cities of St. Augustine or Dante?
5. What method of argument does Justice use to refute the charge that women secretly wish to be raped?

Projects

1. Each portrait of a noble woman is another building stone for de Pizan's City of Ladies. Construct a small portion of a modern City of Ladies; expose as false some misogynist myth by giving brief portraits of contemporary women whose lives refute it.
2. Compare *The Book of the City of Ladies* with contemporary artist Judy Chicago's installation *The Dinner Party*.

MARGERY KEMPE
The Book of Margery Kempe

Margery Kempe's is said to be the first known autobiography written in English. Students may be put off initially by a subject who continually refers to herself as "this poor creature," who has visions, and who describes herself weeping and roaring to a degree that alienated many in her own lifetime. They may need to be convinced that Kempe, unusual though she is, comes within a tradition of married female mystics such as Saint Birgitta of Sweden (1303–1373) and Dorothea of Montau (1347–1394), who weep copiously and seek to live chastely. They may need help to see Margery as a courageous woman seeking to break out of middle-class domesticity into a life that, though fraught with anxiety and danger, allows her the freedom to express her deepest self in prayer, fasting, pilgrimage, and chastity.

It is worthwhile to compare Kempe's feisty account with the measured and meditative autobiography of her Latin-speaking predecessor, St. Augustine, and to ask how each chooses to represent the self, and what sorts of details and episodes each chooses to tell as high points of a life spent seeking God. Inevitably, the theme of pilgrimage also recalls *The Canterbury Tales* and its fictional Wife of Bath, with whom Margery Kempe shares certain characteristics—lust, curiosity, and enthusiasm for life, to suggest a few. Kempe's autobiography gives vivid details about pilgrimage abroad and its rewards and hazards that add to a student's conception of those medieval journeys. Students may be interested to compare her travel accounts with those of other travelers and pilgrims in this volume, including Ibn Jubayr and Sir John Mandeville.

Margery Kempe was several times in her life threatened with being charged with Lollardy; students may look to *The Inferno* for Dante's descriptions of heretics. The strong attraction the world and the flesh exert on souls who aspire to sanctity, a theme that runs throughout many of these medieval texts, is certainly present here, and in delightfully idiosyncratic detail, as Kempe tries to succeed at various business ventures, prides herself on her fashionably slashed tippets, and lusts for a man who is not her husband.

Questions for Discussion and Writing

1. What sorts of things does Kempe omit from her account of her life that we would expect to find in a contemporary autobiography?
2. Why do you think Kempe did not enter a religious order? What are her experiences with members of the clergy?
3. What are the stages by which Kempe and her husband reach a compromise about their married life?
4. Characterize Kempe's visions. What sorts of things concerning Christ and the Holy Family does she visualize?
5. Compare Kempe's account of pilgrimage with the pilgrimage described in *The Canterbury Tales*. Do Kempe's experiences have any secular aspects?
6. How does Kempe's autobiography differ from St. Augustine's? Are they equally self-critical? Do they have the same aim in telling their stories?
7. Compare Kempe with Chaucer's Wife of Bath. What characteristics do they share?

Project

Imagine Margery Kempe as one of the Canterbury pilgrims. How would Chaucer describe her? Write a portrait of her in the style of the Prologue. What sort of tale do you think she would choose to tell?

EVERYMAN

In some ways this is the easiest work to teach in the medieval section. It presents the spiritual journey of humankind through life toward death in a straightforward, accessible way, and it is a simple vehicle through which to explain medieval Christian doctrine. The things of this world are shown to be transitory and even dangerous to the quest for salvation. The frame around the play, in which God sends Death to seek Everyman at the beginning and the learned Doctor arrives to explain what becomes of Everyman's soul at the end, satisfies a need for definition that the modern student may share with the medieval audience. With the headnote, the normalized Middle English text, and the notes, the instructor should be able to present a clear, focused interpretation of the work.

Whatever the truth about the development of medieval morality plays from liturgy to drama, there is a liturgical, devotional quality lying behind the dramatic speeches that make up *Everyman*. It might be worthwhile to stage certain scenes in class, such as the first encounter between Death and Everyman; the arrival of Knowledge, with his promise to stay by Everyman's side; and Everyman descending into his grave, abandoned by Beauty, Strength, Discretion, and Five Wits, but followed by Good Deeds. The stark, simple scenes and the plain, unadorned English stand out better for students if presented in this fashion.

Everyman in some ways perfectly embodies Augustinian theology, which yields to a spiritual interpretation of individual life and counts all worldly affairs from the perspective of salvation. Here as elsewhere, humankind is the *homo viator*, the traveler through life toward the mystery of death. Thus *Everyman* helps to interpret more complicated medieval narrative such as Chaucer's *Canterbury Tales*, as well as Dante's *Divine Comedy*, which applies the same perspective to a dream vision of life after death. It also refers us to later English works such as *Doctor Faustus* and *Pilgrim's Progress*.

The headnote suggests readings to help locate the available scholarship on the medieval church and stage; in addition, it cites three specialized interpretations of *Everyman*. The instructor might also do well to study *Everyman* in the medieval morality tradition. A. C. Cawley's edition, *Everyman and Medieval Morality Plays* (rev. 1974), provides the best text and introduction. Also see Richard Axton's "The Morality Tradition," in Boris Ford, ed., *The New Pelican Guide to English Literature: Medieval Literature*, vol. I, part 1 (1982), 340–52; and Sumiko Miyajima's *The Theatre of Man: Dramatic Technique and Stagecraft in the English Medieval Moral Plays* (1977), a work concentrating on performance, as the title suggests.

Questions for Discussion and Writing

1. Analyze the structure of the play, including the interpretive frame and the action on Earth. Where does the dramatic center appear? Is this any different from the structure of classical and modern drama?

2. Whom does Everyman represent? How is his character developed? In what sense is he individual and in what sense is he typical of all humanity?

3. How are the other characters developed? How much are they individuals? How does the allegory work in the play as a whole? Why do they disappear in the order they do?

4. What scenes are especially powerful? How are they presented? Comment on the effects of language and staging in these scenes.

5. Compare the religious doctrine in *Everyman* with that of St. Augustine's *Confessions*. Where are there clear similarities? Where does the play seem to simplify Christian doctrine? What about justification by faith and justification by works?

6. In what sense does the doctrine of *Everyman* suggest a simple key to Christian beliefs as they affect such larger medieval works as Boccaccio's *Decameron*, Chaucer's *Canterbury Tales*, and Dante's *Divine Comedy*?

Project

Stage *Everyman*, assuming dramatic positions and reading the speeches. Pay attention to particulars in the text, such as Everyman's descent into the grave.

THE KORAN

Despite the importance of Islam in the world, many students are ignorant about the life of Muhammad, the contents of the Koran, and the basic tenets of Islam. A basic summary of these materials is provided in the headnote, but additional research might be necessary to provide a context for reading the Koran, which is difficult for students accustomed to reading the Bible. Generally, the Koran lacks the kinds of biographical, narrative, and historical materials that stimulate interest in the Bible, especially the Old Testament.

Founded in the seventh century, Islam is the youngest of the monotheistic world religions, and it is probably the fastest growing religion across the globe. It is the principle religion in North Africa and in a number of Asian countries, and, in recent years, has become well-represented in Europe and the Americas; fewer than one-fifth of Islam's followers are Arab. Efforts should be made to balance the modern, militant images of Islam in the media with the tradition of morality, piety, and scholarship associated with centers of learning in Cairo, Istanbul, and Damascus.

As mentioned in the headnote, at the core of Islam are five pillars, the *arkan ad-din: shahadah,* stating that "there is no God but God [Allah] and Muhammad is the Messenger of God"; *salah,* praying five times each day; *zakat,* the giving of alms, known as a religious tax; *sawm,* the dawn-to-dusk fast during Ramadan; and *hajj,* a pilgrimage to Mecca during one's lifetime. In addition to these requirements, importance is placed on doing good and shunning evil and avoiding usury, gambling, alcohol, and pork. A word repeated in the media is *jihad,* which on the personal level suggests the struggle to be righteous, but on the communal level connotes warfare against the infidel.

The focus of Islam is, of course, Allah: his will, his teachings, his promises. The most important revelation of Allah's will is the Koran (or Qur'an), which is interpreted by a religious scholar called a *shaykh* or *mullah* and administered by a legal authority, called *mufti,* and a community leader, the caliph. Because of the evolution and growing complexity of Islamic communities, however, the Koran was supplemented by an oral tradition of sayings and interpretations known as the Sunna, and written down as the *Hadrith.* It is within this body of material that serious disagreements arise because a certain amount of leeway is necessary in order to adapt to various social and cultural conditions in countries around the world. Disputants often refer to one of Muhammad's sayings: "My community will never agree in an error."

Other than by length, there is no discernible order to the way the 114 suras, or chapters, are organized. Generally, the shorter suras, the most fervent ones, are the earliest. The longer ones, especially the ones from Medina, follow. Allah speaks to readers in the first person; his statements do not provide historical backgrounds or lengthy biographies of important personages, but instead speak to the interpretation of events, the moral implications of actions and situations.

We have selected suras that delineate central doctrines and suras that contain stories of prophetic figures common to both the Judaic and Islamic traditions.

Questions for Discussion and Writing

1. What seem to be the fundamental beliefs of Islam as revealed in Sura II? Choose a portion of Sura II, such as verses 255–260, and compare the writing style and message to one of Jesus' parables and one of Chuang Tzu's pieces.
2. Discuss the attitudes toward women in Suras II and IV. Why are men given authority over women?
3. According to Suras LV and LVI, what will heaven be like? What important role will women play in the afterlife? How are the Christian heaven and hell different from the Islamic?

4. Sura LV describes the creation of jinn. What are jinn? Are there beings in Christianity that serve a similar purpose to jinn?

5. Compare the story of Joseph in Sura XII with the Joseph story in Genesis.

6. In Sura LXXI, Noah has a much grander calling as a prophet than his role in Genesis. Discuss the similarities and differences in the two accounts.

7. Islam recognizes Jesus as a prophet; how does Sura XIX describe the birth and teachings of Jesus in a manner acceptable to Islam? Compare this account with the stories in the Gospels of Luke and Matthew.

8. When is Ramadan celebrated? What significance does this important event have in the life of a Muslim?

9. Compare the *hajj* to the Christian pilgrimage to Jerusalem. What shrines are important to these pilgrimages?

Projects

1. T. E. Lawrence, in Chapter 3 of *The Seven Pillars of Wisdom,* points out that the three major monotheistic religions of the West all arose from the Near Eastern desert; Lawrence believes that the desert itself, its emptiness and clarity, strongly influenced these religions. After reading Lawrence's observations, investigate the role of the desert in Judaism, Christianity, and Islam.

2. Although both Judaism and Islam recognize the patriarchal role of Abraham, different mothers were involved: Sarah bore the line of Hebrews and Hagar was mother to the Arabs. The story seems to explain the enmity between Israelites and Ishmaelites. With books such as Joseph Gaer's *The Lore of the Old Testament* and Sir James Frazer's *Folklore in the Old Testament,* investigate the folk materials and legends that explain the enmity between these two Semitic peoples. How do modern Arabs and Israelites explain the reasons for their antagonism?

IBN HAZM, USAMAH IBN MUNQIDH, IBN JUBAYR

From the beginning of the eighth century until late in the eleventh century, a glorious intellectual culture flourished in Spain, reflecting the continuity of the Umayyad Dynasty in this western outpost of Muslim control (although it was overturned in the East in 750, this dynasty only relinquished power in Spain in 1031). The major urban centers of Cordova, Toledo, Granada, and Seville held out against barbarian and Christian attacks until the eleventh and twelfth centuries, with the Caliphate of Cordova dominating much of what is now Spain and Portugal until 1002, Toledo holding out until 1085, and the final battle between Christian and Muslim forces taking place at Las Navas de Dolosa in 1212. From this active political and intellectual arena we have selected the work of two important Muslim writers: Ibn Hazm, a scholar of Cordova (994–1064), and Ibn Jubayr, a governmental secretary in Granada (b. 1145).

The power of Islam was firmly established in Baghdad in the East by the victory of the Abbasid dynasty in 750. Contending Muslim leaders fought over control of Baghdad, with the Fatimid caliphate of Cairo in leadership in the late tenth and early eleventh centuries, followed by the Seljuk Turks from the later eleventh to the twelfth century. After Christian victories in the early Crusades, Islam made a recovery in Syria and Egypt and began forcing the Christians back in the late twelfth century. Reflecting this environment, we have selected a chapter from *The Book of Reflections* by the Syrian military officer Usamah Ibn Munqidh (1095–c.1190) commenting on the morals and behavior of the Crusaders he encountered during his long lifetime.

Ibn Hazm's *The Dove's Necklace* is a book on the art of love written by a young man still grieving the sack of his city and the deaths of his father and his first love. Although it contains many commonplace aphorisms, it is also an intensely personal work. The excerpt we have selected both analyzes the emotion of love and expresses the feelings of the author on the subject. There are many such extraordinary passages as this:

> Life holds no joy for me, and I do nothing but hang my head and feel utterly cast down, ever since I first tasted the bitterness of being separated from those I love....I am a dead man, though counted among the living, slain by sorrow and buried by sadness, entombed while yet a dweller on the face of this mortal earth.

The student might compare this passionate entry, written by a brilliant young scholar at the beginning of his career, with the somewhat jaded and ambivalent effect of the treatise by Andreas Capellanus, *The Art of Courtly Love*.

Usamah Ibn Munqidh is an old man reflecting on his younger days, but he still manages to instill considerable vitality into his account of the behavior of the Christian Crusaders. His rhetorical skill is especially impressive, even though it is often understated.

> Franks are void of all zeal and jealousy. One of them may be walking along with his wife. He meets another man who takes the wife by the hand and steps aside to converse with her while the husband is standing on one side waiting for his wife to conclude the conversation. If she lingers too long for him, he leaves her alone with the conversant and goes away.

One feels that Munqidh is very much an old soldier who, having lived among the enemy, feels the need to warn a younger generation of his weakness and perfidy.

Ibn Jubayr is perhaps the best writer of this small group. His work comes in for tremendous praise by his contemporaries and successors. A scholar of the fourteenth century writing a history of Granada says this of Jubayr:

> He was a man of remarkable goodness, and his piety confirms the truth of his works.... His correspondence with contemporary scholars reveals his merits and excellence, his superiority in poetry, his originality in rhymed prose, and his ease and elegance in free prose. His reputation was immense, his good deeds many, and his fame widespread; and the incomparable story of his journey is everywhere related. God's mercy upon him.

The anecdote concerning Jubayr's reason for going on his pilgrimage—it was an act of contrition for having been bullied into drinking a glass of wine by his employer when his religious vows forbade it—is typical of the man. His accounts of the holy places of Mecca are full of his unquenchable piety and integrity.

Taken together, these choices display remarkable literary quality, suggesting the intelligence and culture of the writers. Through excerpts from a manual of love, a book of historical ruminations, and an account of a pilgrimage, the student should learn something of the oriental writer who is, as Edward Said has pointed out in his important work *Orientalism* (1979), still culturally victimized in the West today.

Questions for Discussion and Writing

1. What is gained by Ibn Hazm's injection of himself into his discussion of love in *The Dove's Necklace?* If the piece succeeds for you, comment on the qualities of the writing that save it from being an embarrassment.

2. Compare Ibn Hazm's treatment of love with that of Andreas Capellanus in *The Art of Courtly Love*.

3. What is the effect of the piling on of story after story of the practices of the Frankish Crusaders in Usamah Ibn Munqidh's *Book of Reflections?* Why does Munqidh often tell a story without comment? What is his overall attitude toward the Franks?

4. Compare Munqidh's account of the Franks with the narrative in the *History of the First Crusade*. Can you find common ground in these Muslim responses to the Frankish invaders?

5. Analyze a passage of description from Ibn Jubayr's account of the holy shrines of Mecca. How does his literary style add to the feeling of reverence he wishes to show toward the subject?

6. Compare Ibn Jubayr's account of the journey to Mecca with the account of Jerusalem in *Mandeville's Travels*. What connects the two accounts? How are they different? What would you say about the attitudes expressed by the two authors?

Project

Discuss the idea of civilization as proposed in the West and in the Orient, based on these works: *The Song of Roland, The Book of Reflections,* and the *History of the First Crusade.* Do the Christian and Muslim cultures have different ideas of what makes up a civilization, or do the differences come out in practice?

LI PO
Selected Poems

The differences between Chinese literature and European literature are vast, and range from the very nature of the poetic medium itself—the ideogram, which is both pictorial and phonetic, as opposed to the strictly phonetic alphabet—to the distinctive cultural expectations of the role of the poet. In our postromantic era in the West, poets are often expected to be highly idiosyncratic innovators on tradition, whereas in China the poet has been regarded as the preserver of tradition. Poets of the T'ang dynasty certainly were not outsiders like such poets as Shelley or Baudelaire; rather, more like Chaucer or Montaigne, poets were insiders, privileged members of society who more likely than not were government officials involved in the administration of their country. Indeed, mastery of the Confucian classics and the ability to write poetry were prerequisites for would-be officials, who amounted to an elite class of literati. Even Li Po, who is regarded as somewhat iconoclastic, enhances rather than overthrows traditional forms and conventions, and his poetic skills earned him a court appointment (which he kept only three years) from the emperor himself.

In translation, Li Po's poetry sounds strikingly modern to many readers. This apparent contemporaneity is due, at least in part, to the extensive influence the T'ang dynasty poets had upon modern American poets from Ezra Pound to Gary Snyder. Indeed, the short lyrics and songs, such as "Drinking Alone under the Moon" and "Calling on a Taoist Priest in Tai-t'ien Mountain" are Imagistic, in Pound's sense of presenting "an intellectual and emotional complex in an instant of time." The juxtaposition of images in these poems and the compounding of visual and auditory images heighten the reader's emotional response even as they clarify the scene. Pound and the Imagists sought the same kinds of effects in their poetry, and a useful exercise might be to look at Pound's famous translation of Li Po's "The River Merchant's Wife" to see how he tried to recapture the rhythms of the modulating images from the original (here, "The Ballad of Ch'ang-kan").

As Burton Watson reminds us in his introduction to Witter Bynner's *The Chinese Translations*, although the imagery of the *shih* poetry seems to be captured from the poet's direct experience of a particular moment in a specific natural setting, the imagery in fact draws on widely accepted and highly symbolic conventions, just as in Renaissance lyric poetry. Thus, the splendid and apparently simple surfaces of Li Po's poetry allude to Chinese poetic tradition and have mythic significance. In Watson's words, the T'ang poet's works, "for all their simplicity and apparent realism, move almost always in the direction of the mythic, the timeless." Thus, the two most complex poems in our selection, "The Road to Shu is Hard" and "T'ien-mu Mountain Ascended in a Dream," may be read as spiritual journeys, not unlike those of the European pilgrims, where the book of the world is inscribed with the characters and images of the eternal world. To tease out the importance of the mountain as a symbol in China and the West, one might compare one of these poems with Petrarch's "Ascent of Mt. Ventoux."

The transcendental, symbolic character of Li Po's poetry is especially important to keep in mind when discussing the convivial drinking poems; the apparent *carpe diem,* hedonistic nature of these poems must be qualified by recognizing that "to be drunk forever," as Li Po puts it in "Bring the Wine," is less a call to reckless abandon than to an altered state of consciousness that frees the perceptions from the weight of the world. One can see here why Li Po was so popular in the West during the 1960s. Arthur Cooper's *Li Po and Tu Fu* (1973) offers extensive notes to his translations of the poems that can help unpack the Taoist symbology involved in them.

Questions for Discussion and Writing

1. What are some of the recurring images in the poems of Li Po? What wider cultural significance do these images seem to have for him?
2. In what ways do Li Po's poems invoke a sense of spiritual journey or quest? How does his version of this journey compare with those in Chaucer, Dante, or other Western works in this unit? (The poems of parting and loss, especially the wife's lament in "The Ballad of Ch'ang-kan," may be usefully compared with Petrarch's love poems in the Renaissance section.)
3. What does climbing mountains seem to signify for Li Po? How might "The Road to Shu is Hard" be compared with the "perilous journey" of the Christian writers? Compare Li Po's treatment of mountains with Petrarch's in "The Ascent of Mt. Ventoux."
4. How does Li Po define his solitude? What are its virtues and its costs?
5. Compare Li Po's lyrics with the Latin lyrics or some of the bardic poetry. How would you characterize its distinctiveness? What commonalities can you find to discuss?

Project

Compare two or three different translations of one of Li Po's poems. Discuss the problems that translators of Chinese poetry face and explain how even slight differences in translation might affect our reading of Li Po and hence our understanding of his work and perhaps his culture.

MURASAKI SHIKIBU, LADY MURASAKI
The Tale of Genji

This tale of an ill-fated love affair begins when Genji arrives in a poor district, Gojo, to visit his old nurse on her deathbed. He receives a scented fan on which the young woman Evening Faces has written an intriguing poem. This poem indicates that Evening

Faces is a woman of good taste, even though we learn that she comes from a family that ranks far below the prince. When Genji's reply to the poem is apparently ignored, he goes on to visit his lady at Rokujo, toward whom Genji's affection has begun to cool. When Genji learns from Koremitsu more details about the mysterious author of the poem on the fan—including the fact that she has been seeing To no Chujo, the brother of Genji's first wife, Aoi—his amorous interest is further aroused and a secret meeting eventually takes place. A series of nightly meetings between Genji and the delicate young woman follows. The climax of the story occurs on the night when Genji quietly takes her away to a hidden retreat. Here, just after he is visited in a dream by the spirit of the lady from Rokujo, Evening Faces dies, apparently a victim of the jealous spirit. As Genji reels from his unexpected and sudden loss, the faithful Koremitsu covers for his master and Evening Faces is buried with a simple funeral. After a brief but serious illness, Genji learns about the girl's past from her former servant Ukon, whom Genji has granted a position at Nijo. Eventually his thoughts return to another of his amours, the lady of the locust shell, who is the wife of the governor at Iyo and one of Genji's consorts at Nijo. After celebrating the forty-ninth-day ceremony for the dead girl, Genji's loss increases when the lady of the locust shell leaves Nijo with her husband. The narrator at this point breaks off the story, wondering whether she has revealed too much of the noble Genji's faults.

"Evening Faces" displays the delicate manners, one might even say courtly rituals, observed in affairs of love, and so may usefully be compared with Western stories about love in the Middle Ages such as those found in Chaucer, Boccaccio, and Dante. As a story about the love between a noble prince and the daughter of a mere captain of the guards, "Evening Faces" also raises questions about observing one's allegiances to family and social rank and the way love may transgress social boundaries. Above all, the story centers on loss. Indeed, the tale itself is framed by Genji's visit to his dying nurse. Genji is troubled by, and at the same time drawn toward, the delicacy and apparent frailty of Evening Faces, and the conclusion of the tale focuses on the grief and guilt he feels for being perhaps responsible for her death. Genji is partly consoled by his hope that she has gone on to the Pure Land of Amitabha, to the realm of peace promised by the Amida Buddha. The loss Genji feels may be compared with that found in the poems of lament in the Western texts, and the solace offered by Pure Land Buddhism may be compared with that offered by Christianity in Dante. Finally, the sexual politics of "Evening Faces" may be instructive when compared with that in Petrarch, in particular, but in other European poems and stories about love as well. Evening Faces is valued because of her malleability and delicacy. Indeed, it appears that Genji hopes to remake Evening Faces to serve his own desires. Thus, the representation of women in *The Tale of Genji* and women's status in the court society of Japan offer interesting contrasts and parallels with the European texts that raise similar issues.

Questions for Discussion and Writing

1. What kind of prince is Genji? What do his manners, poise, and romantic interests suggest about court life in Japan during this era?

2. Discuss the elaborate means by which Genji and Evening Faces finally meet one another. What draws Genji and Evening Faces into this relationship? How do these gestures compare with courtly behavior in the West, perhaps such as that described by Capellanus?

3. What assumptions does *The Tale of Genji* make about the relationship between men and women? What does Genji value in Evening Faces? Why is she attracted to him? What is implied about Genji's relationships with other women? about Evening Face's relationships with other men? How does the treatment of women and sexuality compare with that described in *The Decameron* or in Petrarch's lyrics?

4. Compare the religious elements of this story with those in Dante's *Divine Comedy*. Can we read "Evening Faces" as a spiritual pilgrimage through love? Is Evening Faces at all comparable to Dante's Beatrice or Petrarch's Laura? Why or why not?

5. How does Genji cope with his loss?

Projects

1. Write a dialogue between the Wife of Bath and Evening Faces. How would the Wife advise Evening Faces to handle Genji's advances?

2. Examine the Buddhist elements and symbolism of the story. Compare these with the Christian elements that we see in the love poetry of Petrarch or another Western writer.

THE RENAISSANCE

Power
and
Discovery

FRANCESCO PETRARCH
The Ascent of Mount Ventoux
and Canzoniere

Petrarch's poetry appeals to students in its subject matter of the enthralled lover swept by alternating exultation and despair, living out an emotional paradox of ecstatic misery. Students know this person, and they enjoy talking about obsessive love, whether they sympathize with it, mock it, or deplore it. But the *Canzoniere* give us a great deal more than love to talk about. These poems, taken together with Petrarch's letter describing the ascent of Mount Ventoux, provide an excellent way to introduce the major Renaissance themes of personal power and discovery.

THE ASCENT OF MOUNT VENTOUX

A comparison of Petrarch's ascent of the windy mountain with Dante's attempt to scale the "little hill" he encounters in the first canto of *The Inferno* and with his later climb up Mt. Purgatory conveys a great deal about Renaissance artists' increasingly keen delight in the physical world and their eagerness to explore it. It also conveys the Renaissance humanists' interest in linking their own lives to classical and secular models as well as to biblical and Christian ones; Petrarch first resolves to climb Mount Ventoux when he reads about Phillip of Macedon surveying terrain from atop a Balkan peak.

Petrarch's mountain is an actual rugged mountain, and his letter tells of his desire to climb it not just as an act of penance or as an allegorical exercise, but primarily because he wants to see what it's like on top; this is the first time in European literature that someone aspires to climb a mountain simply because it is there. The ascent does, however, take on allegorical overtones; for example, Petrarch's brother Gherardo, a monk steadfast in his vocation, chooses steeper paths and gets where he's going faster. Despite the allegorization, this letter describes the literal ascent of an actual mountain, and the climber's pride in having reached the top is enough to compel him to take a remedial dose of St. Augustine's *Confessions* at the summit.

Mountains are arresting natural features all cultures invest with spiritual and symbolic significance. Students can compare Petrarch and his Mount Ventoux with other climbers and heights they've met. Volume One of this anthology contains Moses on Sinai, the hills of Psalm 121, Jesus tempted by Satan in the high place, Faustus surveying the universe, and Li Po encountering various mountains, especially, perhaps, the hard road to Shu. Which are most allegorical, which more literal, which a blend? Volume Two of this anthology offers fascinating mountain moments with Bashō, Wordsworth, and Thoreau, and with N. Scott Momaday at Rainy Mountain.

CANZONIERE

Petrarch's poems for Laura are obviously in a line of descent from Dante's for Beatrice and from the love poems of the Provençal poets in their themes of human and divine love and the idealized woman. But Petrarch's *Canzoniere* have rather more to do with earthly love than divine, and in both their minute recording of the lover's personal reactions to his plight and in the poet's concern for his vocation as an individual artist with a distinct and significant history, they sound the notes of individuality and secularity that mark the Renaissance. Power is a theme picked up here in the question of which lover is more powerful, and in the poet's attempt to pit his mortal words against Death, the greatest despot of all. Moreover, although Petrarch is not the first to venture the supple and economical sonnet form, he wields it with such mastery that it becomes the most favored of all Western forms for many generations of writers to come.

Our translations do not use the usual Petrarchan rhyme scheme of ABBA ABBA CDE CDE because in English, less richly endowed with rhymes than Italian, such a rhyme scheme often sounds forced and unnatural. Our translations usually rhyme ABBA CDDC EFG EFG. The translations suggest the kinds of strong linkages and antitheses highlighted by rhyming words (i.e., *death / breathe,* or *breached / untouched*). They also preserve the Petrarchan relationship between the octave and the sestet, which Petrarch uses in many ways: to contrast the past and the present, as in 1 and 292; to contrast what does not comfort him with what does, as in 148; or to contrast outer with inner weather, as in 310. Sometimes, as in 164, the two parts of the octave contrast with one another, as do the two parts of the sestet. Sometimes the octave and the first three lines of the sestet set forth an argument or describe a condition that is abruptly reversed in the final three lines of the sestet, as in 3 and 90. Students may enjoy trying their hand at a Petrarchan sonnet, even at translating one of Petrarch's, if you can provide them with a literal word-for-word English transcription. Even if they don't complete the task, they'll gain respect for the difficulty of constructing these poems that often seem so effortlessly graceful.

It's sometimes said that country and western song lyrics are the last great bastion of the Petrarchan conceit. But Nashville is not the only place where Petrarchanism lingers, and students can be encouraged to bring in examples from advertising and popular culture.

Questions for Discussion and Writing

1. Compare Petrarch's ascent of Mount Ventoux with other ascents you have encountered in literature—Moses on Sinai and Dante's "little hill" in the first canto of *The Inferno*

are possible examples. How does Petrarch's climb and his attitude toward it differ from those episodes?

2. Petrarch's brother, Ghirardo, actually did make the climb with Petrarch. What additional literary purpose is served by Ghirardo's presence in the text?

3. What classical and religious authorities does Petrarch cite in this brief account? How do they affect his resolve to make the climb, or add to his experience? What, especially, is St. Augustine's role in the text?

4. What is a Petrarchan sonnet? How, in each of the *canzoni* included here, does Petrarch make the form work to express his ideas?

5. How is Laura presented in these sonnets, alive or dead? Do we get a very clear, realistic picture of her? What sorts of things do these poems tell us most about?

6. What sorts of ideas does Petrarch have about himself as a writer and about the worth of his poetry?

Projects

1. Look in advertising and popular culture of today for echoes of Petrarchan images and ideas about love. Country and western music is a good place to begin hunting.

2. Write a Petrarchan sonnet. Even if you don't come up with a work of art, this exercise will teach you more about the sonnet than any book you could read on the subject.

CHRISTOPHER MARLOWE
Doctor Faustus

Marlowe's *Doctor Faustus,* with its surprisingly contemporary characters and themes, is a delight to teach. Like the mythic plots of Greek drama and the religious stories in medieval plays, the plot of Marlowe's *Doctor Faustus* was familiar to his audience. It is not clear whether a Faust ever actually lived, but rumor, sermons, and numerous books about the magician Faust had created an influential, legendary figure.

In his *Sermones convivales* (1543), Johann Gast, a Protestant minister, maintained that Faust received supernatural gifts from the Devil, who later killed Faust by strangling him. Johann Spies provided his Faust book (Frankfurt, 1587) with a descriptive title: *History of Dr. Joh. Faust, the notorious sorcerer and black artist: How he bound himself to the Devil for a certain time: What singular adventures befell him therein: What he did and carried on until finally he received his well-deserved pay. Mostly from his own posthumous writings; for all presumptuous, rash and godless men, as a terrible example, abominable instance and well-meant warning, collected and put in print. "Submit yourselves therefore to God: resist the Devil and he will flee from you"* (James 4:7). In Georg Widman's Faust book of 1599, Luther needs God's help to fend off an attack by Faust and his magic.

Marlowe's *Doctor Faustus* acknowledges medieval Christianity's moral and religious boundaries—it's a sin to sell your soul to the Devil. Threatened by the Reformation movement and Copernicus' (1473–1543) new cosmology, the Roman Catholic Church promoted the Inquisition, which fed the fires of suspicion and fear, convicting Galileo of heresy in 1630. Protestants were also caught up in superstition; tortured by feelings of sinfulness, Martin Luther (1483–1546) threw his inkpot at the Devil and hurled the Bible at Copernicus, calling him "an ass who wants to pervert the whole art of astronomy and deny what is said in the book of Joshua." The most important handbook on demonology for Christians was the *Malleus Maleficarum (Hammer of Witches,* 1486), which instructed witch hunters about pacts with the Devil, an essential ingredient of witchcraft.

Marlowe, nevertheless, takes the Faustian theme in a new direction by paying tribute to the new cosmological paradigm emerging with Renaissance science. Is Marlowe's Faustus the Christian overreacher who, through his own hubris, sows the seed of his own destruction, or is he the archetypal hero of the new age who risks everything to explore new frontiers and open up new territory? One critic suggests that the conflict between piety and sensuality within Faustus exemplifies the movement from Reformation and counter-Reformation to the Renaissance, with its rediscovered delight in the pleasures and beauties of this world.

The opening scene of the play focuses on the importance of learning. The young Faustus restlessly tries out different fields of study, searching for the one that will put him most on the cutting edge of the research of his day. Although the pact with Lucifer does not really bring the expected intellectual rewards, the basic terms of the play's dialogue are established, with Mephistopheles as the mediator: will Faust bow down to the Church or embrace the world; will he listen to the Good or the Bad Angel? In one of the earlier puppet plays on Faust, a voice offstage on the right cries: "Faust! Faust! desist from this proposal! Go on with the study of theology, and you will be the happiest of mortals." A voice from the left answers: "Faust! Faust! leave the study of theology. Betake you to necromancy, and you will be the happiest of mortals!" The two centers of action in the play reiterate this conflict in political terms: the Church is represented by the Pope's court in Rome; secular power resides in the emperor's court in Germany.

A handy reference book for demonology Devil pacts is Rossell Hope Robbins's *Encyclopedia of Witchcraft & Demonology* (1959).

Questions for Discussion and Writing

1. What does the term *Renaissance* mean to you? What are the various meanings of *Renaissance?*
2. To a certain extent, all innovative scholars and all artists are Faustian. What are examples of this statement? Discuss the similarities between Francis Bacon's intellectual projects and Faust. What are the positive and negative consequences of Faustian enterprises?
3. What does Faustus decide to do with the powers gained through his pact with the Devil? What do these choices reveal about his character?
4. Does Faustus really believe in Hell? What is the evidence for his belief? How is Mephistopheles' answer about the location of Hell particularly modern?
5. If Helen could speak, what would she say to Faustus?
6. Compare the quest for intellectual power in *Doctor Faustus* with the uses of sexual power and control in *The Love-Rogue of Seville*. How are both uses of power connected with the Renaissance?
7. Why doesn't Faustus repent at the end?
8. How do the comic scenes with Wagner, Robin, and Dick mirror Faustus's antics?

Projects

1. The demonic theme of *Doctor Faustus* provides an opportunity for engaging research projects. The sixteenth century was an age of superstition, prophecy, and alchemy. What are the roots of necromancy? Why was necromancy thought to be dangerous? Who was Paracelsus (1493–1541) and why is he so popular today?
2. Pretend that you are a contemporary academic advisor to a modern Faustus and that you are in sympathy with his ambitions. What modern field of study would you advise him to pursue? Was the development of nuclear energy a Faustian enterprise? What might be modern, secular, metaphorical equivalents for damnation and a pact with the Devil?
3. What aspects of this Faustus, compared to Goethe's, reveal the Renaissance character of Marlowe's play?

CHRISTOPHER COLUMBUS
Diario

Students are likely to know something about Columbus's accomplishments, but the actual *Diario* still comes as a surprise to most readers, who are fascinated by Columbus's initial sense of wonder, the baldness of his speculations about the Taino's potential worth as slaves, and the assumptions he blithely makes about the nature of their inner lives and thoughts. Columbus always sees exactly what he wants to see, whether it be signs of abundant gold, clues that China or Japan must lie just over the horizon, or indications that the Taino dwell in a religious vacuum just waiting to be filled by Christianity. In this extraordinary document, one of the most complex and mysterious characters in history describes unguardedly those first days of contact between East and West that were to alter the entire world. The *Diario* is likely to provoke strong and very divergent feelings among its readers, which can make for a lively class.

Teachers might begin by asking questions about Columbus's intentions in keeping the log, its intended audience, and what points Columbus might have hoped to get across to that audience. Other important things to consider are the degree to which Columbus is seeing and hearing what he hopes to see and hear, and how his attitudes change as he spends more time in the Bahamas.

Connections between the *Diario* and other Renaissance texts abound. Columbus can be compared with many other explorers represented here, ranging from Galileo and Kepler speculating about the heavens to John Donne exploring his mistress's body. Students can compare Columbus's initial response to the Taino land and people with the actions and reactions of different members of the court party cast ashore on Prospero's island in *The Tempest,* or consider Montaigne's armchair speculations about cannibals in light of the Taino as seen by Columbus. As an expedition captain and as an invader who bears superior arms, Columbus is a ruler, and his actions can be measured against Machiavelli's advice to princes. Sor Juana's *Loa to The Divine Narcissus* allegorically represents the process of conquest, and one can ask where among those allegorical characters Columbus might locate himself.

Finally, and perhaps most importantly, we can read the *Diario* side by side with the Aztec materials in the World Context section. The mighty inland and urban-centered Aztec Empire obviously differed greatly from the island communities of Taino people, but in the Aztec materials we get a taste of the sort of information the *Diario* omits, for there we glimpse something of the inner life of another Native American people on the eve of conquest.

Questions for Discussion and Writing

1. Why does Columbus falsify his log on the outward voyage?
2. Why do you think Columbus sees few women among the Taino?
3. What are some of the assumptions Columbus makes about Taino life, culture, and character? What leads him to these conclusions?
4. Columbus often describes fairly elaborate exchanges of information between himself and Taino people. Point to instances where it seems to you communication may have actually taken place, and to other instances where it seems Columbus may have been imagining or misinterpreting the information he claims to have received.
5. The Taino who first met Columbus have often been described as naïve, unwary, and helpless. Do you detect any defensive strategies on their part in this account? If Columbus had first landed on the coast of Mexico rather than on this Caribbean island, how might the encounter have differed?

6. What parallels can you find between the reactions and behavior of Columbus and his crew and those of the court party in *The Tempest?*
7. As ship captain and as conquerer of the Taino's island, does Columbus act in accord with any of Machiavelli's advice to princes?
8. In what we can glean from Columbus's account, do the Taino seem to bear out any of Montaigne's observations in "Of Cannibals"?
9. How might Columbus be seen to resemble the ideal of a Renaissance prince?
10. Many readers see Columbus as a villain; others, as a hero. What are the arguments on both sides?

Projects

1. Make a survey of responses to the Columbus quincentennial in 1992, including Native American responses. A good place to find the latter is the anthology *Without Discovery: A Native Response to Columbus,* edited by Ray Gonzales, (Broken Moon Press, 1992.)
2. Imagine a Taino person's account of discovering Columbus.
3. Look at Michael Dorris's *Morning Girl* (1992), a young adult book that recounts Taino life and culture through the eyes of a Taino brother and sister. How does Dorris's fiction fill in areas of Taino life that Columbus perceived as blank spaces?

NICCOLO MACHIAVELLI
The Prince

As discussed in the headnote, Machiavelli's *The Prince* is one of the most controversial of all Renaissance works and directly addresses the question of power—not just political power, but, in the last chapter on Fortune, the power of human beings to control their destiny. Although much of *The Prince* bears directly on the condition of the Italian city-states, especially Florence, during the volatile sixteenth century, Machiavelli's work also addresses more generally the process of overseas discovery and colonization that had been gaining speed since around 1450. *The Prince* also illustrates Machiavelli's genius as a rhetorician. Machiavelli sets up the issues under discussion in such a way that his readers are held to the binary oppositions that frame them, and he strategically uses abundant historical evidence and authority to support his point of view, leading the unwary reader to forget that what he presents is in fact his own interpretation of the past. His prose style and argumentative strategy become more apparent when compared to the very different, more relaxed and exploratory style of Montaigne's *Essays.*

In "Of Mixed Principates" Machiavelli advises the prince how to hold onto colonies taken by force. His discussion of using force, taking up residence in the colonies, and limiting the offenses against the inhabitants while exerting maximum control helps to place other works in this section, especially Shakespeare's *The Tempest,* Montaigne's "Of Coaches," and the Aztec materials, into perspective. Asking students to consider whether Cortés or Prospero behaves according to Machiavelli's principles usually generates a lively discussion on colonization, the rights of native peoples, and the ethical problems posed by conquest. One might also remind students of Plato's "Allegory of the Cave" and ask them to consider how it might relate to Machiavelli's discussion of colonialism.

Chapters 15 through 19 of *The Prince* concern the essential qualities the prince must display in order to retain his power. These chapters raise the familiar ethical question posed by "Machiavellianism"—that is, whether the ends justify the means. As you discuss the reasons Machiavelli gives for whether it is better to be praised or blamed, generous or mean, cruel or merciful, trustworthy or deceitful, you may invite students to think about whether Machiavelli deserves his early reputation as an invidious devil—the Elizabethan "Machiavel" for which he provided the archetype. Moreover, Machiavelli's text encourages us to think about the distinction between personal morality and public ethics. Whereas some students will insist on reading Machiavelli literally, others may wonder whether his apparent pragmatic realism should be read ironically. In the postmodernist age—and in light of the "damage control" experts and image-makers employed by governments and corporations—Machiavelli's emphasis on appearances seems particularly poignant, and we have found that students have little difficulty citing contemporary examples of Machiavellianism at work in our society.

Questions for Discussion and Writing

1. Compare Machiavelli's discussion of colonialism with Montaigne's condemnation of the barbarism of European treatment of the Aztecs in "Of Coaches."
2. Discuss the primary objective Machiavelli sets for the prince: to retain his power.
3. It is often said that for Machiavelli the ends justify the means. Do you agree that this is an accurate reading of Machiavelli?
4. Critics vehemently disagree over the ethical implications of *The Prince*. How does *The Prince* hinge upon a fine line between expediency and efficiency, corruption and competence, personal morality and public ethics?
5. How would you define the qualities, the essential features, of the prince as established by Machiavelli? What figures from this period—either historical or literary—display some of the characteristics of Machiavelli's prince? Describe a modern Machiavellian prince.
6. What are Machiavelli's assumptions about human nature? How does his view compare with those of other writers in the Renaissance?
7. Discuss whether Machiavelli's advice to the prince amounts to a kind of *realpolitik* for early sixteenth-century Florence. If it does, are any of his principles applicable to our political situation today?
8. How would Machiavelli advise Prospero, Columbus, or Cortés? What would Machiavelli say about Sor Juana's Zeal and Religion?
9. How does Machiavelli's discussion of Fortune help us to understand what we mean by Renaissance Humanism? How does his treatment of Fortune differ from that of the medieval writers?
10. How would you define the genre of Machiavelli's *The Prince*? How does it compare to Bacon's *The New Atlantis* or Montaigne's *Essays*?
11. Examine Machiavelli's rhetoric and style. How does he make his argument? How does he use evidence?

Projects

1. Have students stage a conversation about the conquest of the Americas between Machiavelli, Montaigne, Prospero, Columbus, or Cortés and Moctezuma or Caliban.
2. Imagine the ghost of Machiavelli advising an administrator, teacher, or student-government official at your school. What would Machiavelli advise that person to do about a current controversial issue?

MARGUERITE DE NAVARRE
The Heptameron

The Heptameron makes an interesting companion to the other collections of framed tales in the late Middle Ages and the early Renaissance, especially to Boccaccio's *Decameron,* which provided the model for Marguerite's work. Although one tale is a very small sample from a collection of more than seventy stories, the story of Amadour and Florida seems to reveal the author behind the work. The gradual shift of the central focus of the story away from the perfect knight to the woman of conscience turns the story from medieval romance into psychological fiction. What begins, perhaps, as a tale like Boccaccio's ends more like a sketch for Madame de La Fayette's *Princess of Clèves.*

The frame for the tale, which presents a dispute between men and women over the differences between male and female love, sets the story into a context of gendered argument that seems to demand a gendered reading of the story. Not only are we asked to decide who "wins" in the struggle between Amadour and Florida, but we are also asked to decide whether there is more truth in the male assertion that women desire to be sexually overpowered or in the female assertion that women wish to retain control over their bodies and their lives. Although the story may appear to be chivalric costume drama, its issues are remarkably contemporary.

Florida is one of a long line of literary heroines torn between desire and duty, passion and personal integrity. She is a sister to Nora Helmer in Ibsen's *A Doll's House,* Catherine Earnshaw in Brontë's *Wuthering Heights,* and the Princesse de Clèves, who some critics think was inspired by Florida.

Questions for Discussion and Writing

1. Summarize the male and female positions taken by the speakers in the frame narrative. What might Christine de Pizan contribute to this discussion if she were part of the group? How do you think Saffredent would explain a knight's failure to win the favors of a lady? What differences are there between the female and male ideas of love in this discussion?

2. What inequalities between them prevent Amadour from declaring his love for Florida?

3. What are the social rules that make Amadour's initial proposals to Florida "virtuous"? How does his later proposition violate these rules? How does he try to rationalize his way around the rules?

4. How is Florida like the ladies addressed by Renaissance sonneteers, such as Petrarch's Laura? Do the sonnets help to identify the conventions of chivalric courtship in the relationship between Amadour and Florida?

5. Define reason and passion as they are understood in this story.

6. What is Amadour's offense? Is he guilty of deception? assault? rape? What does Hircan mean at the end of the story when he says that Amadour did his duty?

7. Does Amadour change in the course of the story? What causes him to attack Florida? How does he compare to Tirso de Molina's Don Juan as a seducer?

8. Does Florida change from the twelve-year-old she is at the beginning of the story? Is her resistance to Amadour wholly admirable? Why does Florida wound herself? Is she in any way responsible for Amadour's behavior?

9. Does Parlemente's story prove her point? How can Hircan dispute it? Do the men and women of the frame read this story differently?

10. Compare the tale of Amadour and Florida to Boccaccio's tale of Tancred and Ghismonda. Do you find any textual indications in Marguerite's tale that it is a woman's story and in Boccaccio's that it is a man's?

11. Compare the tale of Amadour and Florida to the Wife of Bath's tale. Do they take similar positions on the question of rape? Do you think the Wife of Bath's tale is more hers or Chaucer's?

Projects

1. Make a list of the uses of the terms *service, honor,* and *virtue* in the story. What variety of meanings do these terms take on?
2. Consider Florida in relation to Shakespeare's Miranda in *The Tempest.* Could Amadour be said to play the roles of both Ferdinand and Caliban in this story?
3. Compare the story of Florida and Amadour to the story of the Princesse de Clèves and Nemours. What similarities do you find? What differences? Could this story also be said to be about the conflict between love and duty?
4. In Amadour's voice, write a sonnet to Florida. You may want to consult the headnotes on Petrarch and the Renaissance lyric for information on sonnet form.

MICHEL EYQUEM DE MONTAIGNE
Of Cannibals *and* Of Coaches

"Of Cannibals" (1578–80) and "Of Coaches" (1585–88) come from Books 1 and 3, respectively, of Montaigne's three-book *Essays,* a work that introduces to Western literary history a new form—the personal essay. Although Rousseau complained that Montaigne's *Essays* were not candid enough for his taste, the loose structure, familiar tone, and rhythms of everyday speech that characterize the essays reveal the inquisitive, skeptical, but honest personality of Montaigne himself. Most critics take him at his word when Montaigne writes in "Of Giving the Lie" that he had created "a book consubstantial with its author, concerned with my own self, an integral part of my life." Montaigne's essays explore a vast array of topics drawn from his reading and experience; the various meditations, memories, observations, and opinions hazarded in the three books impress the reader with a sense of the Renaissance desire to explore just beyond the boundaries of tried experience, to try the questions that had once seemed indisputable, and to test the limits—discover the outermost horizons—of the self.

Both essays included here typify Montaigne's desultory style, his unpretentious display of classical learning along with a kind of chatty recounting of everyday experience, his mixing of observations on ancient and recent history with personal reflection, his indirect approach to the ostensible subject of the essay, and his ability to evoke a sense of familiarity even as he observes a fine, perhaps aristocratic, detachment from what may be offensive to his reader or to himself. One way to get started with Montaigne is to compare his desultory prose style to the tightly structured argument of Machiavelli or the clear exposition of Giovanni Pico della Mirandola. Focusing on the differences in style helps to highlight the features of the personal essay, and noting similarities, such as the grounding in classical learning and the appeal to ancient and contemporary history, helps to round out a definition of Renaissance humanism. The description of the making of *Perseus* from *The Autobiography of Benvenuto Cellini* also makes an instructive comparison with Montaigne, whose essays capture the vigorous energy of Cellini's *Autobiography* and display a strong sense of self through the prose, but with a much more even temper, an ironic sense of detachment, and an implicit self-criticism totally lacking in Cellini. This emphasis on the self in the Western texts, the placing of the subject at the center of the text, contrasts dramatically with the communal voice in the works of the Ancient Mexicans.

As discussed in the headnote, "Of Cannibals" and "Of Coaches" are concerned with the New World and the contact between Europeans and indigenous peoples. Whereas the former presents—perhaps only ironically, in the view of some readers—the possibility that Europeans should respect the customs and knowledge of native peoples, the latter condemns the barbarism of the Spanish conquest of Mexico. Both essays take a remarkably enlightened perspective on colonialism and the rights of indigenous peoples, and Montaigne anticipates one of the major features of the Enlightenment discourse on colonialism, with its emphasis on the "noble savage" and the distinction between the artificial and the natural. (See, for example, Denis Diderot's *Supplement to the Voyage of Bougainville* in Volume Two.) His view that only a simple person can give true accounts of travel introduces the question of veracity that plagued writers of exploration and travel narratives throughout the next two centuries. "Of Cannibals," which Shakespeare may have known in the John Florio translation (1603), teaches well as a companion piece to *The Tempest*, and you may ask students to contemplate whether Shakespeare and Montaigne have similar views with respect to indigenous peoples. "Of Coaches," of course, deals directly with the postconquest poems of the Aztecs, and lively discussion arises when students contrast these two perspectives.

Questions for Discussion and Writing

1. What does Montaigne mean by *barbarism?* Does his discussion of the Brazilians anticipate what we would today call cultural relativism? Does the definition of this term change as the essay proceeds? Who are the barbarians of the essay?
2. What exactly does Montaigne find to praise in the activities of the cannibals? Does this suggest that Montaigne may be applying European values to his judgment of the Brazilian natives? Compare Montaigne's evaluation of the Brazilians to Prospero's (or Shakespeare's) treatment of Caliban.
3. Examine carefully the last paragraph in "Of Cannibals." Montaigne seems to close his essay with a declaration of perhaps comic exasperation. Does this statement cause us to question the seriousness of Montaigne's previous discussion? Is he merely being ironic here?
4. Describe the structure of Montaigne's essay. How does he approach his topic? What is the nature of his digressions? How do they relate to the main topic?
5. How does Montaigne approach the main subject in "Of Coaches"? Describe the structure of this essay and explain the relations among its various parts and topics.
6. Compare Montaigne's and Machiavelli's views of the liberality of princes and the uses of a lavish display of wealth.
7. How does Montaigne's account of the contact between the Mexicans and the Spaniards compare to that given in the Aztec materials? Compare his defense of the Aztec religion with Sor Juana's.
8. Compare Montaigne's treatment of people from the New World with Diderot's in *Supplement to the Voyage of Bougainville* in Volume Two. How does Montaigne anticipate the Enlightenment discourse on colonialism? What are some of the differences between his account of the Brazilians or Aztecs and Diderot's account of the Tahitians?

Project

Create a dialogue between Montaigne and either Cortés, Columbus, Prospero, or Sor Juana on the rights of indigenous peoples and the impact of colonization.

MIGUEL DE CERVANTES SAAVEDRA
Don Quixote

Don Quixote is a long, complex novel; any selection is bound to misrepresent the original and neglect some of its riches. In our selection, we have included some of the classic scenes, such as the windmill episode and Quixote's descent into the Cave of Montesinos, but we have made our overall choices primarily to trace the changing relationship between Quixote and Sancho Panza and the story of Sancho's dream of governing an island. Our selections encourage discussion of Quixote and Sancho, what they represent, their world views, how they relate to each other, and how they change. This master–servant relationship can be compared to those between Don Juan and Catalinón, Prospero and Caliban, Faustus and Mephistopheles, and Tripitaka and Monkey in some of the other works in the Renaissance section. These paired characters, in their similarities and differences, reveal each other, open up the multiple plot lines in the works in which they appear, and modulate the tone of the works. For example, the double plot line of *Don Quixote*—the Don's quest for chivalric adventure and Sancho's desire to govern an island—is present in other forms in the contrasting high and low plots in *The Tempest* and *The Love-Rogue of Seville*. Besides raising social issues, these contrasting characters and stories enable the writers to move between the serious and the comic, the sentimental and the satiric, the romantic and the realistic.

Sancho's rise to the governorship of an island provides a variation on the theme of power that reappears in many of our Renaissance selections; in Machiavelli's *The Prince,* the Don Juan and Doctor Faustus plays, *The Tempest,* and the accounts of the conquest of the New World. Quixote's romantic idealism merely seeks to aid those who are suffering or oppressed; Sancho's down-to-earth realism prompts more self-interested and worldly ambitions. Sancho is a fictional cousin to the members of the Renaissance underclass who, like Cortés, took the opportunity for exploration and adventure as a way to rise into a position of power. Thus Sancho's story is part of the Renaissance passion for discovery and conquest and related to the emergence of realistic political theory. The discussions between Quixote and his squire about governing an island and especially the Don's advice to Sancho before he goes off to Baratario can be read in the context of Machiavelli's advice to the prince on conquering and holding a state, and the characters of both the Don and the squire can be considered in relation to Machiavelli's discussion of the virtues of a ruler.

As the first Western novel in the anthology, *Don Quixote,* even in a truncated version, provides an opportunity to consider the central characteristics of the form: its concern with point of view and the reliability of narration, its realism, and its preoccupation with the illusion versus reality theme. *Don Quixote* also has intriguing similarities to *Monkey,* the Chinese novel in this section. Even though the two stories end very differently, both can be read as spiritual quest narratives that pair an idealistic hero with a realistic servant and follow their progress through a loosely connected series of adventures.

Questions for Discussion and Writing

1. How is Don Quixote introduced in Chapter 1? What is the tone of the narrator? What does the discussion of the Don's name tell us about him? What does his physical appearance suggest about him? How does Sancho Panza complement Quixote?

2. The encounter with the windmills in Part I, Book 8 is the single most famous episode in *Don Quixote*. What is the theme of this story? How does the scene enlarge your notion of what it means to tilt at windmills? Describe a contemporary example of tilting at windmills. What other scenes in the novel reveal Quixote's blind idealism?

3. What do Don Quixote and Sancho hope to achieve on their sallies? How do their goals differ? How are the goals of each man appropriate to his character?
4. Dulcinea is related to the chivalric ladies celebrated in romance—such as Florida in Marguerite de Navarre's tale—and to the ladies addressed by the sonneteers, such as Petrarch's Laura. How does Dulcinea differ from these other Renaissance women? Is she a satiric version of them?
5. In Part II, how do Carrasco's presence, Don Quixote's awareness that an account of his exploits has been published, and the translator's intrusions into the narrative complicate the narration?
6. Why does the translator think that Part II, Chapter 5 is apocryphal? Is his judgment of Sancho at this point a sound one? Do you share his opinion?
7. How does Quixote's vision in the Cave of Montesinos reveal a more prosaic and less idealistic side to his character? How does this episode compare to the epic journeys to the underworld?
8. Although Sancho's dream of being the governor of an island comes true only as part of an elaborate practical joke, what kind of governor does Sancho make? Why does he give up the island and return to Don Quixote? How does his experience as a governor change him?
9. Compare Quixote's advice to Sancho in Part II, Chapters 42–43 on how to be a good ruler to Machiavelli's advice to the prince. Is Quixote's advice Machiavellian? Are Sancho's actions as a ruler Machiavellian?
10. How has Quixote changed by the end of the novel? How has the experience in the Cave of Montesinos foreshadowed this change? How do our attitudes toward his idealism change over the course of the story?
11. How does Cervantes' novel help you understand the meaning of the adjective *quixotic?*
12. Cervantes is most often compared to Shakespeare as the other giant of European Renaissance literature (a comparison made even more apt, perhaps, by the fact that both men died on the same day, April 23, 1616). What connections do you find between *Don Quixote* and *The Tempest?* Are Quixote and Prospero in any way alike? What does each work have to say about the power of imagination?

Projects

1. *Don Quixote* is often described as the first novel in Western literature, the work that introduced the fundamental theme of all later novels: the conflict between illusion and reality. Compare *Don Quixote* with another novel—with *The Princess of Clèves* or *Wuthering Heights* in this anthology, for example—as they develop this theme.
2. Imagine Don Quixote and Sancho Panza as members of the expedition of Spanish officer Hernán Cortés as he invades Mexico. How would they respond to being part of the invading forces? Whom would they champion?

FRANCIS BACON
New Atlantis

As an imaginary voyage narrative that discovers a utopian society based on scientific principles, *New Atlantis* is related to such Enlightenment texts as *Gulliver's Travels, Candide,* and Diderot's *Supplement to the Voyage of Bougainville.* But Bacon is not satiric and his respect for traditional religion separates him from the Enlightenment *philosophes,* especially from Voltaire and Diderot. As a vision of an ideal society, *New Atlantis* is more like the

Utopia (1516) of Sir Thomas More than the later Enlightenment works, but Bacon differs from More in his scientific emphasis.

The scientific organization of Salomon's House, the section of the narrative that confirms Bacon's standing as the father of the scientific method, is the part of *New Atlantis* that is most often reprinted. But the first half, describing the religion of Bensalem and the patriarchal rituals of the family, presents a more surprising aspect of Bacon's utopia and prompts us to reconsider just how modern Bacon's scientific world view is. The Christianity of Bensalem rests on an original revelation, inherited scriptures, and established authority. The social organization of the island is hierarchical and patriarchal. Even though it is committed to empirical investigation and the discovery of new knowledge, Salomon's House is also organized on hierarchical principles. Bacon does not appear to have been troubled by the possible conflicts between the revealed religion and the hierarchical organization on the island and its progressive scientific endeavors. He indicates no desire to challenge the church or the political institutions in the manner of Don Juan or Doctor Faustus. The *New Atlantis,* then, links respect for tradition and ancient texts with a belief in empirical investigation and thus represents the Renaissance as a transitional period between the medieval acquiescence to religious authority and the Enlightenment's belief in scientific progress and a utopian future.

Questions for Discussion and Writing

1. What conditions must strangers meet before they are allowed to enter Bensalem?
2. How did Bensalem become Christian? In what ways is this account miraculous?
3. How have the inhabitants of Bensalem managed to keep secret the fact of their existence? What is the purpose of such secrecy? Is the secrecy consistent with the scientific ideals of Salomon's House?
4. What does the Feast of the Family tell us about the social organization of Bensalem? What is the symbolic significance of the various parts of the ceremony; for example, the scroll and the grapes? Would such social arrangements have seemed traditional or progressive in Bacon's time?
5. How does the organization of Salomon's House articulate the principles of the scientific method? In a modern scientific laboratory, what might the various positions described by Bacon be called? Would any of Bacon's functionaries not be included in a modern laboratory? Would we add any positions that Bacon does not include?
6. *New Atlantis* was not completed before Bacon's death. Had he lived, what do you think he might have added to the narrative? Do you think that Bacon could have intentionally left *New Atlantis* "not perfected"? Had he done so, what might its imperfection suggest about utopias? about science?
7. Are the principles of Salomon's House compatible with the traditional religion of Bensalem? How do you think the inhabitants of Bensalem would deal with a scientific discovery that challenged their religion?

Projects

1. How does Bacon make use of the traditional myth of Atlantis, or what he calls "great Atlantis"? Read Plato's account of Atlantis in *Critias*. In what ways is Bacon's story a *new* Atlantis myth?
2. Write the section that you think Bacon would have added to complete *New Atlantis*.
3. Make an organization chart for Salomon's House.
4. You are a wife, daughter, or granddaughter of a New Atlantis family caught up in the frenzy of preparation for your upcoming Feast of the Family. Make entries in your secret diary as that day draws near. (You might want to read Virginia Woolf's

"Shakespeare's Sister" in Volume Two of this anthology, or Margaret Atwood's *The Handmaid's Tale* for ideas.) Or you might write a similar diary from the perspective of one of the male members of the family.

5. Compare the utopian society in *New Atlantis* with a modern utopia such as B. F. Skinner's *Walden II.*

WILLIAM SHAKESPEARE
The Tempest

In the headnote to *The Tempest,* we point out ways in which the play can be read as a study of the duties and responsibilities of the Renaissance prince in a colonial context. Read from this perspective, *The Tempest* has profound connections to Machiavelli's *The Prince* and Montaigne's essays "Of Cannibals" and "Of Coaches." Shakespeare's play, of course, enriches the discourse of power and leads it into areas overlooked by Machiavelli and Montaigne, especially magic, art, and faith. Thus, the play also has direct links to Marlowe's *Doctor Faustus* in that it goes beyond the rational dimension and questions the proper limits of human power. The play's emphasis on the role and power of the artist in the Renaissance also invites comparison with Benvenuto Cellini's account of his making of the Perseus statue, included in the Background Texts section. Cellini's text, despite its braggadocio, gives us a sense of the grandeur of the Renaissance imagination and lets us see how politics and personal rivalries affected the artist's work.

Teaching Shakespeare's works as literary texts without reference to the drama is always reductive, and ideally students should see a performance of the play to help them appreciate Shakespeare's own dramatic magic and to hear for themselves the music of the play's language. Although many versions and adaptations of the play are available on film, it is always possible, and helpful, to have three or four students perform a scene or two for the class. It seems best to get the basic story straight before proceeding to more complex issues. Hence, one might begin by asking how Prospero has come to be on the island, why he's raised the storm to wreck the ship, what his relation is to Caliban and Ariel, and what he hopes to accomplish by scattering the various parties.

As mentioned in the headnote, *The Tempest* raises questions about genre. Although it is often classified as a romance, the play presents a kind of hybrid genre that draws on various literary forms, including a masque that Prospero arranges for Miranda and Ferdinand. Of course, all of Prospero's manipulations—the raising of the storm, the separation of the various parties on the island, the meeting between Ferdinand and Miranda—are the result of Prospero's illusionist art. Like Machiavelli's prince, Prospero is a master of illusion, of creating spectacles to serve his interests. Thus, in the play the boundaries between magic, art, and governance blur, and *The Tempest*—which some critics read as Shakespeare's farewell to the stage—focuses on some of the major issues about power and discovery that we have identified as major themes in the Renaissance. Overall, the play also embodies that sense of wonder that Renaissance exploration introduced to Europe, and which we see in Columbus's *Diario.*

Because Shakespeare has become a kind of cultural institution in his own right, it is often helpful to discuss just what we mean when we say that a work is "timeless." Does Shakespeare's work thrive because it contains immutable eternal truths and psychological insights into some unchanging human nature; or does it thrive because its artistry allows us to adapt his work and reconstruct its meanings to meet our own psychological, aesthetic, and cultural needs? A comparison of interpretations or performances of *The Tempest* over its history may be useful in attempting to answer this larger question, which is really a question about the function of literature and the nature of "great works."

Questions for Discussion and Writing

1. Discuss the major thematic conflicts or oppositions we find in the play—e.g., art versus nature, primitive versus civilized, and revenge versus forgiveness. Other themes to discuss include nature versus nurture, the responsibility of leaders, the nature of freedom, allegiance, the limits of vengeance, and the importance of forgiveness.
2. Discuss the relationship between Ariel, Caliban, and Prospero in terms of master, slave, and servant.
3. Compare Prospero's initial treatment of Caliban to that of Trinculo and Stephano.
4. Compare Gonzalo's response to the possibilities of the island to those of Sebastian, Antonio, Alonso, and Gonzalo. What implications do their responses have in terms of European colonialism and discovery of the New World? Compare these various responses to the New World with that found in Columbus's *Diario*.
5. Prospero, Don Juan, Faustus, and Monkey all use pranks, practical jokes, and games to achieve their ends. How does Prospero's use of jokes and games compare to these other characters'? What's the effect of the comic subplot on our overall reading of the play?
6. Apply Machiavelli's definition of the Renaissance prince to Prospero. Compare Prospero's performance of his princely duties to those of another Renaissance prince.
7. Compare Prospero's use of magic to Faust's. What are the limits of their power? Do they use their power responsibly?
8. What conclusions might you draw regarding colonialism as portrayed in *The Tempest*? Compare Shakespeare's view of colonialism to those of Columbus, Montaigne, Sor Juana, and Machiavelli.
9. Discuss Prospero as an embodiment of Renaissance humanism.
10. Compare Stephano and Trinculo's desire to rule the island to Sancho Panza's desire to rule an island in *Don Quixote*. What do these texts tell us about the growing possibilities for social climbing introduced by the age of discovery, colonization, and exploration? Are these Faustian ambitions?
11. What is the meaning of the word *brave* in the play? How does that term resonate throughout the play, especially in Miranda's "O brave new world"?
12. Discuss the importance of the epilogue insofar as it breaks the spell of the play.

Projects

1. Divide students into small groups and assign to each of them one of the separated parties on Prospero's island—Caliban, Ariel, Ferdinand and Miranda, Stephano and Trinculo, and Gonzalo, Alonso, Sebastian, and Antonio. After some discussion, have them explain to the rest of the class what is happening within their particular party, the internal conflicts among the characters, their objectives, and their relation to Prospero's overall plan.
2. Perform a scene or two from the play for the rest of the class. (A blanket, empty bottle, and a pair of swim-fins are all you need to stage the Caliban/Trinculo/Stephano drunk scene (Act II, Scene 2).
3. Write an act or scene in which Sycorax would speak or take an active part. How might the play change if we could hear her version of the story?
4. Rewrite the story of *The Tempest* from Caliban's point of view. Compare his perspective to that of the Aztecs when Cortés arrives. Is Prospero at all like Cortés or Columbus? How does the Aztec situation differ from Caliban's?

TIRSO DE MOLINA
The Love-Rogue of Seville

Even if they have never read one of the Don Juan stories or seen one of the many Don Juan plays or operas, students will know the Don Juan archetype and have a pretty good idea of the popular conception of Don Juan. They are often surprised to discover that Don Juan was introduced into Western literature by a monk. Rather than disabusing them of an overly spiritual view of the clergy—Boccaccio and Chaucer may have already done that—one might want to explore the religious dimension to the Don Juan story, an element emphasized in Tirso de Molina's version of the legend that is not part of the usual idea of the story. Asked to identify qualities in Tirso's hero that do not appear in the popular conception of Don Juan, students will probably notice that Tenorio is more than a seducer or ladies' man, that these are not the dominant traits in his character, that he is primarily interested in challenging other men and the established order, and that he has no respect for either the political rulers or the Church. It is especially important to notice how central to his character are his rejection of spiritual otherworldliness and his defiance of the Church. His braggart grandiosity, like that of Marlowe's Doctor Faustus, is one expression of the Renaissance's adolescent delight in tweaking established authority.

The *burlas* or practical jokes that engage Don Juan's energies can be read as expressions of the Renaissance excitement over the power of human beings to manipulate the world and determine one's own destiny; in a way, Tenorio's "jokes" are similar to Prospero's elaborate deception in *The Tempest*. But they are also in the tradition of sexual comedy and are related to tricks like those in some of Boccaccio's and Chaucer's tales and to the battle of the sexes that frames Marguerite of Navarre's tales in *The Heptameron*. The Don Juan figure as one whose sexual exploits express a disdain for established authority contributes to Molière's conception of Tartuffe, to Goethe's Faust, and to the philandering protagonist of Carlos Fuentes's "The Prisoner of Las Lomas."

Questions for Discussion and Writing

1. Why does Don Pedro help Don Juan to escape after he rapes Isabela? How do his lies to the king contribute to the way in which the episode is construed by those in authority?
2. How do the men in the play think of women? Are Don Juan's views different from those of the other men?
3. Notice the references to the stories of the Trojan War and Aeneas and Dido. In what contexts do these allusions appear? What do they add to the play?
4. Characterize each of the women Don Juan pursues. What about each attracts him? How do they differ from each other? Are the women individualized characters?
5. What is Catalinon's role in the play?
6. What arguments does Don Juan employ to justify his seductions? How sincere are these arguments? Are his justifications used today?
7. List the uses of the word *honor* in the play. What different meanings does the word take on? What is Don Juan's definition of the term?
8. Is Don Juan guilty of murder or of some lesser crime in the death of Don Gonzalo? Compare this killing to Faust's killing of Valentine in Part I of Goethe's *Faust*.
9. What role does social class play in this drama?
10. How might the strange resolution to the play be explained? Are the living statue and the bizarre banquet to be regarded as supernatural events or as symbolic ways of representing the issues in the story? How could the statue and the dinner be explained symbolically?

11. What brings about Don Juan's final comeuppance? Do the women he has wronged have any influence with the king?
12. Describe the characteristics that you associate with the Don Juan stereotype. How does Tirso de Molina's version confirm or depart from your expectations?

Projects

1. Write the report of Don Juan's psychiatrist after his sessions with Don Juan.
2. If Machiavelli were writing advice to Renaissance Casanovas for the conduct of their sexual affairs, what conclusions might he have drawn from the example of Don Juan?
3. Take one of the upper-class women (Isabela or Doña Ana) and one of the lower-class women (Tisbea or Aminta) and write their accounts of Don Juan and what about him was attractive to them, if anything.

JOHN MILTON
Paradise Lost

Milton remains readable today because of the intensity and drama (even the theatrics) of his story. *Paradise Lost* is dedicated, as he says, to one of the great themes of human history, man's first disobedience and what follows for the human race. It supports not only the sustaining myth of Christianity, but an archetype of innocence and experience deep in the Western psyche. The importance of this theme justifies our study of its supporting doctrine.

Predestination, foreknowledge, and human freedom: The relationship among the three is the key to Milton's moral and ethical system, which is grounded in his theology. By predestination, everything is determined by God before Time begins. By foreknowledge, God already knows what will happen. By human freedom, man has the capacity to choose good or evil. The critical point is that freedom is not extinguished by the existence of predestination and foreknowledge. Thus all the power stays with God, but man is still responsible for his acts. Seldom has the system with its attendant contradictions and reinforcements been so perfectly and geometrically spelled out as in the verses of *Paradise Lost*.

The preceding paragraph uses *man* advisedly, partly because Milton himself would have framed the discussion that way, but also because the dominion of Adam over Eve is clearly established in the text of *Paradise Lost*. The relation of Eve to Adam is one of the great touchstones of this work in the twentieth century. Rather unexpectedly, Milton's concerns intersect with those of modern women, especially in the sphere of law. Milton, after all, wrote a spirited defense of divorce in a time when this was hardly conceivable; and he put speeches in the mouth of Eve that presented, for perhaps the first time in Western literature, a direct challenge to the institution of marriage. (The Wife of Bath criticized its abuses, but that is a different thing.) But Milton's greatest contribution to sexual politics was probably his use of realism. In *Paradise Lost,* he depicts the battle of the sexes in a series of dialogues that remain provocative even today. Eve's brilliant, desperate style of argument and Adam's stupid, stolid common sense ring down through the ages; no Western writer has ever captured the power struggle inherent in the marriage relationship as Milton did. (Ibsen and Tolstoy come close, but on a diminished canvas.) Students should be given the opportunity to read, reflect, and respond.

The principal episodes of the epic that we cover are these:

1. The fallen angels assemble in Hell. Satan leads the debate among them, which determines that he transport himself to Eden and corrupt Eve and Adam. (Books 1 and 2)
2. Satan, "now in prospect of Eden," sees Adam and Eve and falls into doubt; he braces himself, listens to their conversation, and craftily withdraws. (Book 4)
3. Satan appears to Eve in the form of a serpent. He entices her to eat the fruit, then to convince Adam to do the same. Once fallen, the two quarrel and cover themselves. (Book 9)
4. The archangel Michael comes to lead Adam and Eve out of Paradise. (Book 12)

Following the hints we offer in the headnote, the student should pursue Milton's role in the Renaissance as both a progressive and conservative figure. Related to this is his dual interest in the Bible and the Greek and Latin classics. Similarly, his desire to "justify the ways of God to man" must be seen from both a Protestant and humanist perspective. The greatest challenge in teaching Milton is to make him come to life, because if you don't, the text will do it for you—such is Milton's surprising power of attraction, even today. His biography is fascinating; he must be seen in relation to his turbulent times. Then again, like most great literature, *Paradise Lost* is a textured, many-faceted work, with a concern for humanity so tightly woven into its ideological core that the two parts are inseparable.

Aside from the reference works already mentioned in the headnote, the instructor also might consult the standard biography, William Riley Parker's *Milton: A Biography* (2 vols., 1968), and the following works of criticism: G. K. Hunter's *Paradise Lost* (1980), C. S. Lewis's *A Preface to Paradise Lost* (rev. ed., 1960), Northrup Frye's *The Return of Eden* (1965), A. Bartlett Giamatti's *The Earthly Paradise and the Renaissance Epic* (1966), and Diane Kelsey McColley's *Milton's Eve* (1983).

Questions for Discussion and Writing

1. *Paradise Lost* draws on both classical and biblical literature for its backgrounds. Is there conflict between these two sets of sources? How does this dual system of references affect your enjoyment of the poem?
2. Explain the doctrine of free will as Milton understands it. Why is it important that Adam and Eve should freely choose to fall from grace?
3. *Paradise Lost* is an epic, according to Milton; he patterns it after Virgil's *Aeneid*. What major features of Milton's poem put it in the epic tradition? In what way is Adam a hero? Can Satan be said to be a hero too? Why or why not?
4. William Blake said that Milton was of the devil's party without knowing it. In what ways does Milton appear to sympathize with Satan? Where does the sympathy end? How does Satan fare in his attempt to humiliate God by corrupting Adam and Eve?
5. What do you think Milton meant by Satan's saying, "The mind is its own place, and can make / A Heaven of Hell, a Hell of Heaven"? Comment on the meaning of this statement as it appears in the text and as it has meaning in the present.
6. Milton's portrayal of Eve follows Genesis but also offers individualized features. Try to isolate the poet's innovations and comment on his vision of Eve as our first mother. Is his picture sympathetic to women or not? Would you answer this question differently if you were Milton's contemporary?
7. Is *Paradise Lost* a realistic work of art? Does Milton imitate real life in any significant way? Does the poem gain or lose by the way it represents reality?
8. In what sense can our fall from grace be called "fortunate"? What do you think Milton wants us to believe concerning the Fall? According to Milton, should we fatalistically

view our prospects for salvation, or should we hope that our actions might bring us closer to heaven?

Projects

1. Compare *Paradise Lost* with Dante's *Divine Comedy* in terms of the authors' theological beliefs, their literary techniques, and their methods of representing reality. Which work has the greater appeal for you? Why? Refer to the text of the work you favor for support.

2. Compare the marriage of Adam and Eve to your idea of a typical modern marriage (describe and define the latter). What is similar and what is different? Which do you feel stands the greater chance of success? Why? Be as specific as possible, using references from the Miltonic text and examples of modern-day situations for support. This can be an individual or a group project.

SOR JUANA INÉS DE LA CRUZ
Loa for The Divine Narcissus

This *loa*, or playlet, intended to precede Sor Juana Inés de la Cruz's longer allegorical drama *The Divine Narcissus*, is an extraordinary document on several counts. It is that rare thing, a text written by a woman in the colonial Americas; moreover, it is an early sympathetic representation of Native Americans. What is especially remarkable is that the play manages to be sympathetic even while describing wholesale blood sacrifice, the aspect of Aztec culture that most horrified Europeans. To at least some degree, it is a critique of colonialism, of the European rapine of American natural resources, and especially of forced conversion. Although Occident and America become happy Christian converts at the end, it takes no little bravery for Sor Juana to describe Christian Zeal as a "mad, blind, barbaric man" who disrupts native "serenity." Occident and America give an impassioned and moving defense of their culture; "though captive I may moan in pain / Your will can never conquer mine," vows the defeated Occident. It is quite possible that her native characters give voice to Sor Juana's own feelings about her oppression as a woman in orders and her determination to keep her intellect and spirit privately free.

The natural texts for comparison in the Renaissance are of course the writings of the Aztecs themselves, especially the Aztec elders' address to Cortés defending their culture and asking to be allowed to go on with their way of life. One may ask whether Sor Juana's allegorical representation of the Aztec people comes at all near the voices who speak in those texts. Students can also juxtapose this *loa* with Montaigne's "Of Cannibals"; what would he say about the bloody rites of Huitzilopochtli, the God of Seeds?

Questions for Discussion and Writing

1. Why does Sor Juana make Zeal a man and Religion a woman?
2. Is there any discernible difference between Occident and America, other than their gender?
3. What arguments from Religion finally convert Occident and America?
4. What similarities does Sor Juana find between Aztec religion and Christianity?
5. How do Sor Juana's Aztecs compare with the Aztecs we find in the texts in the Ancient Mexicans section of this book?

6. What would Montaigne have to say about the rites used in worshipping The God of Seeds?
7. Compare Occident and America's defense of their religion with Luther's "Here I Stand" speech.

Projects

1. Stage this *loa* in class.
2. Read Chapter 23, "The Float and the Sacrament," of Octavio Paz's monumental biography *Sor Juana; or, The Traps of Faith* (1988). Summarize what Paz has to say about the historical tradition of finding similarities between pagan religions and Christianity.

LYRIC SAMPLER

Although Petrarch has a section to himself as one of the Representative Texts for the Renaissance, it is hard to imagine studying the lyric without him. Almost all Renaissance lyric is somehow in dialogue with Petrarchan conventions, whether it is working within them or revolting against them. It's good to make sure students know what a Petrarchan sonnet looks and sounds like by reviewing sonnet form and Petrarchan devices such as catalogues, antithesis, and hyperbole. This is also a good opportunity to point out the form of the English or Shakespearean sonnet—fourteen lines made up of three quatrains and a final rhymed couplet—and to explore how that structure differs from the Italian or Petrarchan sonnet, especially in the use poets make of the abrupt couplet conclusion.

If you like, you can organize the study of the Renaissance lyric thematically because a number of themes come up in this sampler of lyrics again and again. They include love; attitudes toward women and female beauty; *carpe diem*; the tug between earthly and spiritual concerns; death and mortality; the eroticization of spiritual matters, and, conversely, the spiritualization of *eros*; and the role of the poet and the value of art. As widely separated as these poems are in country of origin, ranging from Russia to Mexico, they nonetheless share these concerns. An interesting enterprise is to compare these European poems with lyrics by Li Po, Nezahualcoyotl, or Bashō to see whether your students discern any universality in the themes of lyric worldwide.

Many Renaissance lyrics were written to music, and it's nice to bring into class a few samples of Renaissance songs on tape. As we suggest in the Projects, musicians in your class might like to learn and perform a piece or two.

Many of the questions we suggest below pertain to specific poems or poets, but with a little adjustment they can often be made to apply to other poems as well.

Questions for Discussion and Writing

1. In Wyatt's "They Flee from Me," in what ways is the woman of the court, thought to be Anne Boleyn, like a hind? Does Wyatt have in mind a deer running free in the wild, or a deer in some other situation?
2. In the first stanza of Wyatt's "They Flee from Me," to what are the human "they" being compared? What is the tone of the last four lines of the poem?
3. Explore how each of the Shakespeare sonnets presented here uses the form of the English sonnet to reinforce the structure of the thought.
4. What attitude toward aging does the speaker take in Shakespeare's Sonnet 73?

5. Can you name a historical or fictional person of the sort Shakespeare is describing in Sonnet 94?

6. In Shakespeare's Sonnet 129, does the final couplet alter your attitude toward the first twelve lines of the poem? Compare its treatment of lust with Saint-Amant's "Go in the Whorehouse."

7. How does Shakespeare's Sonnet 130 mock Petrarchan conventions? In mocking them, how does it praise the mistress? Compare with Michelangelo's exuberant "You have a face that's sweeter than grape mash."

8. Describe the complex triangle situation alluded to in Shakespeare's Sonnet 144.

9. Most Renaissance poems in English are written in iambic pentameter, a ten-syllable line. Nashe's "A Litany in Time of Plague" uses six-syllable lines. What is the emotional effect of these short lines, and how do they complement the theme of the poem? How do Quevedo in his "Sonnet: Death Warnings" and Otradovic in his "Disdain for this Transitory World" treat the same theme of transience? Do any of these poems express love, respect, or regret for those things that are transitory?

10. How do John Donne's poems suggest that they are being written during a time of great geographical and scientific exploration?

11. How do John Donne and San Juan de la Cruz use erotic imagery in religious poems?

12. How does Herbert use the metaphor of business and real estate in "Redemption"?

13. Is it effective to have the surprise conclusion of "The Collar" come so abruptly? What are the dominant themes of the speaker's complaints? Why does the single word God says reduce him to obedience?

14. Sonnets usually have a two-part structure, with some sort of turn, reversal or contrast occurring in the poem. Is there such a turn, reversal or contrast in either of the two Milton sonnets?

15. In Marvell's "To His Coy Mistress," what images does he use to evoke the terror of mortality? Compare this poem to Hofmannswaldau's "The Transience of Beauty"; what is the effect of the final image of the diamond heart in the latter poem?

16. In "The Garden," how does Marvell rewrite the stories in Ovid's *Metamorphoses*? What does the image of the bird in the seventh stanza suggest about the state of the speaker's soul?

17. In Scève's "The day we passed together . . . ," how does the imagery of dark and light function? Why does the speaker image himself as a rabbit? Why is the shade "Egyptian"?

18. Compare Louise Labé's Sonnet 18 to Catullus' 5 (in the Ancient World section), on which it is partly based. Where does Labé differ from Catullus?

19. Why is Diana the goddess present in Labé's Sonnet 19?

20. Compare Pierre de Ronsard's "Epitaph on Rabelais" with the drinking songs of Li Po.

21. In what sense does Revius blame himself for Christ's death in "He Bore Our Griefs"?

22. Compare Fleming's "To My Redeemer" with Donne's "Batter my heart . . . ." How does each poem address God? What does each speaker wish?

23. How does the fact that Saint Teresa's speakers are simple shepherds contribute to "See, His blood He's shedding"? Compare this poem to Faustus's similar vision as he struggles to repent in Marlowe's play. What effect does the blood have on Faustus, as opposed to on Dominguillo and the speaker?

24. It is often said that mystical religious experience is the most difficult of all subjects to write well about. What are San Juan de la Cruz's strategies for conveying such experiences in "The Dark Night of the Soul"? How does darkness function in the poem?

25. What different points does Góngora make by way of the various flowers in "Allegory of the Brevity of Things Human"?

26. In "To Her Portrait," Sor Juana seems to be considering issues of aesthetics, human psychology, and religion. Explore the multiple meanings in this sonnet.

27. In his "On the Painting of the Sistine Chapel," what attitude does Michelangelo take toward the role of the artist? Does this poem surprise you? If yes, in what way?

28. Why does Michelangelo wish to make a statue of Luigi del Riccio instead of making one of his dead lover?

29. Having said that Dante's greatness is indescribable, how does Michelangelo go on to praise his countryman?

30. Compare Lomonosov to John Donne. How does each poet use scientific fact and observation to make his points about divine or earthly love?

Projects

1. Read a fictionalized account of the life and times of a Renaissance poet, such as the opening chapters of Virginia Woolf's *Orlando* (1928), about a young would-be writer in Elizabethan London, or Anthony Burgess's fictional biography of Shakespeare, *Nothing Like the Sun* (1975).

2. If you are a musician, learn and perform for the class a Renaissance song.

THE ANCIENT MEXICANS

By and large, education in the United States has neglected the Mesoamerican civilizations south of the border. For about a hundred years, racist assumptions prevented scholars from deciphering Mayan glyphs; it was assumed that the Maya were incapable of developing a written, phonetic language comparable to the hieroglyphic scripts of the Sumerians, Egyptians, and Chinese. Students might remember something about human sacrifice among the Aztecs, but know little about Mesoamerican art, schools, poetry, books, mythology, mathematics, and astronomy. Usually, an instructor must begin with the basics of history and the physical culture of indigenous peoples. We recommend the use of maps and photographs or slides of the major archeological sites, such as Chichén Itzá, Palenque, Tula, and Tenochtitlán.

The literature of the ancient Mexicans provides an opportunity to make comparisons with the religious documents of Europe and the ancient Near East. Although it is difficult to make accurate generalizations, there are clear differences between the world views of Renaissance writers such as Marlowe or Machiavelli and the world view of Mesoamericans. One way to begin the discussion of these differences is to recognize that the creation stories of the Judeo-Christian tradition reveal that the identity and being of its deity were clearly separate from the world. This separation allowed for differentiation between what is sacred and what is secular, what is under God's dominion and what is under human dominion.

In the creation stories of the ancient Mexicans, several deities provide their bodies to create the world, the sun, and the moon. In this view, the world is a dismembered deity; "godness" is not transcendent and separate, but immanent and integrated. Godness is everywhere, residing in all things. The word *pantheism* could be used if one is careful not to automatically dismiss native religion as pagan and to remind students about Christian angels, saints, and demons—the issue is not monotheism versus polytheism, but the differences between immanence and transcendence. Christians tended to view the life on Earth as a struggle between good and evil, Jesus and Satan, but Mesoamericans strove to balance the forces of light and dark, spirit and material.

84

The meeting of Old World and New World in the figures of Hernán Cortés and Moctezuma reveal other differences as well as similarities. As is detailed in the headnote, several spectacular omens led the Mexicans to expect the return of an important deity, Quetzalcoatl. European explorers often perceived their travels in terms of Christian beliefs: The discovery of Cape Verde in 1445, for example, called into question the mountain of Purgatory in the south. For a time, Christopher Columbus fantasized about the Orinoco River in Edenic terms. Both Spaniards and Aztecs could be warlike and aggressive as well as peaceful and compassionate.

Questions for Discussion and Writing

1. Discuss student preconceptions about the Aztecs and Mesoamericans. What new discoveries about the life and thought of these indigenous peoples do the readings provide?

2. The ancient Mexicans believed that they lived in a world balanced between sky and earth, light and dark, creation and destruction, spirit and matter. How do the creation stories express this view?

3. The ancient creation story of Mesopotamia features a combat between a hero-god Marduk and a water goddess Tiamat; in the writings of the Greek poet Hesiod, the first deities are involved in struggles between fathers and sons; rebellion and murder characterize the first stories in Genesis. Discuss the reasons why the creation of order from chaos might involve violence. What is the role of violence in the Aztec creation stories?

4. How does "The Creation of the Earth" suggest that the ancient Mexicans lived in a volcanic region?

5. Compare the Aztec creation stories with the story of Adam and Eve in Genesis and Milton. How do pain and suffering play important roles in these stories?

6. In the Aztec creation stories, Quetzalcoatl plays the role of a culture bringer, a primeval being who provides the basic necessities of a particular society. What basic necessities of Aztec culture does Quetzalcoatl provide? How do Aztec deities model important behavior for mortals?

7. "The Myth of Quetzalcoatl," as discussed in the headnote, combines the qualities of a deity with those of a cultural hero. What qualities of Quetzalcoatl make him the great, messianic hero of ancient Mexico even though he succumbs to temptation?

8. The Aztec creation stories portray an unstable world, subject to imbalance and even destruction. How are these concerns reflected in Nezahualcoyotl's poems?

9. Discuss the roles of nature in Nezahualcoyotl's poems.

10. Discuss the similarities and differences between Cortés and Moctezuma. How is Cortés's view of the world different from Moctezuma's?

11. Does Christopher Columbus's *Diario* provide insights into Cortés's Renaissance personality and world view?

12. How are the qualities of courage and integrity revealed in "A Defense of Aztec Religion"?

Projects

1. One of the classics of American literature and history is William H. Prescott's *The Conquest of Mexico,* which provides an outsider's description of Cortés's personality and his military expedition. How is Prescott's perspective different from the Aztec account in this anthology? Does Prescott offer any insights into Moctezuma's reluctance to crush the Spaniards?

2. Examine other encounters between Europe and America. Did the world views differ? How might one explain the differences in values? Discuss the psychology of conquerors who presume that they have nothing to learn from the conquered.

3. Does Shakespeare's *The Tempest* raise issues about the relationship of Europeans with native peoples that might be relevant to the experiences of the Spanish in the Americas? One might consult Denis Diderot's *Supplement to the Voyage of Bougainville* in Volume Two of this anthology for a critical comparison of European and Tahitian life-styles.

WU CH'ÊNG-ÊN
Monkey

Although *Monkey* is easy and delightful reading, there is no familiar Western work that is enough like it to show Western audiences how to read it. Like Mandeville's *Travels,* it is an account of an actual journey, the historical trek of Hsüan Tsang to bring the Buddhist scriptures from India back to China, and like Mandeville's work it contains a great deal of nonhistorical, legendary material. But *Monkey* is considerably more fabulous than Mandeville; its fantastic episodes are reminiscent of tall tales such as those recounting the exploits of Paul Bunyan or Odysseus' heroic deeds. The story of a religious pilgrimage, *Monkey* includes comic episodes that make it very different from Dante's deadly serious Easter pilgrimage, and closer to the mixture of the comic and the serious in Chaucer's *Canterbury Tales.* The trickster Monkey, hero of Wu's tale, may be a little like such Renaissance tricksters as Don Juan and Doctor Faustus, and similar to figures such as Coyote in American Indian tales. Prospero's benevolent magic in *The Tempest* also may recall Monkey's magical services for Tripitaka. Among Western works, *Monkey* may be most like *Don Quixote*: Tripitaka's spiritual commitment resembles Quixote's idealism; both narratives are constructed on a loosely connected series of adventures; and although Monkey and Sancho Panza contrast with their masters, both provide necessary common sense and practical support on the journey.

None of these connections, however, gives us a model by which to read the unusual mixture of the serious and the comic in *Monkey.* To us, the work may seem less than literary, closer to superhero comic books than to epics or novels. Monkey's magical needle and his powers of shape changing and traveling between heaven and earth are fabulous and funny as well as supernatural. This unusual combination may bring us closer to something that might be described as comic epic than does Fielding's *Joseph Andrews.* For all their superhuman powers, however, Wu's superheroes—Monkey, Pigsy, and Sandy—are less than perfect. Like the heroes of novels, they must grow during the journey, along with the monk Tripitaka, to merit their role in the spiritual task they have undertaken.

Questions for Discussion and Writing

1. What characteristics of Monkey lead to his quarrel with Tripitaka and his threat to leave his role as a pilgrim?

2. Consider the references to the Jade Emperor and the heaven he administers. What sort of heaven is it? How would you characterize the realm of the gods generally in this story? Is Wu's depiction of heaven satiric? reverential? both?

3. The original title of Wu's narrative translates as *The Journey to the West.* Do you think that Arthur Waley, who titled his translation *Monkey,* would have been truer to the intent of the story if he had kept the original title or titled it *Tripitaka*?

4. Characterize each of the pilgrims—Tripitaka, Monkey, Pigsy, and Sandy—and define what you think the allegorical significance of each is.

5. Compare the story of the King of Crow-cock with *Hamlet* or the story of Orestes. What elements do they have in common? How are they different? What parts of the King of Crow-cock story seem to be serious? What parts are comic? How would you characterize the comedy in this story?

6. How does Tripitaka's pilgrimage compare to Western pilgrimage stories? Is its allegory similar to that in Dante's *Divine Comedy?* If Monkey is Tripitaka's Virgil, what does he represent allegorically?

7. Is the relationship between Tripitaka and Monkey at all like the relationship between Don Quixote and Sancho Panza? What do *Don Quixote* and *Monkey* have in common as novels?

Projects

1. Compare the gods in *Monkey* with the Greek gods in Homer. What similarities and differences do you find?

2. Two contemporary novels that draw on the legends of Monkey are Maxine Hong Kingston's *Tripmaster Monkey* and Gerald Vizenor's *Griever: An American Monkey King in China.* Compare one or both of these novels to *Monkey.* How do these modern writers update the character of Monkey and his story?

3. Recall one of the trickster stories that you may have heard as a child (for example, Brer Rabbit, Reynard the Fox, Aunt Nancy, or Coyote stories). Write a contemporary version of it.

TEACHING WESTERN LITERATURE IN A WORLD CONTEXT

Volume Two
The Enlightenment
through the Present

THE

ENLIGHTENMENT

❧

Reason

and

Sensibility

FRANÇOIS-MARIE AROUET DE VOLTAIRE
Candide

One of the reasons that *Candide* continues to be so popular is that it is so funny and accessible; it is a joy to teach. Although some students might want to dig into Leibniz's thought, it is not really necessary to go beyond the excerpt we have provided in the Background Texts; Voltaire is not so much satirizing Leibnizean philosophers as he is being critical of the Panglosses of the world—people who distort the complexity of problems with oversimplification and glib solutions, whether they are metaphysical, religious, or rational. Candide's journey through various locales is also a passage from innocence to experience, and might be compared to the persona in Rousseau's *Confessions* and the narrator in *Gulliver's Travels*.

Central to Voltaire's writing style is *irony:* irony exists when the suggested meaning of a statement is different from the literal meaning. Voltaire is fond of creating irony through the use of hyperbole and understatement. In Chapter 1, Pangloss's field of study is an exaggerated metaphysico-theologo-cosmolo-nigology, but description of the lustful encounter between Cunegonde and Candide later in the chapter is described with incredible restraint and feigned tastefulness. Irony regularly attends the exploration of a central philosophical theme of theodicy, the attempt to reconcile an all-powerful, good God with the existence of evil in the world. When disasters strike, Pangloss springs to life with a positive explanation justifying pain and suffering: Everything is for the best in the best of all possible worlds.

Questions for Discussion and Writing

1. Does Pangloss represent the ivory tower philosopher? Who represents philosophical views different from his?
2. How does Voltaire turn serious actions such as murders, the Inquisition, and earthquakes into events for satire and even humor?
3. What kinds of evil does Candide encounter among the Bulgarians, in Holland, and in Lisbon? Does Voltaire use understatement or hyperbole in his depictions of priests?
4. Discuss how Cacambo is a foil to Candide.
5. What makes El Dorado a utopia? Does Voltaire imply that the utopian El Dorado has a negative side to it?
6. What philosophical position does Martin represent? How does Martin contribute to the development of Candide's character?
7. Compare Voltaire's treatment of his own country of France with his treatment of other countries.
8. Does Candide learn anything from his adventures or does he essentially remain the same throughout the novel?
9. Discuss the possible meanings of Candide's culminating observation, "We must take care of our garden." Do you think that Voltaire is recommending a retreat from social involvement?

Projects

1. In the Enlightenment, rationality was applied to all aspects of society, including religion. Compare the ways in which religion is treated in *New Atlantis, Tartuffe, Candide, Supplement to the Voyage of Bougainville,* and *The Narrow Road through the Provinces.*
2. The great European explorations of the globe stimulated wide-ranging searches for the original Garden of Eden or its secular equivalent. Compare the utopian El Dorado with Bacon's New Atlantis, Diderot's Tahiti, and Swift's land of the Houyhnhnms. Where would you prefer to live?
3. Compare the uses of satire in *Candide, Tartuffe,* and *Gulliver's Travels.* What are the similarities and differences in these works? How does the fact that *Tartuffe* is a play make a difference in the nature of its satire?

JEAN-JACQUES ROUSSEAU
Confessions

In the headnotes to the Enlightenment and to Rousseau, we've discussed how the *Confessions* marks a shift in emphasis in the eighteenth century from reason to feeling, but it is worth reminding students (and ourselves) that the passions were always a concern for Enlightenment thinkers before Rousseau; likewise, although he objected to being called a *philosophe,* Rousseau shared their skepticism about deductive reasoning and metaphysics and their basic meliorism. In some ways, his attention to matters of the heart and of the development of the self results from subjecting those entities to an empirical study—here in the form of an autobiography. As Rousseau declares in the opening paragraph, his *Confessions* amounted to "an undertaking, hitherto without precedent," although he was certainly aware of Augustine's *Confessions* and seems even at times to allude to it. What makes Rousseau's autobiography unique—its focus upon the inner self, the way events shape the emotional composure of a person—may be readily seen by comparing his *Confessions* to Augustine's (in Volume One), or to the autobiographies of his contemporaries that we include here: Benjamin Frankin's *Autobiography* and Olaudah Equiano's *The Interesting Narrative of the Life of Olaudah Equiano.* Unlike the *Confessions,* these works focus primarily on events that affect the development of their authors' moral character. Although Franklin makes something of a spectacle of his "errata," his approach to them remains less than candid and avoids investigating their emotional consequences—to himself or to others. Rousseau, on the other hand, relishes his "unworthiness and imperfections"—some of them, such as his masochism and petty thievery, are rather startling. Rousseau focuses primarily on the feelings aroused by incidents in his life, and he shows how these feelings leave a lasting impression on his character. Rather than draw lessons about morality, Rousseau's *Confessions* strives to attain another kind of truth, one about feeling, about the formation of subjectivity, of individuality. For this reason, Rousseau has been seen as the precursor to romanticism, and the *Confessions* invites comparison with the selections from Wordsworth's autobiographical *Prelude* in the next unit.

We include all of Book I to give students a sense of Rousseau's style and the organization of the *Confessions.* Book I begins with a series of claims about Rousseau's unique character, his difference from other men and women, and his commitment to complete honesty in recounting his innermost secrets before the public. Book I then presents a succession of key events from his childhood. One way to approach the text is to think of these events as what Wordsworth calls "spots of time"—memories of moments invested with intense feeling that have had a lasting effect on his character. The key incidents in Book I include reading books in his father's library, being falsely accused of breaking Mlle. Lambercier's comb, building the aqueduct for the walnut tree, stealing M. de Franceuil's money, and finally leaving Geneva. He also tells the story of his first love affairs—with Mlle. de Vulson and Mlle. Goton. Each incident offers a focus for class discussion and helps to differentiate the kinds of feelings that Rousseau deals with in Book I. For example, from his reading of books Rousseau claims to have gained a spirit of independence and pride; from his wrongful punishment over Mlle. Lambercier's comb he traces his strong contempt for injustice and his loss of innocence. Rousseau describes his transformation during his apprenticeship to M. Ducommun, the engraver, as a descent "from the sublimity of heroism to the depths of worthlessness." Students may follow the emotional track through Book I and find some faint parallels with the story of the expulsion from the garden of Eden or with the loss of the Golden Age, for Rousseau's is a story of loss. Rousseau's view of childhood anticipates the celebration of innocence that becomes a major feature of romanticism, and you might discuss how Rousseau defines childhood as a golden age and sees the development into adulthood as a steady erosion of happiness, innocence, imagination, and even individuality. Here comparison with Wordsworth's "Ode: Intimations of Immortality" and with Voltaire's *Candide* may be helpful.

Questions for Discussion and Writing

1. How does Rousseau describe, overall, his childhood? What does he gain and what does he lose as he grows older?

2. Is Rousseau somewhat disingenuous when he says that he will disclose everything about himself, to enumerate truly every feeling? What signs do we have that he may or may not be completely honest?

3. Why does Rousseau tell us about his masochism—his fondness for spankings? How has that shaped his character or had a lasting impact?

4. Consider the incident of false accusation and punishment for breaking Mlle. Lambercier's comb. What does Rousseau learn from this event? Was his experience wholly negative? Discuss how in many of these incidents Rousseau displays mixed feelings and seems to find some compensation for his apparent losses.

5. Compare Rousseau's love for Mlle. de Vulson and Mlle. Goton.

6. How does Rousseau respond to the tyranny of M. Ducommun, the engraver to whom he is apprenticed? Why? Discuss how he generalizes principles from his experience, here and in other incidents.

7. Wordsworth describes childhood as an apprenticeship to love and to fear, to the beautiful and the sublime. Do these terms apply to Rousseau's account of his childhood? Compare Rousseau's loss of innocence to Candide's.

8. Discuss Rousseau's characterization of his childhood development as a downward spiral "from the sublimity of heroism to the depths of worthlessness." What does he mean by the "sublimity of heroism"? Has he gained anything from this decline?

9. Compare the tone and voice of Rousseau's *Confessions* with Franklin's *Autobiography,* Equiano's *Life,* or Bashō's *The Narrow Road through the Provinces.*

10. Discuss the apparent modernism of Rousseau's *Confessions* in contrast with other works of the Enlightenment. Does Rousseau seem closer to us than Voltaire or Diderot?

Projects

1. Write a chapter of your own *Confessions,* focusing on a few incidents from your childhood that seem to have left an enduring impression on your character.

2. Michel Foucault describes the post-Enlightenment era as the age of the confession, where the institutions of psychoanalysis, criminal justice, government, the family, and education demand from us an accounting of our innermost feelings, thoughts, and actions. What cultural, economic, and social changes during the eighteenth century might begin to explain why Rousseau would feel the need, as he puts it, to let "the countless host of my fellow-men . . . hear my confessions, lament for my unworthiness, and blush for my imperfections"?

JEAN-BAPTISTE POQUELIN MOLIÈRE
Tartuffe

Comedies often use stock situations within the framework of a standard plot structure, which is summarized here by Northrop Frye in the *Anatomy of Criticism:*

> What normally happens is that a young man wants a young woman, that his desire is resisted by some opposition, usually paternal, and that near the end of the play some twist in the plot enables the hero to have his will. In this simple pattern there are several complex elements. In the first place, the movement of comedy is usually a movement from one kind of society to another. At the beginning of the play the obstructing characters are in charge of the play's society, and the audience recognizes that they are usurpers. At the end of the play the device in the plot that brings the hero and heroine together causes a new society to crystallize around the hero. . . .
>
> The appearance of this new society is frequently signalized by some kind of party or festive ritual, which either appears at the end of the play or is assumed to take place immediately afterward. (p. 163)

The *comedy of manners,* which pokes fun at the affectations, manners, and conventions of society, uses a number of conventions such as stock characters: foolish old men and women, the jealous husband, young naïve lovers, the clever maid, the hypocrite, and the buffoon. Stock situations involve missed communication, misunderstandings, deceit, and trickery. These comedic conventions make it easy for the audience to recognize the main characters and the overall plot of the play; after all, the main thrust of a comedy does not rest with depth of character or with *whether* the impostor will be unmasked, but with clever twists and turns in the action, with *how* the world will be restored to balance and harmony.

The world at the beginning of *Tartuffe* seems hopelessly ensnared in the chicanery of hypocrisy; Orgon, the gullible fool, and Tartuffe, the impostor, are blocking figures whose maneuvers hopelessly frustrate the courtship between Valère and Mariane. The key to hypocrisy is the discrepancy between appearance and reality; Cléante describes this in the first act:

> Is not a face quite different from a mask?
> Cannot sincerity and cunning art,
> Reality and semblance, be told apart?
> Are scarecrows just like men, and do you hold
> That a false coin is just as good as gold?

Not only does the impostor depend upon situations where his victims confuse appearance and reality, but delight and satire are the byproducts of this confusion. Underneath the comic devices and situations is the sober realization that innocent people can be hurt by bad judgment and evil schemes. Mariane might be forced by her father's pigheadedness into a disastrous marriage. Self-deluding characteristics have been passed down from Mme. Pernelle to her son, Orgon, and from father to Damis and Mariane. In the comic scene between Valère and Mariane in Act II, appearances confuse reality as communication fails and a breach opens in the relationship.

By the end of the play, however, the complications are resolved by the almost artificial intervention of the king; a most hospitable social situation emerges, which is symbolized by the marriage of Valère and Mariane.

An excellent way to begin the discussion of this play is to select certain scenes, divide up the speaking parts, and read these selections out loud, in order to learn about Molière's skill as a dramatist: the economy of his language, the cleverness of his plot twists, and the wit of his satirical thrusts.

Questions for Discussion and Writing

1. How does Molière use small details to pinpoint his characters?
2. One of the funniest scenes in all comedy is in Act I, Scene 4 of *Tartuffe,* in which Orgon responds to Dorine with "And Tartuffe?" What does the dialogue reveal about Orgon and why is it so funny?
3. One of the prime targets of satirists in the Enlightenment was intellectual pretension. Discuss the different uses of reason in *Tartuffe* and *Candide;* Dorine, for example, seems to use common sense and represent practical reason. Are there characters who use theoretical reason? Which characters are humorous because of their intellectual airs?
4. We live in an age that has developed a language of family systems: family dynamics, healthy boundaries, codependency, open communication, conditional love, and so forth. Discuss the dynamics of Orgon's family. What characteristics of this family are common today?
5. Discuss the roles of women in *Tartuffe.* How do Dorine and Elmire display both intelligence and independence?
6. Discuss how the scene between Elmire and Tartuffe (Act IV, Scene 5) makes use of slapstick.

7. Discuss the resolution of the play in Act V. What effect does the king's intervention have on the meaning of the play? Is it back to normal for the patriarchal social structure?
8. Both *Tartuffe* and *The Love Suicides at Amijima* deal with questions of honor or duty to one's family and to society. Although *Tartuffe* is a comedy of manners and *The Love Suicides at Amijima* a tragedy, what do they have in common?

Projects

1. Discuss the variety of perspectives on sexuality in *Tartuffe, Candide,* and *Supplement to the Voyage of Bougainville.*
2. Compare the roles of women in *Tartuffe* with other Enlightenment texts dealing with gender roles. How do the women in these works both fit and exceed typical stereotypes for women before and after the Enlightenment?

MARIE DE LA VERGNE DE LA FAYETTE
The Princess of Clèves

The historical setting of *The Princess of Clèves* is important to the novel, but the many names and relationships may be daunting to students, particularly to those with little knowledge of European history. Most students merely need to know that many of the characters are historical figures from a period a century or so earlier than the time of the writing and that the central character, the Princesse, is a wholly fictional creation. For students who are interested in history, the novel provides numerous opportunities to compare Madame de La Fayette's fictional characters with their historical originals and to speculate on her reasons for choosing to set the story in the court of Henry II.

The historical setting is also significant for understanding the ways in which politics and love are linked, both in the court of Henry II and in that of Louis XIV, of which Madame de La Fayette was a member. *The Princess of Clèves* is more than a costume drama or historical romance; the love story is also a political story and the duty for which Madame de Clèves sacrifices her passion extends beyond personal considerations to include political and social dimensions. It is useful when considering the concept of duty in the novel to relate it to the ideals of reason, order, and decorum during the period.

Although the novel is set in the court of Henry II and includes many important historical figures, it does not focus on these grand people or on the politics of the day. In its time, it was a radical departure from the grandiloquent romances that preceded it, for it focuses on the character of the Princesse. In narrowing her subject to her heroine's psychology, Madame de La Fayette produced what is sometimes described as the first psychological novel or the first novel of character in French literature.

The character of the Princesse has been controversial from the beginning. Madame de La Fayette's contemporaries argued about the wisdom or foolishness of her confession to her husband and whether her scrupulousness was believable in the context of the manners of the court. Modern readers have been more bothered by her refusal to marry Nemours after the death of Clèves. By resisting the pressures of the court and the pull of her own passion, however, the Princesse takes control of her life and maintains her personal integrity. The importance that the novel gives to these psychological issues gives them a primacy over the external politics of the court. Although her decisions seem to affirm reason and restraint over passion and personal indulgence, the paradox at the heart of the story suggests that the Princesse can only fulfill herself and achieve personal autonomy by denying her passion.

1. What details in the description of Henry II's court that opens the novel are particularly relevant to the story of the Princesse de Clèves? What are the qualities most admired in courtiers? By what rules does the court operate? How do the manners of the court conceal what is going on behind the scenes? What is the point of view of the narrator in the opening scenes of the novel?

2. What indications are there of the naïveté of the Princesse at the beginning of the novel? Why does she marry Clèves? What signs are there as the story goes on that she is no longer as naïve as she was earlier in the story?

3. How is love "always mixed with politics and politics with love" in this novel? In what ways is the Princesse's marriage political?

4. What do the stories told within the novel—for example, the account of the relationship between the King and Diane de Poitiers, Clèves's story about Madame de Tournon, and the story of Nemours's "courtship" of Elizabeth I of England—contribute to the story of the Princesse de Clèves?

5. Why does the Princesse confess to her husband that she loves another man? Is her action believable in the story? Does she do the right thing?

6. What does Nemours's spying on Madame de Clèves say about the life of the court? about Nemours? about the inner desires of the Princesse?

7. Why does the Princesse not marry Nemours after her husband's death?

8. *The Princess of Clèves* is often described as a novel that explores the conflict between love and duty. What constitutes duty in this novel? In what ways is the conflict between love and duty related to the conflict between reason and emotion that is treated in other Enlightenment works such as *Tartuffe, The Rape of the Lock,* and *The Love Suicides at Amijima?*

9. Can *The Princess of Clèves* be considered a feminist novel?

10. Marguerite de Navarre's story of Amadour and Florida is sometimes considered a source for *The Princess of Clèves.* Compare the two stories; especially compare Florida and the Princesse. Are the two works enough alike to consider them related or so different that the comparison obscures the virtues of each?

Projects

1. Compare the Princesse de Clèves to Catherine Earnshaw in *Wuthering Heights* and Nora Helmer in *A Doll's House.* How are the situations that all three women face similar and different? Do the class differences between the three women change their situations? How do they resolve the conflicts they face?

2. Read up on the courts of Henry II and Louis XIV, the Sun King. In what ways were the two eras similar? How might Madame de La Fayette have been using Henry's court as a way of talking about Louis's court, of which she was a part?

MARY ROWLANDSON
Narrative of the Captivity and Restoration of Mrs. Mary Rowlandson

The *Narrative of the Captivity and Restoration of Mrs. Mary Rowlandson* was meant to be read as a demonstration of "the sovereignty and goodness of God," as its full title suggests, but we read it today more for what it tells us about the encounter between cultures in seventeenth-century New England and for the glimpse it affords of a colonial woman's physical and psychological endurance under duress. Rowlandson had no notion when she wrote that her narrative would be read by anyone who might take a more sympathetic view toward her captors than she; she feels no need at all to persuade us of the Indians' inherent viciousness nor of the distastefulness of their way of life. The fascination of the *Narrative* partly lies in how Rowlandson tells us more than she intends to about the Native Americans' bravery, stamina, common sense, compassion, and commitment to sharing what resources they possess.

From our vantage point, we know certain things that Rowlandson did not; we are aware of the high rank Rowlandson's "mistress" Weetamoo held among her own people, for instance, and we know that Algonquin captives, unless they were somehow troublesome, were usually well-cared-for and ransomed or adopted into the tribe. But even in her ignorance and understandable prejudice, expecting the very worst, Rowlandson tries to tell as straight and fair a story as she can, praising individual Indians for their kindness and remarking with some wonder that no one attempts to rape any of the captives and no one ever seems to go hungry as long as there is any food to share.

Rowlandson herself is compelling to observe throughout the *Narrative*. As she moves beyond the shock and grief of her capture and her child's death, she gradually recovers her natural feistiness and discovers how to make a place for herself in an alien society. Students may be interested in comparing Rowlandson's account with Sarah Winnemucca Hopkins's to see how an American Indian culture is viewed by an insider.

Questions for Discussion and Writing

1. Trace the stages by which Rowlandson recovers from her initial devastation. The single greatest blow is her child's death; how does she manage to continue? Does she receive any help from her captors in this crisis?

2. How does Rowlandson enter into the economic life of the Algonquins? How would you describe their attitude toward her?

3. What are Rowlandson's assumptions about American Indians? Do any of her assumptions seem questionable, given the evidence she herself presents? Does her own attitude change in the course of the narrative?

4. How does Rowlandson view the relations and power balances between the sexes among Native American men and women?

5. To what parts of biblical history does Rowlandson liken her own plight?

6. How do you think Mary Rowlandson would respond to Mary Astell's *A Serious Proposal to the Ladies*?

7. Compare Rowlandson's *Narrative* with Sarah Winnemucca Hopkins's *Life Among the Piutes*. What different things is an insider such as Winnemucca likely to talk about? What changes have occurred in Indian–Euro-American relations in the years that separate these two narratives?

8. Contrast Rowlandson's narrative with Equiano's or Jacobs's. What are the differences between a white captivity narrative and a black slave narrative?

9. Many European authors in this anthology see American or South Seas places as either primitivist utopias or dangerous savage wilds. How do Montaigne's, Bacon's, and Diderot's ideas about native places and peoples hold up in the light of Rowlandson's first-hand account? Does her experience challenge, reaffirm, or disturb the European notions of America?

10. Compare Rowlandson's narrative with Lady Mary Wortley Montagu's description of the time she spends among the Turks. Do the women have anything in common as observers?

1. Write an account of Mary Rowlandson's captivity from the point of view of Weetamoo, her "mistress."
2. Read several other captivity narratives, such as those in Frederick Drimmer's *Captured by the Indians: Fifteen First-Hand Accounts, 1750–1870* (1961). What features do they share with Rowlandson's *Narrative?*

JONATHAN SWIFT
Gulliver's Travels

Students may be dismayed or disgusted by *Gulliver's Travels,* especially if they've previously encountered only watered-down retellings of Gulliver's visit to Lilliput, but they seldom fail to become engaged with this book. The text is so readable that it often seems like an easy text to students, and they may need the instructor's help to realize just how elusive, complex, and fast-moving Swift's satire actually is. Reading closely, as a class, one of Swift's particularly dizzying passages—the four concluding paragraphs of Book IV, for example—is a worthwhile exercise. It is important to get students thinking about Gulliver's reliability as a narrator. Like all readers, students will want to know with a certainty that is sure to elude them exactly where Swift stands on the matter of Houyhnhnms, Yahoos, and human beings as we know them. Are Yahoos human, or degenerated descendants of humans, or something else altogether; in particular, how close does Swift actually think human beings are to his noxious creatures? Are the Houyhnhnms really Swift's idea of an ideal society? How close is Swift's view to Gulliver's? Students are often surprised by the wide divergence of opinion among themselves on these questions, and surprised as well to understand that an author can be as deliberately ambiguous as Swift, and that a text can propose problems without providing definitive answers.

One obvious strategy for teaching Books III and IV is to compare the various scientific and social utopias in the anthology with one another—Laputa and Houyhnhnmland, for example, with Bacon's New Atlantis and with the Academy envisioned by Mary Astell. Houyhnhnmland also can be compared to Diderot's South Seas island, Voltaire's El Dorado, and tribal woodlands life before the coming of the Europeans, as the Micmac elder describes it. Students can explore how these texts valorize or sharply criticize what is defined by Europeans as reasonable and civilized in matters of government, family life, education, sexuality, scientific learning, and religion.

Questions for Discussion and Writing

1. What contemporary scientific research might Swift satirize in a twentieth-century account of Laputa?
2. What do the experiments undertaken by the projectors of Laputa have in common?
3. Are there any points of comparison between the House of Saloman and Laputa's academy?
4. How close are the Yahoos to human beings?
5. Would you like to be a Houyhnhnm? Why or why not? What would you miss from your normal life if you lived among them?
6. What aspects of European society is Swift satirizing in his account of the Yahoos?
7. Swift's work is insistently scatological. What does the emphasis on the Yahoos' physical filthiness add to the text?

8. Compare Houyhnhnmland with other utopias you have encountered in this course. Which, if any of them, would you prefer to live in, and why?
9. By the end of Book IV, what is your assessment of Gulliver's psychological state?
10. How does the presence of Captain Pedro de Mendez in the narrative add to the text?
11. How would a Houyhnhnm judge the Princesse de Clèves or Chikamatsu's lovers? What figures of Enlightenment literature that you have read would they most admire?
12. *Gulliver's Travels* imitates the popular genre of the travel narrative. One of the problems for authors writing about visits to fantastic places, real or imagined, is that they must convince us they have actually seen and done the wondrous things they tell us about. How do Swift, Equiano, Montagu, Bacon, and Diderot handle the problem of making their narratives sound valid?

Projects

1. Why does Swift choose to make the Houyhnhnms horses? What animal or being might a contemporary satirist choose to be the inhabitant of his utopia?
2. Imagine you are Gulliver transported to this time. Write the account of your trip to a compelling contemporary place such as Las Vegas, Washington, D.C., Silicon Valley, or your own city or institution.

ALEXANDER POPE
The Rape of the Lock *and* An Essay on Man

Pope's is a complex and mannered society, and he depicts his world in the highly structured form of the heroic couplet: pairs of rhymed and end-stopped iambic pentameter lines. Beginning students of eighteenth-century literature often do not find Pope as immediate or accessible as Swift, Voltaire, Molière, or Franklin. But reading Pope, as a teacher who loved him was once heard to remark, can be "like running barefoot through Tiffany's," a sensual and intellectual delight made up of many small surprises.

In order for Pope to work well in a classroom, students must understand the jokes and appreciate the heroic couplet. Obviously, neither is best accomplished by the teacher laboriously explaining every joke and poetic device. The fun is probably best conveyed by a skillful reader of comic verse. Engravings by Hogarth and other contemporary artists may help evoke Pope's milieu. As for the heroic couplet, one strategy is to pick out five or six especially tasty couplets, divide your class into groups, and let each explore how their assigned couplet works to comic effect—what are the rhyme words, and how might they be related to one another? Does the word order set up and then undermine any expectations? What things are incongruously juxtaposed or made to seem equal by being listed in a series? The excerpt from *An Essay on Man* gives students a small taste of the philosophical Pope, here using his matchless skill in the couplet not for comic ends but to manipulate argument. Nothing will convey more to your students about the art and the degree of difficulty of the heroic couplet than trying to write a few themselves. (You might make a rhyming dictionary available to your class and spend fifteen minutes with teams vying to write the best couplets on some matter of current concern.)

We are assuming that students will already have some knowledge of the epic and be able to recognize the epic machineries Pope is bringing to bear on Belinda's self-involved little society in *The Rape of the Lock*. But you may want to call attention to specific allusions and compare, for example, Ariel's descent into the Cave of Spleen with other epic underworld visits, or Pope's battle-scene of Book IV with those in *The Iliad*.

The Rape of the Lock gains much if students are able to see beyond its sparkle and froth to a hint of the darker waters below, and what the poem has to say about women in a patriarchal society that gives them no encouragement to develop their minds or their spirits and that values them most for beauty and virginity, stock that is certain only to lower in value as they age.

Questions for Discussion and Writing

1. Compare the epic devices in *The Rape of the Lock* with similar moments in other epics you've read. Compare, for example, Belinda dressing with Achilles arming for battle in *The Iliad,* or Pope's sylphs and gnomes with Milton's angels and fallen angels.
2. What sorts of psychological attitudes and social behaviors does Pope seem to encompass in the word *spleen*? Does any modern term seem to be a close equivalent?
3. How does Pope's dictum "Whatever is, is right" stack up against Pangloss's theory that this is the best of all possible worlds? Does Pope support his argument convincingly?
4. What serious issues underlie the playfulness of *The Rape of the Lock?*
5. Do any of the observations Marie Le Jars de Gournay or Mary Astell make about women seem to be borne out by Belinda and her friends?
6. Choose one couplet from *The Rape of the Lock,* another from *An Essay on Man,* and explore how each makes effective use of its form to comic or serious effect.
7. Many critics view the Baron's act as symbolic of an actual rape, or bodily violation of some sort. How is the topic of rape or violence against women treated by Christine de Pizan, Marguerite de Navarre, and Emily Dickinson (in Poem 512, "The soul has bandaged moments")?
8. What does the elaborate description of Belinda's room tell us about Belinda and her world? What other characters are associated with other sorts of emblematic details?

Projects

1. Attempt a poem in heroic couplets that satirically presents some local or national issue of current interest that seems to you to have been overblown.
2. Research the rules for Ombre and play a hand.

BENJAMIN FRANKLIN
Autobiography

In the Enlightenment section, we have included a number of autobiographical or semiautobiographical texts, and students may be asked to compare Franklin, Rousseau, Rowlandson, Bashō, and Equiano in terms of how they present themselves, what sorts of things they think are important to tell, and what sorts of information they are content to leave out of their accounts of their lives. (Other autobiographical texts in Volume Two are by Harriet Jacobs, Sarah Winnemucca Hopkins, Henry David Thoreau, N. Scott Momaday, and Elie Weisel.)

Franklin's eminently practical and rational approach to life can be compared with the attitude of other Enlightenment figures toward various projects; his own life and the society in which he lives are projects he is bent on improving through cleverness and hard work. His printer's metaphor of "errata" implies both that wrong moves, misjudgments, and unhappy events are totally the result of human laziness or carelessness, and that they can be erased. What is most interesting of all is what Franklin does not emphasize or omits altogether from his account of his life—most of his family life, his romantic entanglements, indeed most areas of life that have high emotional content. In the debate between reason and sensibility, there is little doubt which side Franklin takes.

In this prototype of self-help manuals, the virtue chart is a graphic example of Franklin's cheerful attitude toward human perfectability. Students can ask themselves what doesn't appear on the chart that they might consider worth working toward in their own moral, ethical, social, or spiritual lives. Charity? Open-mindedness? Inner peace? (We want to warn you, though, that unless you can get your students to approach this with somewhat light hearts and active imaginations, this assignment can result in some of the deadliest essays you'll ever see, full of earnest resolves to improve study habits and nutrition.)

The *Autobiography* is easy and engaging reading, but it is easy for students to miss Franklin's irony and to overlook the fact that Franklin is capable of poking fun at himself and his own attitudes, as he does in the tale of the farmer and the speckled axe.

Questions for Discussion and Writing

1. How does Franklin depict himself as a child? What traits are revealed in the boyhood incidents he relates?
2. How does Franklin's trade as a printer befit his character and interests?
3. What does Franklin mean by *errata?* What is the significance of this term?
4. What sorts of things does Franklin omit from his account that you might expect to find in a modern autobiography?
5. Compare Franklin's autobiography with Rousseau's and at least one other Enlightenment autobiography. Have they anything in common? What does each choose to emphasize? Who are their imagined audiences? What might account for the differences in style and focus?
6. Compare Franklin with Bashō or Equiano as travelers.
7. Franklin is definitely a positive thinker. What, if anything, saves him from being a Pangloss?
8. What features of this autobiography make it seem fitting that its author will go on to be a framer of the Declaration of Independence?

Projects

1. In his lifetime, Franklin was a great ladies' man, and in his old age, much of it spent in France, many young women treated him as their confidant. How would Franklin advise Pope's Belinda or the Princesse de Clèves to conduct their lives?
2. Design a chart to help improve yourself. What qualities or habits will you choose to work on acquiring? Don't be afraid to make your chart more lighthearted than Franklin's; you may really feel that you need to work more on daydreaming or on your rollerblading technique.

DENIS DIDEROT
Supplement to the Voyage of Bougainville

Throughout the age of discovery, but especially in the eighteenth century, European writers used native peoples (both real and imagined) as standards (both positive and negative) against which to measure and test the moral, social, and political behavior of Europeans. In its use of Tahiti as a site of sexual freedom and its portrayal of the Tahitian as a "noble savage," Diderot's *Supplement to the Voyage of Bougainville* is linked to other works such as Shakespeare's *Tempest,* Montaigne's "Of Cannibals" (included in Volume One), Defoe's *Robinson Crusoe,* and Rousseau's *Discourse on the Origin of Inequality,* in which non-Europeans appear primarily to shed light on Europeans. Like Rousseau, Diderot sees in the native people a vestige of the Golden Age, a society untainted by the alienating forces and customs of civilization. This early version of the "decline of the West" among the *philosophes* was reinforced in part by scientific theories, especially Buffon's *Natural History of the Earth* (1749–1778), which introduced the possibility of geological and biological decline.

Diderot's Tahiti, like Rousseau's "state of nature," depicts a unity between humanity and nature that has been lost in the West during the process of civilization, which introduces false desires, false customs, and false standards of morality. This separation from nature results in a tension between the "natural man" (we use the term *man* advisedly) and the "artificial man." Thus, the *Supplement* celebrates the robust vigor of the Tahitians, their energetic and uninhibited display of sexuality, which is consistent with the highest *natural* morality. Diderot's work participates in an Enlightenment discourse on the "noble savage" that envisioned the South Sea islands as a contemporary version of the Blessed Isles, a place where people living with impunity in idleness enjoyed a superabundance of natural delights. Although Diderot shows the familiar Enlightenment contempt for religious hypocrisy and the introduction of false sensibility that Rousseau associates with *amour propre,* he avoids a total idealization of the Tahitians by alluding to some negative qualities, such as cannibalism, infibulation, and infanticide. He thus introduces an element of realism into the spectacle of the exotic in this Enlightenment version of the Golden Age—a contemporary utopia lying just beyond the borders of the West.

Diderot's attack on moral and religious hypocrisy invites comparison with Molière's in *Tartuffe* and Voltaire's in *Candide;* its apparent, if qualified or cautious, relativism also looks back to Montaigne's "Of Cannibals" and "Of Coaches" (Volume One), and forward to Lessing's "The Parable of the Rings" from *Nathan the Wise.* Here, the clerical restrictions on sexuality are shown to be incompatible with the natural law that Diderot believes governs human actions and desires. The doctrine of chastity denies the most basic of natural desires, and marriage denies the individual the opportunity to participate in the inevitability of change. Thus, both religious law and civil law are inconsistent with natural law. For Diderot, this incongruity leads to hypocrisy and to unhappiness, for people are forced by natural impulses either to act against their religious and civil imperatives or to keep up appearances of following those imperatives while secretly fulfilling their natural desires (the subject of Diderot's gothic–erotic novel, *Le Religieuse*). To facilitate the discussion over natural law, you might begin by asking students to discuss Diderot's division of law into three kinds—natural, civil, and religious—and the relations among them as portrayed in the *Supplement.* In Diderot's opposition between the natural and the artificial, students may see the struggle between id and superego with which they may be more familiar. Indeed, Diderot describes the struggle between the natural and the artificial as a kind of civil war within the European psyche.

Questions for Discussion and Writing

1. Discuss the way Diderot opens the *Supplement* with a frame story. Why does he create layers of narrative? What is the relationship between the dialogue of A and B, the Old Man's testimony, and the frame story?
2. How does Diderot describe the European contact with the South Seas? Does his account here amount to an attack on colonialism? Consider here the testimony of the Old Man and compare his account of the French to the historically authentic Micmac elder's account of Europeans in "You Tell us that France is an Earthly Paradise."

3. How does Diderot use the *Supplement* to criticize European values? What are some of the differences between European and Tahitian culture, in his opinion? What basic assumptions in each culture underlie those differences?
4. Compare Diderot's critique of European hypocrisy to Montaigne's, Voltaire's, or Molière's.
5. Diderot's essay focuses primarily on the vital sexuality of the Tahitians. Why does he choose this passion for the basis of his analysis?
6. What happens to people who try to deny the dictates of natural law? How has the repression of natural law in European society created an artificial, alienated culture? How has it affected the European psyche?
7. Compare Diderot's presentation of the Tahitian "noble savage" to Rousseau's treatment of childhood innocence in the *Confessions*. Are they similar?
8. Study the concluding paragraph of the *Supplement*. Like the last paragraph of Montaigne's "Of Cannibals," Diderot's conclusion seems to destabilize his critique of sexual hypocrisy by making a joke that relies on a typical European view of sexuality. How does this joke affect your reading of the *Supplement* as a whole? What does it tell us about the limitations of Diderot's critique?

Projects

1. Look through accounts of other cultures in back issues of *National Geographic* or similar magazines. What point of view do these accounts take on the cultures they describe?
2. Select a place that you associate with values very different from your own. Write a travel account in which you compare the different sets of values.

GOTTHOLD EPHRAIM LESSING
Nathan the Wise

The Parable of the Rings is one episode from a much longer work, a work that Lessing described as a "dramatic poem." The larger work tells the story of Nathan, a Jewish merchant in Jerusalem, and his adopted daughter, Rachel. When the girl wishes to marry a Knight Templar who has come to Jerusalem as a crusader to fight Saladin, the Sultan of Egypt and ruler of Jerusalem at the end of the twelfth century, the romantic story becomes entangled in the religious differences between the three major Middle Eastern religions: Judaism, Christianity, and Islam. The differences between the three religions that have led to the crusades are philosophically resolved by the wise Nathan in the Parable of the Rings, which suggests that all religions are part of a larger truth. In the romance, the religious differences between Rachel and the Knight become moot when it is discovered that they are brother and sister, the children of Saladin's lost brother and his German wife.

Although Nathan's story of the three rings is only one episode from a much longer play, the parable is self-contained. It allegorically presents the central themes of the play and some key ideas of the Enlightenment. Saladin's certainty that Nathan's wisdom derives from having arrived at rational religious beliefs sets up one of the central issues of the period: whether religious beliefs could be discovered through reason. Nathan's solution to Saladin's challenge embodies the Enlightenment's conviction that truth is not absolute and that there is some truth in all religions. The test for truth articulated by the judge in Nathan's story is a pragmatic one: The ring that produces love and tolerance in its owner will over time prove to be the true one.

Questions for Discussion and Writing

1. Does Nathan prove that he is wise or just shrewd? What's the difference between the two?

2. What sort of person is Saladin? What does his framing of the question tell you about him?

3. In the parable, what does the father represent? Is he an allegorical version of God? How do you explain his "pious frailty"? What does the judge represent?

4. How does Nathan answer Saladin's objection that the identical rings are unlike the three major religions, which are not identical?

5. Why does Nathan say that history is not helpful when trying to decide which of the three rings is the true one?

6. What criteria does Nathan's story suggest for establishing truth? On the basis of the story, how would you define truth?

7. Basing your answer on the parable, how many authentic rings can there be? none? one? three? more than three?

8. One of the judge's criteria for testing a ring is that the actions of the ring's owner demonstrate the authenticity of his ring. If this test is applied to religions today, is there any religion that seems to possess an authentic ring?

9. Would Nathan's ideas on religion be shared by the framers of the Declaration of Independence?

Project

Compare Lessing's version of the story of the three rings with The First Day, Third Tale in Boccaccio's *Decameron*. In what ways is Lessing's an Enlightenment story and Boccaccio's a medieval one?

MATSUO BASHŌ
The Narrow Road through the Provinces

Bashō's *The Narrow Road through the Provinces* is an excellent text for highlighting some differences and similarities between Eastern and Western literature and thought. First a disclaimer: We begin this process of making comparisons with the assumption that we will need to modify and correct our generalizations as we try to refine our observations and learn more about the texts and cultures involved.

Whereas Voltaire's *Candide* and Molière's *Tartuffe* are concerned with social issues and changing or correcting society, Bashō's writings are very personal and involved with the transformation of his individual consciousness, having some affinities with Rousseau in the *Confessions*. One way to describe Bashō's goal is to say that he is concerned with fully realizing in the present moment the significant connections in his life: his relationship with nature, history, and other poets. On one level, he is like a tourist who visits interesting places in the northern part of his country, carrying a journal rather than a camera. But on a deeper level, the writing describes a pilgrim who deliberately leaves home in order to seek a spiritual goal. Through travel, Bashō attempts to leave behind all that inhibits his enlightenment. Passing through the barrier gates symbolizes rites of passage or stages in the pilgrimage; the shrines themselves are places where previous individuals have realized important connections. Shrines are like lightning rods where a person's experiences coalesce. Paul Reps in *Zen Flesh, Zen Bones* describes enlightenment in rather simple terms:

> It can happen to you. In a flashing moment something opens. You are new all through. You see the same unsame world with fresh eyes.
> The universe-renewing power comes by grace, not logic.

These issues of consciousness or the spirit are difficult to talk about in ordinary language; for this reason, a mixture of prose and poetry is used to suggest the desired transformation of consciousness. *The Narrow Road through the Provinces* is not simply a travel journal that describes tourist attractions; it is also the skillful, imaginative evocation of the journey for the reader, whose consciousness might thereby be changed; the mixture of prose and poetry provides in itself the potential for transformation, a changed consciousness through a new way of perceiving a particular place.

One problem for the Western reader, of course, is unfamiliarity with the places visited by Bashō. We recommend using slides or photographs of Japanese shrines to help students envision the places in Bashō's writings. Comparing several translations of the same haiku provides an entrée into the nature of haiku and the difficulties of translation.

Questions for Discussion and Writing

1. Two closely related terms for describing Bashō's travels are *pilgrimage* and *shrine*. What do they mean? How are they relevant to Bashō's journey?
2. Discuss the meaning of the various barriers. What does passing through the barriers symbolize?
3. The seventeenth and eighteenth centuries in Europe are often described as the Age of the Enlightenment, by which is meant an age awakening to the uses of reason. Through his travels, Bashō seeks enlightenment. Discuss the different meanings of enlightenment as they apply to different situations and places.
4. What information does Bashō provide about the particular traditions concerning *how* and *when* one should view individual shrines: which angle? which time of day? which season?
5. What does the moon symbolize and what role does it play with certain shrines?
6. What role is played by Sora, Bashō's companion?
7. In the United States, we do not normally think about disciples gathering around a poet. What did Bashō's disciples hope to learn from him?
8. Travel literature was common during the Enlightenment. Discuss the differences and similarities between Bashō's travels and the travel accounts by Swift and Diderot.
9. Discuss and compare various translations of Bashō's poems. Translators include Earl Miner, Sam Hamill, Cid Corman, Maeda Cana, and Nobuyuki Yuasa.
10. Compare Bashō's concern with the transformation of consciousness with Rousseau's psychological concerns in the *Confessions*.

Projects

1. Take a walk through a place that is special to you; write haiku along the way.
2. One of the best ways to appreciate Bashō's writing is to write a series of haiku. After explaining how verses might be linked to one another, divide the class into pairs and have each pair write an "anthology" of haiku. It is easiest to begin with a theme, such as "love in the spring." One student begins by writing down three lines and reading

them out loud; the second responds with two or three lines; then back to the first, and so forth. Be loose about this poetic form; for example, about the exact number of syllables for a traditional haiku. Another form to explore is the *tanka,* with thirty-one syllables in four lines.

3. Other than geography, are there significant differences between Bashō's pilgrimage and the pilgrimages in the West? Compare *The Narrow Road through the Provinces* with the medieval pilgrimages described by Chaucer and Mandeville in Volume One of this anthology. What shrines exist in the United States that might be compared to the ones visited by Bashō? Consider the shrine to Elvis Presley in Memphis, Tennessee, and the memorials to Lincoln, Washington, and Vietnam veterans in Washington, D.C.

4. Earl Miner includes *The Narrow Road through the Provinces* in *Japanese Poetic Diaries,* an anthology that represents a tradition of journal writing. A research project might involve Miner's book and others.

CHIKAMATSU MONZAEMON
The Love Suicides at Amijima

Although Chikamatsu's play was written for the puppet theater (hence the need for a narrator to describe facial expressions and settings), it may have presented more problems for its earliest performers than for the modern reader. As Donald Keene points out in his introduction to *Major Plays of Chikamatsu* (1961), "Chikamatsu's ability to create complex, evolving characters was no asset in the puppet theater" with its fixed number of puppet types representing traditionally good or bad characters. Indeed, modern readers will be comfortable with the middle-class character, Jihei, and the major conflict he faces—his incompatible love for the courtesan, Koharu, and for his wife, Osan. More like a Willy Loman than a Hamlet, Jihei represents the concerns of the common merchant class—the petit bourgeois, if you will—who, like Chikamatsu's character, were sometimes distracted by the enticements of the pleasure quarters from their routine business and domestic responsibilities. As mentioned in the headnote, the dramatic situation in the play is not unlike that in Madame de La Fayette's *The Princess of Clèves* or in Goethe's *Sorrows of Young Werther.* Despite what we might call the uneven development between Japan and Europe and the nearly complete isolation of Japan in the Tokugawa period, both Japan and Europe were emerging from feudal societies and the economic and cultural pressures of the rising middle classes created similar conflicts as private interests often ran counter to traditional social expectations.

Students in the age of television and movie docudramas may be interested to know that Chikamatsu's play is reputedly based on the actual story of a love suicide that took place in 1720. Keep in mind that Chikamatsu, like any other artist, takes great liberties with the base material from which his plays are made. In his important essay on the art of *joruri,* the puppet stage, Chikamatsu cautions: "In writing *joruri,* one attempts first to describe facts as they really are, but in so doing one writes things which are not true, in the interest of art." Strict realism, he adds, "would permit no pleasure in the work." Chikamatsu emphasizes in his discussion of *joruri* the importance of the poetic effect of the dialogue, the need to evoke feeling even in descriptive sections of the play, such as the *michiyuki* (the journey, as in Act III, Scene 2 of our play), and the importance of stylization, by which he means something equivalent to what the formalists call defamiliarization—creating resemblances but not copies of the real. In this way, the monotony of the everyday appears fresh and renewed so that the reader is astonished by the familiar. Much of that stylization, of course, is necessarily lost on Western readers of a translated work, but it is important to emphasize that Chikamatsu's portrait of Japan in the eighteenth century is no more unaltered or transparent than Shakespeare's view of Denmark in Hamlet's time.

We begin our approach to *The Love Suicides at Amijima* by setting up the basic conflicts in the play—Jihei's love for Koharu and Osan, the competition between Tahei and Jihei for Koharu's affection, Jihei's struggle between love and *giri,* or obligations to one's family and friends, and the lovers' sense of leaving behind the material world that tries to keep them apart for a spiritual world where they may be united forever. Despite its innocent appearance as a domestic tragedy, this is a disturbing play, and many readers will react strongly to the graphic suicide scene at the end. This scene may usefully be compared to the suicide in Goethe's *Sorrows of Young Werther* or to the deaths of Catherine Earnshaw and Heathcliff in *Wuthering Heights* (which are sometimes described as suicides) to contrast Western attitudes and literary uses of suicide and to open discussion on this sensitive and important issue.

Questions for Discussion and Writing

1. Magoemon, Jihei's brother, has come to Sonezaki New Quarter to disrupt the affair between his brother and Koharu. What values does he represent? What right does he have to meddle in his brother's affairs?
2. What obligations do Koharu and Jihei have to other people that threaten to stand in the way of their love? In what way does Jihei's rivalry with Tahei affect his actions with regard to Koharu?
3. What is the relationship and what are the mutual obligations between Koharu and Osan, from whom the former has received a letter (see Act I, Scene 2 and Act II)? Discuss Osan's reactions to her husband's affair with Koharu. Why would Osan give up her possessions and raise money to help Jihei ransom Koharu?
4. What do Koharu and Jihei hope to achieve through suicide? How is this attitude toward suicide similar to, or different from, Western views of suicide?
5. Discuss the conflict between commercial and spiritual values in the play. In what way are they dramatized in various characters?
6. Discuss the manner in which Mogoemon and his aunt, Osan's mother, point the blame for Jihei's dissipation at Koharu and Osan. Are women often blamed for the faults of their lovers or husbands in Western culture as well? Discuss Chikamatsu's treatment of love, sex, and marriage and compare it to that in one of the Western texts in this unit.
7. Examine the language of the *michiyuki,* or journey scene (Act III, Scene 2). Why does the language become so densely poetic and symbolic here? How does this kind of language transform the action—the journey toward the love suicide—into a kind of spiritual journey? You might compare the language here to Bashō's.
8. Discuss the meaning or significance of the death of Koharu and Jihei. Does it appear that they are self-mystified or does Chikamatsu treat the suicide as a holy ritual without irony?

Project

Read Goethe's *Sorrows of Young Werther* or Shakespeare's *Romeo and Juliet* and contrast their use of love suicide to Chikamatsu's. Research the cultural attitudes toward suicide in Japan and explain how these are handled in the play. Keep in mind that the Japanese authorities banned these suicide plays to discourage young people from imitating them, as people did in Europe after the popularity of *Werther.*

OLAUDAH EQUIANO
The Interesting Narrative of the Life of Olaudah Equiano, or Gustavus Vassa the African

Although both American and English literary historians have claimed Equiano as their own, Equiano insisted to the end of his life that he was African. By placing him in our World Context section, we take Equiano at his word while acknowledging that his work exerted a major influence on slave narratives in both England and the United States. A hybrid form of autobiography and travelogue, Equiano's *Life* introduced what would become characteristic features of the slave narrative, beginning with an account of his life in Africa and his capture and captivity and culminating in the account of his emancipation from slavery. The traces of the structure of biblical captivity narratives here are not accidental, and like many of the slave narratives of the next century, Equiano's *Life* draws heavily, both rhetorically and philosophically, on biblical sources from which Equiano drew strength to endure his misfortunes, to serve as an outspoken witness for the misery of other slaves, and to censure the complacency of his European readers and move them to remedy the horror of slavery by outlawing it altogether.

Equiano wrote his *Life,* he says, not to gain literary reputation but to move his readers to support the abolition movement to put an end to slavery. Part of the brilliance of the narrative is Equiano's mastery of rhetorical strategies that appeal to both the feelings and the intellect of his readers. In the portrayal of Africa at the beginning of the tale, Equiano paints a picture of happiness and near innocence, but he does not overly idealize his homeland and does not hide the fact that the Ibo themselves had slaves. His capture uproots him from this state of innocence, and Equiano creates moving scenes, such as when he is briefly reunited with his sister, that invite the reader's sympathy. With his detailed, first-hand accounts of the horrible treatment of slaves, such as his description of conditions in one of the infamous slavers (the death ships employed in the African slave trade), Equiano appeals simultaneously to his readers' sympathy and sense of justice. At times, he pauses from the narrative to reflect, sometimes in a kind of prayer and at others in a brief sermon, to remind his Christian readers that God judges these actions and, by extension, their silent complicity in them. In our experience, Equiano's narrative captivates student readers, who are sometimes shocked by his graphic accounts of brutality and who are often eager to learn more about the plight of slaves in the eighteenth and nineteenth centuries. For content, tone, and technique, it is very interesting to compare Equiano's tale of actual suffering to Voltaire's fictional *Candide* or to Rousseau's story of his experience of injustice. Students sometimes find Equiano's tale more compelling because the hardships he endured were more palpable than those imagined by European writers.

Questions for Discussion and Writing

1. Discuss Equiano's *Life* as a story of the fall from innocence into experience (similar in pattern to Rousseau's *Confessions*). Does the fact that this is a true account of enslavement make his story more compelling than a fictional story of misfortune, such as Voltaire's *Candide?*

2. Compare Equiano's account of his first encounter with Europeans with the Micmac elder's or with the Old Man's in Diderot's *Supplement to the Voyage of Bougainville.*

3. Compare Equiano's love of liberty and the circumstances that arouse that love with Rousseau's hatred of tyranny and the circumstances that led to it.

4. What is the image of slavery depicted in the *Life?* How does Equiano use the descriptions of brutality against slaves to elicit compassion from the reader?

5. How does Equiano's *Life* appeal to readers' feelings and their sense of justice? Do you think the *Life* would lead some of its readers to act against slavery?

6. Equiano attributes his emancipation to the grace of God. What role does Christianity play throughout Equiano's life? Do you find Equiano's humility and gratitude believable? Discuss the effect this tone might have had on readers in the 1790s.

7. Examine the opening and closing paragraphs of the narrative. Why does Equiano make these disclaimers about his intentions and his artistry?

Project

Analyze the structure and basic rhetorical strategies in Equiano's narrative and compare them with those in Harriet Jacobs's *Incidents in the Life of a Slave Girl*. What common features can you identify? You might also compare her account of her slavery with Equiano's account of his to discuss the differences in their experiences. How does gender exacerbate the conditions of slavery, if it does?

THE
NINETEENTH
CENTURY

❧

The Romantic Self
and Social Reality

JOHANN WOLFGANG VON GOETHE
Faust

Many of our students find *Faust* the most difficult work we teach in the second semester of our course. The poetry alone puts off some of them. The philosophic content of the play and its intertextuality also make it difficult for students with little or no literary background. We continue to teach it, despite these challenges, because it is so central to romanticism. Nearly every work of European romantic literature has ties to *Faust*. Its quest romance, beginning in dejection and despair and seeking fulfillment through an immersion in experience; its romantic hero, the imperfect Faust whose Napoleonic desires anticipate the Nietzschean superman; its exploration of the dark side of human nature and its Walpurgis-nacht journeys into the irrational and surreal; its expressive use of literary forms, producing a wide range of different poetic lines and stanzas in the poem; and the importance it gives to the feminine in Faust's quest for wholeness: these central features of Goethe's dramatic poem make it historically and thematically the paradigmatic romantic text.

Two approaches to the poem make it less intimidating: a comparison with Marlowe's version of the story and a study of the characters. The differences between Marlowe's and Goethe's versions are apparent from the beginning. Goethe's Joblike "Prologue in Heaven" sets a very different context for the story, and his transformation of the bargain in Marlowe's play into a wager are important points of difference between the two. One can also consider the difference between the power Marlowe's hero bargains for and the experience Goethe's hero seeks. Such considerations naturally lead to an analysis of other

111

characters. Wagner, Martha, and, especially, Margaret are interesting in themselves and for the ways they reveal different aspects of Faust and Mephistopheles, the two characters who evoke the most discussion.

In light of the Prologue, one must consider just how devilish Mephistopheles is or whether he is in fact one of God's servants. Looking at the various guises in which he appears is a good way to get at some of the richness in his character. The division within Faust's soul between the worldly and the spiritual, which Faust describes beginning with line 1112, is a good starting point for analyzing his character. This can lead to a discussion of the intellectual life that he is rejecting and the experience that he is seeking with Mephistopheles. Part II, Act V, Faust's project to drain the marshes for a housing development, has usually been viewed as an altruistic endeavor that leads to Faust's final redemption. To contemporary readers, these scenes are considerably more problematic. Faust's imperialist ends run roughshod over the past and lead to the deaths of the old couple, Baucis and Philemon. The death of this old couple is emblematic of the death of the pastoral as industrialism and urbanization destroy the old way of life, a theme also explored in Pushkin's *Bronze Horseman*. We are likely to be far more critical of Faust at this point than his nineteenth-century readers were. In any case, Faust's final redemption is not so much something earned by this project, but rather a result of his attitude of mind, his continual seeking.

Faust defines many of the themes that reappear in the literature of the nineteenth century. The divisions between mind and body, the spiritual and the physical, inform such works as the poems of Blake and Keats, Brontë's *Wuthering Heights*, Flaubert's "A Simple Heart," Tolstoy's *Death of Ivan Ilyitch,* and Tagore's *Broken Ties*. The romantic journey into the realm of the unfamiliar and dangerous, into the dark side of the psyche, most explicit in the Walpurgisnacht episode in *Faust*, reappears in Hoffman's "The Mines at Falun," Coleridge's "The Rime of the Ancient Mariner," and Tagore's *Broken Ties*. Goethe sees this journey, in part, as an exploration of the feminine, as Faust leaves his rationalism behind to seek the hidden truths from the Realm of the Mothers. This exploration of the feminine can be found in many other nineteenth-century texts, in Brontë's *Wuthering Heights* and Tagore's "Hungry Stones," as well as in such feminist works as "The Yellow Wallpaper" and *A Doll's House*. Nearly all of Faust's romantic successors experience the instability of imperfection and are threatened by the dangers of self-consciousness. Such self-absorption can result in the obsessive confessional of an Ancient Mariner or in the celebration of self as in Whitman's *Song of Myself.*

Questions for Discussion and Writing

1. What does the Prologue in Heaven add to the play? How would you characterize God and Mephistopheles in this scene? Are they enemies? On the basis of the dialogue between them, would you say that Goethe believes in the existence of evil? How are Mephistopheles' guises later in the play consistent with the figure who appears in the Prologue?

2. For what reasons is Faust dissatisfied with his life? What does he feel has been lacking? What is Wagner's role in the opening scenes of the play?

3. What causes Faust to give up his suicidal thoughts?

4. What is the bet Faust makes with Mephistopheles? If this is a "bargain," what is Faust's obligation in the deal? How does this wager relate to the understanding between God and Mephistopheles in the Prologue?

5. Why is Margaret so attractive to Faust? Are Mephistopheles' strategies to win her for Faust appropriate ones? Why is Faust not more active in courting her? How is Faust's interest in Margaret different from the interest of Marlowe's Doctor Faustus in Helen of Troy?

6. Would you describe Part I of *Faust* as a tragedy? If you do, whose tragedy is it? Faust's? Gretchen's?

7. Many critics see Part II of *Faust* as the story of Faust's redemption. In the excerpts from Part II included in the anthology, what part does nature play in Faust's restoration? How could Faust's project in Act V be seen as redemptive? What aspects in these sections suggest that Faust is not changed and is not redeemed?

8. Consider Faust's project to drain the marshes in the light of Pushkin's *Bronze Horseman*. Is a noble vision for such a project sufficient to atone for the costs of implementing it?

9. Characterize Faust as a romantic hero. Is he a sympathetic figure? What are his strengths and weaknesses? How does he change over the course of his life? What qualities of Faust are implied in the adjective *Faustian*? Read Madame de Staël's account of Napoleon in the Background Texts section. In what ways might Faust be described as Napoleonic?

10. Does Mephistopheles win his wagers with God and Faust?

11. What do you think is the significance of the Walpurgisnacht scene? Does it belong in the plot where it appears? How does it resemble the epic journeys to the underworld or Marlow's trip up the Congo in Conrad's *Heart of Darkness*?

12. Consider *Faust* in light of Blake's distinction between innocence and experience. What parts of *Faust* might be considered songs of innocence? What parts are songs of experience?

Projects

1. Compare Marlowe's *Doctor Faustus* with Goethe's *Faust*. Are both heroes seeking the same things from Mephistopheles? How do they differ as characters? How does Goethe change the Faust story told by Marlowe to fit the needs of the nineteenth century?

2. Retell the Faust legend for the 1990s. What would be the profession of a contemporary Faust? What would he sell his soul for? Would our definition of *Faustian* differ from that of the nineteenth century?

3. Imagine the Faust story—either in the nineteenth century or in our own time—with a woman in Faust's role. How might this change the story and the character of Faust? In pursuing this project, you may want to look at *A Woman's View of the Faust Legend: The Seven Strings of the Lyre* (translated 1989), George Sand's version of the Faust story with a woman as a central figure.

EMILY BRONTË
Wuthering Heights

Wuthering Heights is usually considered either as an intensely realistic, even naturalistic novel or as an example of gothic fantasy. Its realistic elements include its detailed descriptions of Yorkshire, its portrayal of the natives as products of a particular and peculiar natural environment, its narrative strategy that effaces the author, and its use of dialect and native customs. Its gothic features include its remote setting, its use of dreams and hallucinations, and its suggestions of supernatural aspects to the events in the story. In either version, Heathcliff has a central role. Realists cast him variously as an outcast gypsy or an exploited Irish laborer. In the gothic version, he becomes a conflicted Byronic hero, larger than life and simultaneously threatening and attractive.

Heathcliff is a charismatic and enigmatic figure. His origins are mysterious and the reasons for Mr. Earnshaw's kind treatment of him are not told. If his plot to secure Wuthering Heights from Hindley can be explained as a revenge story, his undying passion for Catherine and his extreme behavior, especially at the time of her death, complicate the conventions of such a story. He may, as various critics have suggested, be the dispossessed natural heir to Mr. Earnshaw's estate, a representative of the oppressed working class in early Victorian England, or the male double to Catherine, expressing the alienation of the feminine in a highly patriarchal culture. He is a captivating presence at the center of the novel, but *Wuthering Heights* is at least as much Catherine's story as his. Approaching the novel as Catherine's bildungsroman locates the central conflict in her psyche. The narrative frames Brontë uses suggest Catherine's importance: Lockwood's interest in Wuthering Heights is spurred by reading her books and by encountering a nightmare vision of her in his dream. Of all the characters in the story, Nelly Dean is most closely associated with Catherine. Approaching the story through Catherine, then, gives some psychological context for the apparently supernatural elements in the novel.

The narrative frame offers opportunities to study the point of view of the novel, a limited narration that some critics have considered problematic. Nelly certainly has reasons for telling the story in the way she does, but she may not be trying, as at least one critic has argued, to gain control for herself of both Wuthering Heights and Thrushcross Grange. Emily Brontë may not include her as the hidden villain of the story, but rather as a sensible person whose down-to-earth narration may give credence to a bizarre tale. Her narration thus gives realistic coloring to a romantic story. But Emily Brontë further complicates Nelly's tale by having Lockwood retell it to the reader. His initial judgment of Heathcliff as a misanthropist much like himself suggests that he is not an especially astute judge of character. The effect of the double narrators is to hide completely Emily Brontë's perspective and to objectify the tale. The careful structuring of the novel and its multiple narrators make Brontë, like Flaubert, nowhere visible in her story but present everywhere.

Catherine possesses many of the characteristics of the romantic hero. Like Faust, she is divided between worldly and otherworldly impulses, between the civilization of Thrushcross Grange and the elemental passion of Wuthering Heights. Unable to fulfill both of these contradictory directions within herself, Catherine chooses one and denies the other, the crucial moment coming when she decides to marry Linton and reject Heathcliff. If Faust's choice to pursue experience destroys others—notably Margaret and her family—Catherine's choice is self-destructive. Starved of her love for Heathcliff, she ultimately starves herself. Her anorexic death is a kind of suicide, as is Heathcliff's death many years later. The difference between Faust's story and Catherine's may be the difference between male and female versions of the romantic search to overcome self-division. Faust's quest leads to grand adventures and to tragic suffering for others; Catherine's quest leads to self-destruction, for she is unable to escape the controlling power of the patriarchy. Her dilemma is similar to that of Nora Helmer in *A Doll's House* or that of the imprisoned wife of "The Yellow Wallpaper." She and Heathcliff, in their mutually self-destructive love, might be compared to the lovers in Chikamatsu's *Love Suicides at Amijima,* or her "suicide" to that of Werther in Goethe's *The Sorrows of Young Werther.* Goethe's Faust is saved from suicide by hearing the Easter bells; in this more naturalistic story, there are no bells to save either Catherine or Heathcliff from the elemental forces that finally destroy them.

The settings in *Wuthering Heights* are especially important in articulating the central conflict. Each of the novel's two houses is associated with one of Catherine's lovers, Thrushcross Grange with the cultivated Edgar Linton, Wuthering Heights with the elemental Heathcliff. Although supernatural and frightening events such as Lockwood's nightmare in the coffin-like bed occur, these are not the mansions of gothic horrors. They are realistically described; even the occasionally gruesome surprises seem to belong to a natural world where one season and one generation passes into the next. In the end, the settings in the novel are less like the romantic palace in Tagore's "The Hungry Stones" and more like Félicité's realistic rooms in Flaubert's "A Simple Heart."

Comparing the novel to the 1939 film adaptation starring Merle Oberon and Laurence Olivier raises many questions, especially about the ending. Is the image of Catherine and Heathcliff as resident spirits of the moor an appropriate note on which to end the story? Or should the younger Catherine and Hareton be seen as the more appropriate conclusion, as they recall the original pair, reduced by the losses that have been incurred to a realistic pair of country people? The younger generation may even be redeeming the excesses of the past as Catherine teaches Hareton his letters—reminiscent of Faust redeeming the marshes from the sea for a housing development. Yet they suggest just how much has been lost in the destructive series of events that leads to this realistic and deflationary ending.

Questions for Discussion and Writing

1. What sort of person is Lockwood? How does his own experience color his account? Is his illness related to his visits to Wuthering Heights?
2. How do Wuthering Heights and Thrushcross Grange differ as physical places? What do these differences suggest about their symbolic role in the novel? Is it reasonable to characterize them as opposites?
3. Characterize Nelly Dean. Why do you think Emily Brontë chose to have her tell the story? Do you think Nelly misrepresents or leaves important information out of her account? Does she cause any of the significant events to happen?
4. The novel covers a long period of time, over three generations of the families involved. What does Emily Brontë do to focus and unify her story?
5. What mysteries are there about Heathcliff and his origins? What possible explanations might there be for Mr. Earnshaw's fondness for him? What is there about Heathcliff that attracts Catherine to him? What might Heathcliff represent in the novel?
6. Why does Catherine marry Edgar Linton? Does Catherine's explanation to Nelly of her different feelings for Linton and Heathcliff indicate that she knows that her marriage to Linton is a mistake?
7. Both Catherine Earnshaw and Faust are divided figures, conflicted within themselves. Are their divisions similar? Is Catherine a Faustian figure?
8. What is the effect of tracing the story of the Earnshaws and Lintons into a third generation? Would the novel have been more effective if it had told only the story of the generation of Catherine and Heathcliff?
9. Joseph is a difficult person in the novel, difficult to get along with and, for most readers, difficult to understand. What is his role in the story? What would be missing if he were left out?

Projects

1. Rewrite, from Heathcliff's point of view, the scene where Catherine tells Nelly of how her love for Linton differs from her love for Heathcliff.
2. Get at least two of the many movie versions of the novel and compare them as adaptations of the book. Among the versions you may want to consider are the 1939 classic with Merle Oberon and Laurence Olivier, the 1970 version with Timothy Dalton as Heathcliff, or Luis Buñuel's Spanish version, *Abismos de Pasion* (1953).
3. Write a treatment for a film version of *Wuthering Heights* set in the present. Indicate where you would set the story and how you would adapt it to fit the present time.

WILLIAM BLAKE
Selected Poems

William Blake's poetry embodies many of the concepts traditionally associated with romanticism, including the celebration of childhood as a time of uncorrupted energy, innocence, imagination, and genius. Blake contrasts these values with the passivity, corruption, rationality, and dullness associated with adulthood. More than the other romantic works represented here, Blake's poetry is directly polemical, and even the most innocent works, such as the Introduction to *Songs of Innocence,* anticipates the critique of reason and the fall into division and separation more fully articulated in *The Marriage of Heaven and Hell.* Blake does not hesitate to name the institutions perpetrating corruption—not just political corruption, but the religious corruption that legitimates the political and material exploitation of the innocent—in "London" and in the "Holy Thursday" and "The Chimney Sweeper" poems. The history of that corruption or perversion of religious feeling and the domestication of the prophetic vision of which Blake believes everyone is capable is told in *The Marriage of Heaven and Hell,* plate 11.

In addition to presenting these thematic issues, Blake's poetry encourages discussion about literary form. The lyrics and some of the poems in *Songs of Innocence* and *Songs of Experience* are written in the ballad stanza, which students readily associate with nursery rhymes and children's songs. Yet beneath the simplicity of their surfaces, these poems are deeply ironic and present a tragic picture of innocence undone and liberty stolen, as in "How sweet I roam'd from field to field" and "The Sick Rose." From these lyrics, we move to *The Marriage of Heaven and Hell,* which combines many traditional forms into a complex satire. Of course, these texts are further complicated when seen in their original form, for the engraved images often further ironize the text, as in "The Tyger," where the ferocity of the tiger that emerges from the text is ironically undercut and complicated by the somewhat silly-looking tiger of the plate. This plate represents one of the most dramatic tensions between image and text in Blake's work, and so serves as a useful teaching tool. One of the most common teaching strategies for Blake's early poems, one that draws out the ironies of the poems and clarifies Blake's social vision, is to compare and contrast the companion poems from the *Songs of Innocence* and *Songs of Experience.*

Satire, jeremiad, autobiography, and manifesto, *The Marriage of Heaven and Hell* is a difficult poem to teach, but more than any other poem it presents the essential Blake. As it parodies Swedenborg's *Heaven and Hell,* Blake's poem engages in a ruthless satire on the repressive institutions that have evolved in the West, attacks the Enlightenment faith in reason, celebrates the power of imagination, and announces Blake's arrival as the prophet of the New Jerusalem. Its diversity of form and themes initially presents difficulties, and students who attempt a literal allegorical reading of the text will be frustrated by the poem's refusal to make neat closures. Nonetheless, students are often intrigued by Blake's radical turning of the world upside down, and, as he would have hoped, students enjoy memorizing some of the Proverbs of Hell and find amusing the exploits of Blake's devil—a sort of Mephistopheles—as he torments the somewhat dimwitted angel who represents convention and order. If they understand that Blake set out here to shock and to provoke his readers to generate their own ideas, students may put up less resistance to the text.

Questions for Discussion and Writing

1. What expectations does the ballad stanza—as in "How sweet I roam'd from field to field" and "To the Muses"—usually evoke? How do Blake's poems subvert those expectations?

2. In the "Introduction" to *Songs of Innocence,* Blake's piper gives up his music for writing so that his songs can be disseminated more widely. Is this a wholly positive transformation? (Consider, for example, the resonance of "stain'd" in the final stanza.) What is gained and lost?

3. Discuss the mother's advice to her son in "The Little Black Boy." Does Blake really believe that only the eradication of physical difference can produce harmony among the races? Consider this poem in relation to the role religion plays in Harriet Jacobs's life.

4. Compare the two "Chimney Sweeper" or the two "Holy Thursday" poems. How has the perspective of the speaker changed in the later poems? From this contrast, consider what Blake means by *innocence* and *experience.*

5. Compare "The Lamb" with "The Tyger." Notice how the first poem brings about closure by offering a reassuring answer, whereas the second remains open-ended. What does this tell us about the difference between innocence and experience?

6. Consider "The Tyger" as a poem about the nature of good and evil. Does the poem suggest that the tiger is intrinsically evil, something to be feared, or does the poem suggest that the tiger's value is subject to our perception? How does this poem anticipate the discussion of good and evil in *The Marriage of Heaven and Hell?*

7. Discuss the "Argument"—plate 2—as a condensed history of civilization. What tone does the speaker of the poem take here? What does this prophetic voice suggest about how we should read the poem? Is that voice sustained throughout the poem?

8. Discuss Blake's treatment of heaven and hell in plates 3 through 6. How does he overturn convention here? How do we know that he has, like Milton's Satan, taken evil to be his good? How does this section repudiate the Enlightenment faith in reason?

9. Choose a few of your favorite Proverbs of Hell and discuss how they present a challenge to conventional ways of thinking. One could compare some of these to the aphorisms of Benjamin Franklin to characterize the radical difference between Blake's visionary iconoclasm and the pragmatism of the late eighteenth century. (Some Franklin sayings are God helps them that help themselves, a sleeping fox catches no poultry, little strokes fell great oaks, a stitch in time saves nine, and a penny saved is a penny earned.)

10. Discuss Blake's description of the history of religion in plate 11. Compare this to Wordsworth's description of growing older in "Tintern Abbey" or to Blake's own comparison of childhood innocence to adult experience.

11. What does Blake mean by "sensual enjoyment" in plate 14?

12. Plate 15 is usually read as a loose allegory of Blake's own methods of printing. What do you make of the final stage of this process—the books being arranged on library shelves. Compare this process to the process of writing in the "Introduction" to *Songs of Innocence.*

13. Who are the Prolific and the Devourers? Why are they both necessary?

14. Discuss the interaction between the Angel and Devil in the "memorable fancies"— plates 17 through 25. (The "memorable fancies" directly parody Swedenborg's "memorable relations" from his *Heaven and Hell;* these were reportedly accounts of Swedenborg's conversations with spirits.) What is Blake trying to tell us about the nature of reality here?

15. What is the tone of the "Song of Liberty"? Why does Blake end with this prophetic anticipation of a revolution?

16. Blake pokes fun at Voltaire and Rousseau in "Mock on Mock on Voltaire, Rousseau." What, if anything, does Blake have in common with these writers?

17. Compare Blake's definition of the poet and the poet's role to Wordsworth's, Baudelaire's, Whitman's, or Dickinson's.

Compare Blake's devil with Faust's Mephistopheles. Is Blake's devil more like Wagner or Mephistopheles?

Projects

1. Invent some of your own proverbs from hell.
2. Make an illustration in the manner of Blake about another poet's poems.
3. Look at Blake's illustrations to the works and discuss them in relation to the poetry.

WILLIAM WORDSWORTH
Selected Poems

Wordsworth's poetry allows students to recognize that romantic poetry is not a poetry of nature, but a poetry of the relationship between mind and nature. Moreover, the "Ode: Intimations of Immortality" and "Tintern Abbey" show that romanticism's celebration of childhood innocence does not so much involve a simple nostalgia for a golden age of unconscious bliss, but a complex relationship of present consciousness with the past. For Wordsworth, emotions and incidents recalled from childhood foster in the adult a deep sense of loss from which, as he explains in "Ode: Intimations of Immortality," he or she develops the "philosophic mind"—a sense of compensation for loss in a redeeming understanding of the necessity of suffering and the hope for some future felicity, as Meyer Abrams might put it. Of course, as many contemporary critics of Wordsworth's poetry have noted, this sense of compensation involves an act of faith that many readers may not accept on Wordsworth's word, and so his poetry allows us to discuss both the positive and the negative aspects of romanticism—its explicit faith in the power of imagination to create a world of harmony, and its implicit skepticism that such a world may be a hopeless illusion. The poems we include here are preoccupied, above all, with the mapping of the self and its boundaries, with tracing the development of the self over time, and with sorting out the external and internal agencies that have shaped the poet's consciousness.

It may be helpful to begin a discussion of these poems by outlining the structure of what Meyer Abrams calls the "greater romantic lyric." Such poems usually begin with the speaker in the present visiting a particular landscape; something in that landscape reminds the speaker of the past, and the speaker engages in a sustained meditation on the significance of temporality and loss. Finally, the speaker's thoughts return to the present scene, usually with some sense of compensation for what has been left behind or a sense of renewal in what has been gained over time. Using this structure helps to clarify the distinction between "Tintern Abbey" and "Ode: Intimations of Immortality," for the first vividly recalls the scene as viewed from above the banks of the Wye and the latter invokes a more conventional, abstract setting to set out its more generalized philosophical position.

Useful comparisons may be drawn between Rousseau's autobiography and the autobiography in "Tintern Abbey" and the section from *The Prelude* we include here. Like Rousseau, Wordsworth focuses in the boat-stealing episode on a moment of transgression, which both writers see as formative moments in their character. Wordsworth says that he "grew up / Fostered alike by beauty and by fear," represented in this seminal episode as the desire for some forbidden trespass onto the lake, followed by the threat of punishment—in this case, from the mountain peak, which represents the stern authority of the father. Not at all the unrepentant revolutionary Blake was, Wordsworth here suggests that transgression has a dire cost. This passage may be read in terms of the sublime and the beautiful, or as a prefiguration of the Oedipal scene, with the lake as an embodiment of maternal nature and the mountain as the symbol of the father. Students often find it amusing to reflect on the Freudian implications of Wordsworth's "elfin pinnace." Above all, this scene constitutes what Wordsworth calls a "spot of time," a formative moment in the development of the self. The boat-stealing episode may be usefully compared with the poet's return to the scene above Tintern Abbey, for both passages show the way in which Wordsworth believes that consciousness and identity depend on a reciprocal relationship between past and present. Again anticipating Freud, Wordsworth acknowledges that the present self is a composite of both past and present experience, and he presents the past and childhood innocence not as places to recapture unmediated, but as scenes to revisit from the changed perspective of the adult consciousness.

Questions for Discussion and Writing

1. Describe the structure and the setting of "Tintern Abbey," "Ode: Intimations of Immortality" or the boat-stealing episode from *The Prelude*. What is the speaker's initial relationship to the landscape he describes? How does this relationship to the landscape—that is, his perspective on the past and the present—change over the course of the poem?

2. Discuss the balance between the speaker's loss and gain in "Tintern Abbey" and in "Ode: Intimations of Immortality." In the words of the latter, Wordsworth claims to have found "strength in what remains behind." What has in fact remained behind and how does it compensate for the loss of childhood innocence and bliss?

3. In Wordsworth's view, of what value is primary experience of nature? How do "Tintern Abbey" and the section from *The Prelude* describe the importance of remembered scenes and incidents? Can you think of scenes from your own experience that similarly impressed themselves on you through beauty or fear?

4. What does Wordsworth mean by "glory" in "Ode: Intimations of Immortality"? Discuss the various resonances within this term and how they are teased out in the course of the poem.

5. In "Tintern Abbey" Wordsworth celebrates the power of the eye and ear, for what they "half create, / And what perceive." How does Wordsworth here define the relationship between the mind—or imagination—and nature? Compare his view of the imagination and the role of the senses with William Blake's view.

6. Discuss how Wordsworth describes his relationship with his sister in the concluding lines of "Tintern Abbey."

7. Describe Wordsworth's view of the child and what happens to the child as he or she adapts to society's expectations. Compare his view of childhood to Blake's.

8. Describe the structure of "Ode: Intimations of Immortality." When does the tone shift from being elegiac to being celebratory? What is the meaning of this shift in tone?

9. Can you detect a difference between the childhood experience of fear and the adult's recollection of that fear in the boat-stealing episode? Discuss this distinction as an example of the philosophic mind.

10. Compare Wordsworth's experience of terror and beauty in the mountains with Thoreau's in Ktaadn.

11. Discuss the significant differences between Wordsworth's emphasis on mountain experiences and Hoffmann's emphasis on subterranean ones. Does this distinction help to characterize distinctions between English and German versions of romanticism? Also compare Goethe's *Faust*.

12. Discuss the differences in the language, tone, and style of Wordsworth's poetry compared with Blake's, Whitman's, or Dickinson's.
13. Discuss the characteristically rural atmosphere of Wordsworth's poetry in contrast to the urban atmosphere in Blake or in the Symbolist poets.
14. Compare Wordsworth's view of the relationship between mind and nature with Bashō's.

Projects

1. In his early years, Wordsworth was very much caught up in the enthusiasm for the French Revolution. Like other English liberals, however, he was disappointed by the brutal turn of events during the Reign of Terror, and he ultimately lost faith in the principles of the Revolution. Discuss "Tintern Abbey" and "Ode: Intimations of Immortality" as elegies for the revolutionary hopes of his youth.
2. Give an account of incidents in your life that you might consider to be "spots of time," that is, key formative moments that have shaped your personality. Discuss the difference between the way you think about them now and the way you first experienced them.

SAMUEL TAYLOR COLERIDGE
Selected Poems

Coleridge claimed that "Kubla Khan" originated from an experience in 1797, when, having taken an anodyne for an illness, he fell asleep while reading from *Purchas his Pilgrimage* (1613). He awoke with a vision for a poem and wrote down the lines we now have, but was interrupted by a visitor. By the time he went back to writing, he had lost the inspiration, and left the poem incomplete. A comparison of Coleridge's lines with the following lines by Purchas provides some insights into the creative process;

> In Xamdu did Cublai Can build a stately Palace, encompassing sixteene miles of plaine ground with a wall, wherein are fertile meddowes, pleasant Springs, delightfull Streames, and all sorts of beasts of chase and game, and in the middest thereof a sumptuous house of pleasure, which may be removed from place to place.

The actual poem builds on this beginning; the patterns of images and symbols interweave nature and psyche with sexual overtones; Coleridge is particularly skillful in this poem and "The Rime of the Ancient Mariner" at creating images of nature that mirror internal, psychological states. The music of the lines, the rhymes and the alliteration, create a rich tapestry.

Nature and supernature merge in "The Rime of the Ancient Mariner." The ancient mariner interrupts ordinary reality; he interjects himself into workaday consciousness, just as the supernatural intersected the mariner's expectations at sea. Beneath the vivid images of distant seas and perishing sailors, Coleridge constructs a moral lesson about paying attention to the natural world and the taint of corruption that attends the most sacred of events, even a marriage. Humans and nature are a single web; the blaspheming of this certainty demands penance.

It is convenient to divide this long poem into parts for discussion: "The Rime of the Ancient Mariner" divides easily into five parts: Shooting the bird, Becalmed, Ghost ship, The Blessing of the Snakes, and The return.

1. Images in "Kubla Khan," such as caverns, chasms, moon, river, and others, are applicable to the unconscious. Discuss how this poem might be read on at least two levels at the same time. Compare the images of the unconscious with the psychological symbols in Hoffmann's story.

2. What exotic associations with the historical Kubla Khan might pertain to the figure in Coleridge's poem?

3. If "Kubla Khan" is about creativity and the imagination, discuss how the poet might build "That sunny dome! those caves of ice!" What kind of powers does Coleridge associate with the poet? Compare his idea of the poet with those of Blake, Baudelaire, Whitman, and Dickinson.

4. Who is being commanded in the lines, "Weave a circle round him thrice, / And close your eyes with holy dread"?

5. Does it make any difference that "Kubla Khan" is called a fragment?

6. Why did the mariner shoot the albatross in "The Rime of the Ancient Mariner?"

7. What is the significance of the setting of the wedding for telling the tale? What kind of person needs to hear the mariner's tale? Are you such a person? What kind of storyteller is the old mariner?

8. Romantic writers were interested in psychology and exotic states of mind; compare the psychological extremes in Coleridge's poems with the portrayal of Heathcliff in *Wuthering Heights*.

9. What is the role of the supernatural in Coleridge's poems included here?

10. How does the blessing of the water snakes serve as a turning point for the ancient mariner?

Projects

1. Compare the ancient mariner's need to tell his story with the therapeutic role of storytelling in Freud's writings. How is the mariner similar to Marlow in Conrad's *Heart of Darkness?*

2. Draw the scene in "Kubla Khan."

3. Investigate the tradition surrounding the traveler with a story to tell, such as the "Wandering Jew" and "The Flying Dutchman."

E. T. A. HOFFMANN
The Mines of Falun

"The Mines of Falun" underscores the attractiveness of darkness, the underworld, and the supernatural in romantic literature. Keats's "Ode to a Nightingale" and "La Belle Dame sans Merci"; Brontë's *Wuthering Heights* with its fairy cave and beckoning female ghosts; and Tagore's *Broken Ties,* which also combines the themes of woman and cavern, all deal with similar themes.

Students usually respond eagerly to Hoffmann's storytelling voice, although he surprises them by delivering a darker romantic folktale than they may expect. The story almost begs for psychoanalytic interpretation, and students who are uncomfortable with the supernatural will immediately want to get down to the business of deciding what the story is "really" about. This involves discussing what Elis may be repressing or feeling guilty about, what the story has to say about young men and their father figures and mother figures, and what it means to make a journey to the underworld. A Jungian approach, which sees the Metal Queen as Elis's *anima,* may be fruitful. But the story should also be allowed to work its magic on its own terms of mysterious messengers, shining gems, secret underground chambers, and towering female divinities.

This story provides a good opportunity to examine the fatal woman convention of romantic literature and to ask what fears of women and of sexuality lie behind that figure. In this volume, Catherine Earnshaw of Brontë's *Wuthering Heights,* the Eternal Feminine that attracts Goethe's Faust, Keats's "La Belle Dame sans Merci," and the Priestess of Conrad's *Heart of Darkness* are all different sorts of fatal women; Dickinson's poem "My life had stood—a loaded Gun—," Charlotte Perkins Gilman's nameless heroine in "The Yellow Wallpaper," and most especially Adrienne Rich's poem "I Dream I'm the Death of Orpheus" in one way or another all supply commentary on that image of the devouring and draining woman who holds men in thrall.

Questions for Discussion and Writing

1. What effect does Elis's prior history have on the events of the story, especially his family history?
2. What are some of the traditions associated with the sea and sailors, and with mines and workers in metal? Is there any symbolic significance in switching from one profession to the other?
3. What does Elis seem to be seeking in the opening pages of the story? What is his state of mind at the story's opening? Why does the young girl affect him so deeply? What seems to stir him in the things Torbern tells him?
4. What sort of being is the Metal Queen? What other figures in myth or literature might she be compared to?
5. How much of Elis's experience do you think Hoffmann wants us to understand as subjective?
6. What goes wrong in the relationship between Elis and Ulla?
7. How would the speaker of Adrienne Rich's "I Dream I'm the Death of Orpheus" interpret this story?

Project

Imagine that Steven Spielberg's next project is a film version of "The Mines of Falun." You are the casting director. Which contemporary actors will you choose for the major roles? Where will you film? Will you leave the story as a nineteenth-century piece, or translate it to another time? Write the screenplay for one scene of the production.

JOHN KEATS
Selected Poems

The sensuousness of visual and auditory imagery in Keats's poems usually appeals to students. The youthful themes of his poems cluster around variations on the transience of life: the disillusionment exacted by mortality; the flower that inevitably fades versus the immortality of a work of art; the world weariness resulting from impermanence; the sense of pathos, even tragedy, that attends the fading of youth and the loss of creative energy. Only the young and the subjects of country and western songs enjoy the luxury of pining away in the field, "alone and palely loitering."

We recommend beginning with close readings of Keats's poems, paying particular attention to the wide range of imagery and the rich mixture of sounds. The brevity of suggestions for teaching Keats does not imply a lack of importance, but rather his accessibility.

Questions for Discussion and Writing

1. Romantic literature is characterized by passion, spontaneity, and imagination. How are these qualities expressed in Keats's poems?
2. Romantic writers often use external nature to reflect internal moods. Discuss the relationship of nature and mood in Keats's poems. Compare Keats's use of nature with that of Coleridge, Wordsworth, Goethe, Brontë, and Bashō.
3. What really happened to the knight in "La Belle Dame sans Merci"? Is the knight a reliable narrator? What gothic elements does Keats use in this poem?
4. "Ode on a Grecian Urn" compares the transience of life with the permanence of art. What are the characteristics of both, and which is preferable? What is the significance of the scenes on the urn? Discuss the similarities between the Grecian urn and the nightingale in "Ode to a Nightingale." Compare the urn to the statue of Peter in *The Bronze Horseman*.
5. What common themes and structural patterns unite Keats's odes?
6. How does Keats mix joy with suffering in "Ode to a Nightingale"? Why is it important that it be dark in this poem, beyond the fact that nightingales sing at night? What role does death play in this poem? How is Keats's flirtation with death a rather naïve, youthful indulgence?
7. Discuss the pattern of the flight of the imagination and the fall into the world in "Ode to a Nightingale" as a common romantic theme.
8. Does the personification of Autumn in "Ode to Autumn" deepen the poignancy of this season and its passage into winter? Discuss how each stanza moves the reader closer to winter. What feelings result from Keats's treatment of the transience of life in this poem?
9. Would Keats share Faust's desire for eternal experience?

ALEXANDER PUSHKIN
The Bronze Horseman

The Bronze Horseman was written in 1833, published in a censored version in 1841, and not in its original version until 1904. Considered one of the great masterpieces of Russian literature, the poem is based on the story of the devastating flood of 1824, which left much of St. Petersburg—especially the low-lying suburbs where many of the poorer people lived—in a shambles. Pushkin uses the occasion of the flood for a Byronic meditation on the grandeur of human aspirations and the transitory nature of human accomplishments, as well as a consideration of the tragic cost of the achievements of the great. Beginning as a paean for Peter the Great and the city he founded on the Neva, the poem shifts focus to the story of Yevgeni, whose simple dream is swept away in the fate of St. Petersburg itself. At the conclusion of the poem, the statue of Peter the Great rises above the disaster that has befallen both the city and Yevgeni. Pushkin presents this apparent triumph within the context of the downfall of the little man, thus vexing critics (and possibly disarming the censors under whose scrutiny he knew the poem would fall) up to the present.

As discussed in the headnote, *The Bronze Horseman* was first read in terms of a struggle between the collective and the individual will, although considerable disagreement arose over whether Peter or Yevgeni personified the individual will, depending on whether or not one stressed Yevgeni's victimization or his defiance—however hopeless and ineffectual that may be. If one chooses to emphasize the links to nineteenth-century literature, however, Pushkin's poem helps to demonstrate the link between romanticism and realism (or even naturalism). *The Bronze Horseman* ultimately tempers the romantic idealism embodied in Peter's vision with a naturalistic pessimism—if not a Nietzschean nihilism—in the utter helplessness of the clerk who succumbs to the overwhelming power of nature and empire, symbolized by the endurance of the Falconet's statue of the city's founder. At the same time, however, the poem may level the social distance between the two protagonists, for the flood that destroys Yevgeni's unrealized dream also has shown the possible vulnerability of Peter the Great's accomplished one.

Another issue raised by the poem is Russia's very relation to the West. In lines 11 and 12 of Thomas's translation, Peter muses that "By nature we are fated / To cut a window through to Europe." Pushkin added a note to these lines, writing "Algarottie said somewhere: 'Petersbourg est la fenêtre par laquelle la Russie regarde en Europe,' " (Petersburg is the window through which Russia beholds Europe). Of course, for Slavophile Russians, their country's relation to the West was by no means settled, and so the poem implicates the westernization of Russia in the downfall of Yevgeni. This issue may interest students, some of whom tend to link Russian with Western European history and culture. Mori Ōgai's "The Dancing Girl" raises the same question about Japan's relation to the West, though more directly than Pushkin's poem.

Translations of poetry always present difficulties for the editor, teacher, and student. Pushkin's *The Bronze Horseman* appears in rhymed tetrameter in the original Russian, and D. M. Thomas, whose translation we've used here, renders the poem in blank verse because, in his words, "It struck me . . . as fitting that, for this central work of Russian literature, our natural and national English metre, blank verse, should replace Russia's, the rhymed tetrameter." To dramatize these differences, you might have students compare the Thomas translation to Charles Johnston's translation (available in his *Narrative Poems by Alexander Pushkin and by Mikhail Lermontov,* 1983), which preserves the rhymed tetrameter. Johnston translates the first few lines from Part 1 thus:

> On Petrograd, the darkened city,
> November, chill and without pity,
> blasted; against its noble brink
> Nevá was splashing noisy billows;
> its restless mood would make one think
> of sufferers on their restless pillows.

As with other poems in translation, it is always interesting for students to compare different translations, if for no other reason than to give them a sense of what is lost in the process, and perhaps to motivate them to learn a second language.

Questions for Discussion and Writing

1. What is Pushkin's attitude toward the founding of the city, the realization of Peter's dream? What motives does he assign to Peter for founding the city?
2. Does the statue of Peter the Great change through the poem? Discuss the significance of the statue as a sign of the endurance of Peter's dream of the empire.

3. What kind of character is Yevgeni? Discuss the significance of the difference in stature and vision between Yevgeni and Peter the Great and explain how their fates are connected.

4. How does Yevgeni's story undercut or call into question the mythic stature of Peter the Great and his legacy? How does his story affect our reading of Pushkin's apparent praise for Peter the Great and St. Petersburg?

5. Pushkin presents the Neva as a willful perpetrator of disaster, a major character in the drama of destruction. What effect does this have on the story? What powers does the Neva represent?

6. After the flood, Yevgeni is "neither beast nor man." Does he symbolize the fate of all human beings, or does he stand for a particular class? What is the significance of his defeat?

7. Discuss Yevgeni's reproach to the statue and his subsequent fear of it. Why does he fear the statue but not the flood? What does this suggest about Pushkin's view of the power of the state (or empire) as opposed to the power of nature?

8. Is Yevgeni a victim of Peter's grandiose plans, or is he a heroic figure whose defiance represents the voice of the "little man" overpowered by the great?

9. Pushkin wrote *The Bronze Horseman* knowing full well that the poem would be subject to the scrutiny of censors. Does or should this knowledge affect the way you read the poem?

10. Compare Pushkin's celebration of Russia with Whitman's celebration of America. How does each poet qualify, if he does, his love of his country? How do the poems, if they do, transcend mere nationalist propaganda?

Projects

1. Examine a photograph of E. M. Falconet's statue of Peter the Great, the statue to which the poem refers, and compare Pushkin's treatment of the city's founder to the sculptor's equally ambiguous treatment of him.

2. Pretend you are a Russian censor of Pushkin's time. Present a case against the poem.

3. How does the poem treat the issue of class? How would Marx, or a Marxist literary critic, read the poem?

HARRIET A. JACOBS (LINDA BRENT)
Incidents in the Life of a Slave Girl

In its assertion of human rights and women's rights, its condemnation of a patriarchy that supports slavery and enforces sexual double standards, and its realistic depiction of grim scenes calculated to arouse the reader's social conscience, Jacobs's autobiography shares much in common with other nineteenth-century texts in our anthology. One obvious teaching strategy is to ask in what way this is especially a woman's slave narrative; another is to compare it to the other nonfiction texts about slavery or coercion or captivity by Equiano, Hopkins, and Rowlandson. Teaching actual slave narratives along with Euro-American works that use words such as *freedom* and *slavery* in often rather metaphorical senses—as in Blake, Goethe, Hoffmann, Dickinson, Whitman, Brontë, and Gilman—is an exercise that causes one at the very least to reevaluate some of the romantic cries for liberty of the spirit.

Readers, even if they have read other slave narratives such as Frederick Douglass's, are usually surprised and moved by Harriet Jacobs's account of her life in slavery. Jean Fagin Yellin's 1986 edition of *Incidents in the Life of a Slave Girl* is an invaluable teaching aid, with its photographs and documents, its maps of Edenton, North Carolina, and the surrounding area, and in particular its reconstruction of Molly Horniblow's house and its attic crawlspace where Jacobs lay in hiding for seven years.

It took an act of great courage for a nineteenth-century woman to speak as frankly about her sexual history as Jacobs does here. Other slave narratives of course allude to sexual coercion, rape, and double standards. But Jacobs dares to tell of these abuses in detail. She describes her persecutor, "Dr. Flint," and his myriad strategies; she explains how, denied marriage to a freeman, a slave woman might choose to take a white lover; she analyzes trenchantly the effects on the black and the white community alike when white men are allowed to hold black women in concubinage. She also speaks with great detail about the supportive network of African-American women, slaves and freedwomen alike, who keep her and others like her alive with practical aid and love and faith.

Questions for Discussion and Writing

1. Characterize Jacobs's grandmother and explain her part in Jacobs's life.
2. What role does literacy play in Jacobs's story?
3. How does Jacobs depict the Christian church? What does the visiting minister mean when he refers to slavery as "a beautiful patriarchal institution"?
4. How do her gender and her motherhood affect Jacobs's life story?
5. Hopkins, Gilman, Nora Helmer, and Jacobs are all women who have stories to tell of confinement in small spaces. What use does each woman make of that space, and what are her emotions toward it?
6. How does Jacobs analyze the effects of slavery on slaveholders' white families?
7. What are some of the reasons that Jacobs is able to survive her ordeals?
8. Whom does Jacobs imagine as her audience? How does she appeal especially to that audience?
9. Compare Jacobs's account of her enslavement with those of Equiano and Rowlandson. What differences do you see in how they regard their audience, their captors, their self-worth? In each case, what is their aim in telling their stories?

Projects

1. Write a few pages of Mrs. Flint's diary.
2. Research the life of Lydia Maria Child, one of the women who helped Jacobs to get her story in print.
3. Research the Nat Turner rebellion of 1831, the effects of which are felt in Edenton.

WALT WHITMAN
Song of Myself

Whitman's intense interest in the self and its infinite potential, his democratic idealism, his interest in realistic urban scenes and in natural speech, and his sheer love of revolutionary daring (in his case, primarily in matters of style, vocabulary, and subject matter) make him unmistakably a nineteenth-century figure. Faust, Blake, Wordsworth, and Rousseau are all of his company; he and Harriet Jacobs share a subject in their passionate condemnations of slavery. But oddly enough, he may most resemble Emily Dickinson, the writer here who on the surface sounds least like him. Both share a facility and an interest in juxtaposing cosmic images and concerns with homely natural details of the most minute sort; they see the connections between the wheeling galaxies and the blade of grass.

Whitman still sounds fresh and brash to modern ears, a century and a half after he wrote. Readers may be faintly appalled at some of his high-handed commandeering of their attention, his posturing, and his open sexuality, but they usually end up loving him. He celebrates his own individuality, the worth of every person, the worth of every part of creation, and not only the roses and noble stags and diamonds that abound in other poetical poets: Whitman hymns mullein and pokeweed, ants and alligators, granite and gneiss. He especially celebrates the American diversity of terrain, climate, ethnic groups, regional culture, social classes, and occupations. Reading him aloud is very important, especially in conjunction with some of the poetry popular in the United States at his time, such as a sample of Longfellow or Whittier, so students can appreciate the distance, both moral and musical, between them and Whitman.

Song of Myself has so many delightful catalogues and accessible passages such as Section 6 ("A child said, What is the grass?"), that it's easy to forget that it is a very difficult and ambiguous poem in spots. It is also easy to lose sight of the design of the whole, which follows a definite movement. In the sections we present here, Whitman first declares his purpose (Section 1); he evokes all the senses, especially the more primitive ones of odor, taste, and touch, and promises the readers that the validity of their own personal experience will be respected (Section 2); he describes in homoerotic imagery the early experience of discovering his own soul, an experience that translates instantly into a feeling of oneness with all creation (Section 5). The oceanic sense of immortal community is reaffirmed by the grass of Section 6 and again in 16 and 17, as he turns specifically to his own country, the "Nation of many nations." In 20, he envisions himself as a kind of Rabelaisian giant Walt, "hankering, gross, mystical, nude," all unstoppable will and healthy appetite, and mightily pleased with himself; more softly, in 21, he identifies with all polarities, for he is the poet of body and soul, man and woman, day and night, addressing a tender canticle to his voluptuous lover, the Earth. In 24, he explains matter-of-factly and explicitly just how he is a poet of the body. This boldness may be a kind of whistling in the dark, though, for in 28 comes one of the major crises of the poem, in which the speaker is terrifyingly overpowered by some sort of sexual experience. The poem here is so ambiguously worded, we are unsure whether Whitman is referring to an experience as mild as a caress, or to masturbation or even to rape. Whatever the case, here the speaker must make good on his boasts about his sexual openness in order to achieve the paradisiacal homoerotic vision of 29, with its "landscapes projected masculine, full-size and golden." In 30, he continues his wonderfully surrealistic (and comic) vision of himself incorporating All, but in 32 comes one of the darker passages of the poem, in which the great Democrat and lover of humanity allows that humans can be tiresome compared to the dignified simplicity of animals. This segues into Section 33, another wonderful animal-filled catalogue of American scenes. Section 50 reaffirms the speaker's democratic vision, which includes a God democratically indwelling in all creation, and accordingly dismisses death as unfrightening, a sort of process of God returning to God; he speaks here, as he does in 49, of the peacefulness at the center of his being. The poem begins in the morning as he awakens beside a loving bedfellow, and now in 51 and 52, Walt bids farewell as night draws on, cautioning us that he'll always be just underfoot or just ahead, waiting for us. After a few days spent with Whitman, my class and I often do have an eerie feeling that he's somewhere in the shadows at the back of the room.

127

1. By the second line of *Song of Myself*, Whitman is addressing you, the reader, very personally. How do you feel about the way he talks to you throughout the poem? How do Whitman and Baudelaire differ in their attitudes toward the reader?
2. Whitman packs Section 2 with images of smell and touch—the smell of dry leaves and salt air, the feeling of the air on one's naked body. Do these senses differ from sight and hearing? What are your own earliest sensual memories?
3. What kinds of things does grass represent for Whitman? How is it a democratic image? How is the grass metaphor developed in Section 6?
4. What does Whitman mean when he says in Section 21, "I show that size is only development"?
5. What do you think Whitman is describing in Sections 28 and 29? Why is this such a crisis for him, given his persona earlier in the poem?
6. How would you describe Whitman's theology? Whitman and Blake are both characterized as radicals; have they anything in common?
7. *Epic* has been defined as "for every given era, the most significant person performing the most significant action in a setting that encompasses the known world." By this definition, is *Song of Myself* an epic?
8. How are Whitman's language and subjects appropriate to his vision of the United States?

Projects

1. Both Whitman's and Dickinson's poems name many plants and creatures. Scan some anthologies of American poetry before the twentieth century to see what plants and creatures are most frequently mentioned in titles and first lines. What sorts of creatures and plants do Whitman and Dickinson like to talk about, and why?
2. In the spirit of Walt Whitman, write a catalogue of some sort. It could be just a list of what happens in your household in a day and night, or of what happens in your community day to day; it could be a description of all the patrons and activities going on in a lively bar. All it really need do is organize itself by line beginnings that repeat for a few lines, (*I hear, I see, Over, Where*, etc.; see Sections 16 and 33.)
3. Compare Whitman, Bashō, and Dickinson as poets of nature.

GUSTAVE FLAUBERT
A Simple Heart

"A Simple Heart" is a quintessential example of literary realism. Its commonplace heroine, objective narration, and predictable plot can make this story seem inconsequential and boring to students. Its use of the conventions of the saint's life may even reinforce this initial judgment and make the story appear trite as well. The power of the story is in the simplicity of Félicité, and in the details with which Flaubert reveals the extraordinary and miraculous in the life of a most common woman. Flaubert's project in this story—to present a convincing portrayal of simple goodness—is one that intrigued many nineteenth-century authors. Félicité is related to Dickens's Little Dorrit and to Dostoevsky's "idiot,"

Prince Mishkin, as one of God's fools. She is like Gerasim, Ivan Ilyitch's caring servant; her unselfconscious devotion to others makes her biography a saint's life. In an increasingly industrial and urban world, such simplicity was rare, almost as if it were a strange vestige from a less complicated age when faith was not undermined by Darwinian doubt.

By his detailed descriptions of people, places, and, especially, buildings and rooms, Flaubert makes Félicité's world solid and real. These details of her world and her life enable her story to transcend the conventions of the saint's life and give meaning even to the banal events of her narrow existence. Félicité's losses—her family, Theodore, Virginie, Madame Aubain, Loulou—and her suffering, especially in the scene where she is whipped by the coachman, make her much more than a representative of the common people or a case study. These scenes elicit the reader's sympathy for her. Flaubert's careful presentation of the details of her life also elevates her beyond her common station. In the scene in Part 3 where Félicité is in the church, she is linked to the figure of the Virgin in the stained glass window and her thoughts about the Holy Ghost as a bird of fire prepare us for Loulou's elevation to holiness. The description of her room in Part 4 echoes the description of the church, and Loulou's stuffed body, elevated to a bracket on the wall where his colorful feathers catch the morning light, turns her common room into a sanctuary. By such echoing detail, Flaubert is able metaphorically to consecrate Félicité and reveal the surprising truth about his common heroine.

Questions for Discussion and Writing

1. How is Félicité different from Madame Aubain? How do the reactions of the two women to the same events help to develop Flaubert's portrait of Félicité? How does the relationship between the two women change in the course of the story?

2. Characterize Félicité's religion as it is described at the beginning of Part 3. How do the details in the description of Félicité's room at the end of the story recall details in this description of the church? What do these echoes contribute to the story?

3. Is Félicité courageous in the confrontation with the bull? Is Madame Aubain? Does Madame Aubain view Félicité's fronting the bull as heroic? Does Félicité? Does Flaubert?

4. In what ways is Félicité simple? Trace the various uses of the word *simple* in the story. What variety of meanings does the word take on?

5. Discuss the significance of the details that Flaubert gives when Victor leaves from Honfleur. What does the laundry episode contribute to the account of Félicité's reaction to Victor's death?

6. What happens in this story? Are there any surprises? Is the ending of the story in any way unexpected?

7. What is the significance of the parrot? How does it become linked to the Holy Ghost? Do you think Flaubert is being ironic and suggesting that Félicité is ridiculous by believing in a stuffed parrot as the Holy Ghost?

8. Why is Félicité whipped by the coach driver? How does the scene affect your attitude toward her?

9. Make a list of all of Félicité's losses. How does she react to them? Compare her reactions to those of Madame Aubain.

10. Compare "A Simple Heart" to Kate Chopin's "The Story of an Hour." How are the two stories similar? How do they differ?

11. Compare Flaubert's evocation of place to Kawabata's in "The Moon on the Water."

12. "A Simple Heart," Chopin's "The Story of an Hour," and Ibsen's *A Doll's House* are all examples of literary realism. What do these three works have in common that you think might describe realism?

Read a traditional saint's life. What episodes in "A Simple Heart" recall standard episodes in a saint's life? Is Flaubert's story a saint's life?

FYODOR DOSTOEVSKY
The Brothers Karamazov: The Grand Inquisitor

Although "The Grand Inquisitor" is a relatively short piece, it is potentially explosive in the classroom because it still raises controversial philosophical and religious issues. Ivan, the narrator of the story, calls it "a poem in prose," and, like a fine poem, it deserves several readings.

The Inquisitor maintains that most people are not ready for freedom and that "real" Christianity is not for the masses, who prefer "bread" (material goods and security) to individual choice. An excellent place to begin teaching this piece is with the Inquisitor's analyses of the three temptations of Jesus (recorded in both Matthew and Luke of the New Testament); they form the core of the work and raise questions about the meaning of individual freedom and the need for institutional controls. Through the voice of the Inquisitor, Dostoevsky seems to develop the position that Jesus advocated a freedom of choice not available within the legalistic framework of Judaism, but that Christian institutions such as the Roman Church undermined this freedom by instituting a whole new system of hierarchical controls.

In fact, Dostoevsky does not provide answers in the piece; the voice of freedom is silent, as if Jesus were depending on totalitarianism to convict itself. Dostoevsky leaves it up to his readers to arrive at their conclusions about these issues; we are free to choose. Students might be asked to compare their images of Jesus with the picture presented in "The Grand Inquisitor."

Questions for Discussion and Writing

1. Ivan calls his story "a poem in prose"; what are its poetic qualities?
2. What is the relevance of the historical setting (time and place) of this work?
3. Why does the Grand Inquisitor arrest Jesus?
4. Discuss the mixture of sympathetic and evil qualities in the character of the Inquisitor. What are the contradictions in his speeches to Jesus? What do these contradictions signify? Does the Inquisitor symbolize Protestant as well as Roman Catholic authority?
5. How does the Grand Inquisitor use the temptations of Jesus to support his argument? The first temptation pits freedom against bread, the second temptation involves the attraction of miracle and mystery, and the third temptation focuses on authority.
6. How does the figure of the Inquisitor prefigure dictators and totalitarian movements in the twentieth century?
7. What evidence is there in modern society that people prefer material possessions to personal freedom?
8. Some social and religious movements maintain that hungry people need to be fed before they are educated in morality and political freedom. Discuss the pros and cons of this position.

9. How would you describe the kind of radical freedom that the Grand Inquisitor ascribes to Jesus? Do you think you would be capable of exercising this kind of freedom? Do you know anyone who has become *free* by following Jesus' teachings?

10. Discuss the portrayal of Jesus in "The Grand Inquisitor"; which of his biblical qualities are used by Dostoevsky? Why doesn't Dostoevsky allow Jesus to answer the Grand Inquisitor? What is the impact of Jesus' silence?

11. What is the meaning of the final kiss? Is it at all related to Judas' kiss in the Gospel of Matthew (ch. 26)?

12. Does Ivan's atheism reveal itself in the portraits of either the Grand Inquisitor or Jesus?

13. Some critics have maintained that Dostoevsky was a prophetic writer who was a significant precursor to modernism. What qualities of "The Grand Inquisitor" connect it to early twentieth-century literature and writers such as Kafka, Rilke, Conrad, and Camus?

14. How does the Grand Inquisitor reflect an acquaintance with the basic principles of Machiavelli?

15. Compare the inquisitor in *Candide* with Dostoevsky's Inquisitor. Does Voltaire show some sympathy with the inquisitor? Is Nietzsche's superman similar to Dostoevsky's Inquisitor?

Projects

1. The history of the Inquisition provides an excellent research topic.

2. Students might want to read *The Brothers Karamazov* and analyze the character of Ivan, an exceedingly modern protagonist. What is the role of "The Grand Inquisitor" section in the larger work?

HENRIK IBSEN
A Doll's House

A Doll's House is by a male author who denied that he was consciously presenting women's issues. Ibsen stated: "I . . . must disclaim the honor of having consciously worked for women's rights. I am not even quite sure what women's rights really are. To me it has been a question of human rights." Nevertheless, *A Doll's House* is Nora's play. It traces her transformation from the child-wife of Act I through the transformation in Act II, which builds to the climactic tarantella where Nora dances out of Torvald's control, to the woman who challenges the hypocrisy and dishonesty in her marriage and finally acts to free herself from its constraints. As she closes the door on her marriage, Nora emerges as one of the "new women" of late-nineteenth-century literature, women who represent women's issues from the woman's point of view.

Although the issues may at first seem hackneyed to contemporary students, the details in the play give them particularity and life. The contradictions in Nora's character are brilliantly balanced. She is a resourceful woman who manages her household budget and deceives her husband while making him think she is the frivolous little wife who appears incapable of taking anything seriously. The foils in the play, especially Kristin and Krogstad, whose relationship counterpoints that of Nora and Torvald, bring out the facets of Nora's character and highlight the shifts in her consciousness. In the confrontation between Torvald and Nora in Act III, Ibsen's observation of the dimensions of Torvald's unconscious oppression of his wife is still compelling. If Nora slamming the door at the end is not as shocking to us as it was to the Victorians, Torvald's inability to comprehend Nora's situation and his utter bewilderment at the end of the play can still unsettle contemporary readers with its incisiveness.

A Doll's House is concerned with some of the same issues as *Faust*—for example, with the ways in which social conventions stultify self-fulfillment. But the drama of the two plays is very different. *Faust*, a romantic dramatic poem, ranges over the earth and ventures into realms beyond ordinary experience, covering in the process nearly the whole of Faust's long lifetime. Faust, too, is an extraordinary hero, a man of high accomplishment in many endeavors. *A Doll's House*, in prose rather than poetry, confines itself to a few rooms in Torvald Helmer's house and a few days in the lives of Nora and her husband, a fairly typical bourgeois couple. With their contrasting heroes, subject matter, and dramatic techniques, the two works represent some of the essential differences between the romantic and realistic impulses in nineteenth-century literature.

Although the two works contrast so markedly in technique and scale, the relationship between Faust and Margaret has some intriguing similarities to that between Torvald and Nora. Both women are victims of male power: Margaret becomes a plaything in Faust's quest for experience, Nora a doll in the house of a social-climbing banker. Both women are confined: Margaret in the prison where she dies, Nora in the doll's house of the suffocating constraints of bourgeois marriage. The difference between the endings of the two women—Margaret's death and Nora's liberation—marks one of the important changes in the literature of the nineteenth century. *Faust*, despite its celebration of the eternal feminine, is firmly grounded in a male consciousness. The feminine is useful in defining Faust's incompleteness, but the play does not get inside a feminine point of view. It remains a male quest story. *A Doll's House*, despite the disclaimer of its author, tells a woman's story from the woman's point of view.

Questions for Discussion and Writing

1. What do the nicknames Torvald uses to address his wife indicate about their relationship? Compare these epithets to the ones John uses in "The Yellow Wallpaper." Compare these two husbands. In what ways are they alike? In what ways is Torvald a more fully realized character?

2. In what ways is Kristin different from Nora? How does Ibsen use Kristin to help reveal Nora's character?

3. What are Nora's reasons for not telling Torvald why she wants to go to Italy?

4. Why do you think Ibsen set the play at Christmas? Describe how elements of setting—the house, the clothing, the season—reinforce the conflicts in the play.

5. What is the significance of the title of the play? What lines in the play help to make clear the import of the title?

6. What is the tarantella? Is it significant that the dance is from Capri and that Nora is "capricious" when she dances it? Why does Torvald want Nora to dance? What does the rehearsal scene tell you about each of them and about their relationship? Why does Torvald bring Nora home as soon as she finishes dancing?

7. What is the "wonderful thing" that Nora wishes would happen in the final act? If the wonderful thing had happened, would it have changed the outcome of the play?

8. Do you believe that Nora is telling the truth in the final act when she says that this is the first serious conversation they have had in eight years of marriage? Why or why not?

9. Does Torvald understand why Nora is leaving him? Compare his situation at the end of the play with John's at the end of Gilman's "The Yellow Wallpaper."

10. Why does Nora leave at the end of the play? Do you think she will return to Torvald later on? Why or why not? Is this play, finally, a comedy or a tragedy?

1. Write an essay in which you consider Nora Helmer in relation to some of the other heroines of nineteenth-century literature. You may want to compare her to Catherine Earnshaw, Harriet Jacobs, or the wife in "The Yellow Wallpaper."
2. Describe how you would modernize the plot of *A Doll's House* to fit a contemporary situation. What crime might a contemporary Nora commit rather than taking out a loan on her own? Would a contemporary version of the play end with Nora leaving or with some other resolution?

LEO TOLSTOY
The Death of Ivan Ilyitch

With apparent simplicity and directness, Tolstoy's *The Death of Ivan Ilyitch* tells a story about a man who, at the height of his career, develops a terminal illness that dramatically changes his life. All—or almost all—of the people and institutions that should provide aid and comfort to Ivan fail him. Beneath the surface, then, is another story that shows how Ivan's career influences the adoption of a life-style that gradually isolates him from his inner life, his family, his clients, and his colleagues. Ivan does not appear to be malicious or evil; he is a conscientious official—recognizable in every corridor of our own society—who gets trapped by the superficial veneer of job and social class and somehow misses out on the substance of life. The story is a good example of nineteenth-century realism and can be compared with other realist texts such as Flaubert's "A Simple Heart" and Ibsen's *A Doll's House*.

From their own life experiences, students easily connect to the major themes of this portrait: the effects of bureaucracy on human relationships, the compartmentalization of personal and public roles, the lack of substantive communication in families, the role of denial during crises, the isolating effects of illness and disability, and the horrendous fears surrounding death. In other words, this story taps into strong, emotional issues for most of us.

Questions for Discussion and Writing

1. Who tells Ivan's story? What tone does this narrator use? Why is Ivan Ilyitch's death announced at the beginning of the story?
2. Does it make any sense to say that *Ivan Ilyitch* is not about death, but about dying? Why or why not? Does Ivan's life have a focus or meaning before his illness? If not, why not?
3. Explain the irony involved with Ivan Ilyitch being a judge.
4. What are some of the literary and psychological devices Tolstoy uses to make Ivan's death a premonition of our own?
5. How does Tolstoy develop sympathy (or even empathy) for Ivan? Is he a man for whom we would usually have sympathy? Is he a typical representative of his class? How does his illness gradually lead to relative isolation?
6. What is the role of Gerasim, the servant boy? Why might a servant connect more readily to a dying person than a member of the upper classes would?

7. What is the role of love and compassion at the end of the story? Does Christianity provide consolation to Ivan? How does Ivan's son assist Ivan in coming to terms with his life and death?

8. Elisabeth Kübler-Ross enlarged our present understanding of the dying process in *On Death and Dying* (1969) by describing the typical states that a dying person goes through: denial, anger, bargaining, grieving, and acceptance. Does Ivan Ilyitch go through any of these stages?

9. Have you had experiences with death that might contribute to an appreciation of *The Death of Ivan Ilyitch*?

10. Compare the death of Ivan to that of Félicité in Flaubert's "A Simple Heart." What do these two realists have in common in their approach to death and its meaning? Do you think Tolstoy and Flaubert held similar views on the meaning of life and death?

Projects

1. The kernel for this story was reported to Tolstoy from the brother of an Ivan Ilich Mechnikov; Ivan was a judge at Tula where he died in 1881. Tolstoy planned to write the story as the diary of a man struggling with death. Write diary entries for poignant scenes in *The Death of Ivan Ilyitch* from the point of view of Ivan's wife or son.

2. What are our contemporary attitudes toward dying and death? Some historians maintain that when most of the populace lived on farms, death was accepted as a natural part of life, but as people became urbanized, death became unnatural and frightening. Discuss the roles that environment might play in one's attitudes toward death. Do we—as a culture—avoid the reality of death? How are our attitudes changing?

3. What roles do funeral homes and cemeteries play in our society?

EMILY DICKINSON
Selected Poems

Emily Dickinson, like many other nineteenth-century authors, is concerned with the difference between surface and reality, especially among the middle classes, where materialism, social climbing, and bourgeois niceness have replaced honest communication. Tolstoy's Ivan Ilyitch and Brontë's Heathcliff and Catherine would agree with Dickinson when she says, "I like a look of Agony / Because I know it's True" (241). She writes about natural beauty, but like Thoreau, Hoffmann, Wordsworth, and Brontë, she knows and thrills to the powerful and threatening side of nature. Above all, she shares with many authors here—Brontë, Jacobs, Whitman, Flaubert, Ibsen, Chopin, and Gilman—a keen sense of the constraints laid on women by a patriarchal society.

Dickinson usually teaches very well, especially in a survey course, where students often find it a relief to stop galloping through great swaths of material and concentrate on some small, self-contained texts such as these poems. Some of Dickinson's poems are immediately accessible, hence her frequent appearance in children's anthologies, even though there may well be complexities beneath the surface. "Wild Nights—Wild Nights!" (249), for example, is not a poem students will have much trouble understanding. Other poems of hers are complex and ambiguous enough to have provoked long critical essays, even whole books; "My Life had stood—a Loaded Gun—" (754) is one such poem. Students need to be reassured that many of Dickinson's poems baffle and engage gifted critics as well as beginning students of literature. It may help to begin with Dickinson's own great anti-analysis poem "Split the Lark—and you'll find the Music—" (861). Most of us have experienced the feeling of having reduced something alive and lovely to a bloody corpse, or of having watched a professor commit that act. Speaking those feelings aloud clears the classroom air.

Dickinson's poems are ideal for close reading, and most of our suggested questions and projects are directed toward that. But it's also good to try to convey something of the cultural and social world out of which these poems grow. You can bring into class pictures of nineteenth-century valentines, funerary art, and New England house interiors; for this purpose, Polly Longsworth's *The World of Emily Dickinson* (1990) is an invaluable teaching tool, though relevant illustrations can be found in many coffee-table books. The Emmaline Grangerford chapter in Mark Twain's *Huckleberry Finn* is a hilarious parody of the sort of lugubrious amateur elegy tradition Emily Dickinson rises out of and utterly transcends. Being able to belt out a standard hymn or two in order to demonstrate that Dickinson indeed uses common measure or hymn meter is a good standby skill; one of the editors of this text sometimes teaches her class to sing "I never lost as much but twice" (49) to the tune of "Oh God, Our Help in Ages Past."

Questions for Discussion and Writing

1. In "I know that He exists" (328), in what sense is God hiding? What are some conventional notions about what a good Christian might expect to see at the moment of death? How does this poem subvert those ideas when it pictures God as a sadistic playmate at hide-and-seek who refuses to come out when the game's over?

2. In "I never lost as much but twice" (49), what does Dickinson mean by losses "in the sod"? What is implied about the third, most recent loss? How does this poem comment on the text often incorporated into the burial service, "The Lord giveth, and the Lord taketh away; blessed be the name of the Lord"? Why does the speaker address God as a banker and a burglar?

3. "Have you prayed about it?" is a question people in Dickinson's society would often ask someone who was perplexed or in pain. What is the speaker's exasperated response in "Of course—I prayed—" (376)? How is the frequently voiced idea that "God's eye is on the sparrow," that he keeps watch over the least of his creatures, dealt with in the first stanza? What do you envision when you hear Dickinson's phrase, "the atom's tomb"?

4. In poem 986, what aspects of the snake does Dickinson concentrate on? What does the phrase "zero at the bone" suggest to you?

5. What do the poems "They shut me up in Prose—" (613), "I tie my Hat—I crease my Shawl—" (443), "My Life had stood—a Loaded Gun—" (754), and "The Soul has Bandaged moments—" (512) suggest about middle-class white girls' and women's lives in the nineteenth century? Compare Dickinson's visions of repression, servitude, confinement, deprivation, and assault to Charlotte Perkins Gilman's and to Harriet Jacobs's and Sarah Winnemucca Hopkins's.

6. What do you think are the literal events in women's lives that are being symbolically envisioned in poems 754, 1670, and 512?

Projects

1. Write an imitation of an Emily Dickinson poem. *Suggestions:* One of her most common forms consists of two four-line stanzas, alternating iambic tetrameter and trimeter. One of her favorite kinds of poems is the definition poem, such as 435, "Much Madness is divinest Sense—." One strategy is to pick a word such as *justice, logic, delight,* or

procrastination and then define it in very concrete terms. ("Delight's the Morning Glory's theme— / Her bumptiousness of Blue—" etc.)

2. Examine collections of Victorian valentines or funerary art. How do Dickinson's love poems or poems on death resemble these? How do they differ?
3. Look at pictures of typical Euro-American middle-class interiors from the mid to late nineteenth century; get pictures of Dickinson's own house, if possible. What characterizes decor during this era? Note the reluctance to leave any space blank, the penchant for swathing every possible surface with drapery, the abundance of bric-a-brac and decorative moulding, and the interest in assembling together styles from a wide variety of times and places—China, ancient Egypt, Turkey, classical Greece, and India. What does this tell you about contemporary tastes and interests? How are those tastes and interests affirmed or set aside in Dickinson's poems?

KATE CHOPIN
The Story of an Hour

"The Story of an Hour" is marked by the influence of Chopin's mentor in short story form, Guy de Maupassant. Chopin translated several of Maupassant's stories into English and she wrote about him as a writer who created "life, not fiction." In the terseness of the storytelling, the carefully observed details, the surprise ending, and the ironic point of view, Chopin acknowledges her mentor. Notable among the telling details in the story are the descriptions of the rooms in Mrs. Mallard's house, the view from the bedroom window, and her vision of weeping over her husband's body. The objective narration gives us an unmediated impression of Mrs. Mallard's mind as she responds to the news of her husband's death. It also surprises us with two unexpected events at the end of the story: Mallard's return and his wife's death. The dramatic irony in this surprise ending is matched by the more subtle irony of the doctor's conclusion, for by the end of the story the reader knows enough about Mrs. Mallard's mind to know that her unconventional response to the news of her husband's death makes the doctor's conclusions especially banal.

Although this is a very short story and would not seem to warrant extended historical and cultural discussion, it reinforces the women's issues presented in other late nineteenth-century works such as "The Yellow Wallpaper" and *A Doll's House.*

Questions for Discussion and Writing

1. How does the story make ironic the "great care" with which Josephine and Richards break the news of her husband's death to Mrs. Mallard?
2. What does the view outside the bedroom window tell us about Mrs. Mallard's state of mind?
3. What is the significance of "Richards' quick motion" at the end of the story?
4. What is the most surprising thing in the story?
5. Discuss the significance of the title.
6. Compare Mrs. Mallard's sense of her marriage with Nora's sense of hers in *A Doll's House* and that of the wife in "The Yellow Wallpaper." In what ways are their views of their situations alike? How do they differ?

SYMBOLIST POETRY

Rather than assemble a minianthology of the many poets who may be considered symbolists, we have focused on three French poets of the mid-nineteenth century—Baudelaire, Rimbaud, and Mallarmé—in whose work can be traced the shift from romanticism to symbolism (by no means an even or organic development) and who arguably have exerted the most influence on modernist poetry. The shepherd's nature of Wordsworth's poetry gives way to a tough-minded urbanity in Baudelaire, Rimbaud, and Mallarmé, whose poetry marks a major shift in consciousness in the mid-nineteenth century as these three poets confronted the shock of the city—its excess, fragmentation, and alienation. Baudelaire, whose poetry vividly depicts the stench and stain of urban life, has much in common with the realists and naturalists who visit the same streets, but in more accessible language. Hence, it is helpful to compare his vision of life with that, say, of Flaubert, Chekhov, or even Ibsen. Like them, Baudelaire feels the pulse of the feebling hypocrisy and the hopeless materialism of the bourgeois world; in poems such as "To the Reader" and "Spleen" he faces directly the *ennui* that is the product of that miserable life. Rimbaud also knows the zone of *ennui*. A poem similar in theme to Baudelaire's "The Voyage," *The Drunken Boat* records Rimbaud's vexed attempt to break free from the smear of commerce and trade, but Rimbaud rejects the elegiac longing and detachment of Baudelaire and opts for a poetry of immediacy that insists on an identification between the reader and the "I" in the poem who desires escape. In contrast to these two poets, Mallarmé seems closer to the modernism of James Joyce or the early T. S. Eliot, who claim that an author should be totally absent from his or her work. Although the tormented poet lingers in "Windows" and "Azure," the most Baudelairean of his poems, the subject is altogether missing from "The Afternoon of a Faun," which represents the purest symbolism of our selections. The latter poem's formalistic detachment and allusive density will present difficulty for students.

Because symbolist poetry has a reputation for being difficult, many students may resist attempting to understand it at all. As one of our preliminary reviewers put it when recommending we exclude symbolist poetry altogether, "I've never understood it myself, so I never try to teach it." Students should recognize even before approaching the poetry that these poets, especially Rimbaud and Mallarmé, were deliberately evasive in their work. Rather than delineate a position, they sought to evoke a feeling, to suggest ideas that were in themselves ineffable—that defy utterance, much less paraphrase. Keeping in mind the attempt on the part of Mallarmé and Verlaine to use language as music, it helps to ask students to read less for getting meaning from the text and more for registering their own responses to the poetry. Ask them to become Baudelaire's *hypocrite lecteur*, to record ideas that the poems *suggest* to them rather than ideas the poems *convey* to them. In many ways, the symbolists anticipated a response-oriented criticism, and it is no accident that the famous "death of the author" was announced by a philosopher very much influenced by the French symbolists. Rimbaud's attempt to scramble the ordinary, to disorient and estrange, also anticipates the Brechtian and formalist notion of defamiliarization. If these critical methods are only partly successful, it may be useful to set aside poet Kenneth Rexroth's admonition to the contrary and get students interested in the lives of Baudelaire and especially Rimbaud, whose efforts to cultivate a decadent Bohemianism will remind contemporary readers of popular lyricists, such as Jim Morrison of The Doors and Kurt Cobain of Nirvana.

Questions for Discussion and Writing

1. How do Baudelaire's "To the Reader" and "Spleen" affront the reader's sensibility and confront his or her conventional beliefs about evil and sin?

2. Discuss what Baudelaire means by *ennui,* or boredom, and why it may be a greater evil than, say, murder. In his attack on *ennui* and apathy, does Baudelaire show certain affinities to Goethe's *Faust,* with its emphasis on actions or deeds?
3. Explain how Baudelaire defines the social position of the poet and the role of poetry in "The Albatross" and "Correspondences."
4. Compare Baudelaire's "The Voyage" to Rimbaud's *The Drunken Boat.* How would you characterize the difference between the two poets, both in terms of their treatment of the theme of the voyage or journey and in terms of their style?
5. The French word for *swan, le cygne,* closely resembles the word for *sign, le signe.* Discuss how you might read "The Swan" as an extended meditation on language and poetry.
6. Compare Baudelaire's "The Swan" with Mallarmé's "The Afternoon of a Faun." How would you characterize the differences between the two poets? Explain how Baudelaire anticipates the symbolism of Mallarmé.
7. Discuss Rimbaud's allusions to colonialism and trade in *The Drunken Boat.* What do these allusions suggest about Rimbaud's perception of Europe? of himself?
8. Baudelaire's "Correspondences" and Rimbaud's "Vowels" are often seen as major precursors to, even major founding statements of, symbolism. Examine the poems to justify this point of view.
9. Discuss the Baudelairean elements of Mallarmé's "Windows" and "Azure." How do Mallarmé's poems move further toward symbolism than Baudelaire's?
10. How are some of Baudelaire's poems and Mallarmé's "Windows" and "Azure" linked to realism and naturalism as well as to romanticism and symbolism?
11. Discuss Mallarmé's use of color in "The Afternoon of a Faun." You might consider how the technique of the poem may be related to movements in nineteenth-century art, such as symbolism and impressionism.
12. Discuss the problems involved in reading a poem such as "The Afternoon of a Faun." How does it, for example, defy the reader's desire for closure and elude fixed meanings? Discuss this poem as an example of symbolism in its most refined form.
13. Compare the atmosphere, tone, and subject matter of the symbolist poets with that of the romantics. Discuss how the symbolists explore new or different states of consciousness that emerge from their primarily urban experience.

Projects

1. Listen to Claude Debussy's "L'Après Midi d'un Faune" and compare the composition to Mallarmé's poem.
2. With colored pencils, try drawing the images that come to you as you read a symbolist poem. Don't worry about the accuracy of your drawings; rather, try to capture the tone or mood of what you hear, see, or feel.
3. Listen to the lyrics of some popular rock bands, such as The Doors, Pearl Jam, and Nirvana. What do the symbolist poets have in common with these groups, if anything?

ANTON CHEKHOV
The Cherry Orchard

Chekhov's plays deal with turn-of-the-century themes arising out of fundamental social change: the demise of the upper class, the rise of a bourgeois middle class, and the apprehensions about the quality of the world taking shape on the horizon. But Chekhov was not a reformer; he did not bring a particular social agenda to his plays in the way that Ibsen did. He was not like Dostoevsky, who took the great ideas and cataclysmic passions of his time and clothed his characters with them, nor like the elder Tolstoy, who conceived of art as serving religious ends.

Chekhov's brilliance lies not in the complexity of his ideas, but in his dramaturgy, the *way* he creates lifelike characters in lifelike situations who struggle with contemporary issues. In *The Cherry Orchard*, he explores the suffering and faint hope that attend the demise of the landed gentry and rise of middle-class entrepreneurs, but he is not so much concerned about the social philosophy of his characters as their perceptions of themselves, their moments of self-consciousness when they are honest and vulnerable. We really do not see these characters in their best lights, but in situations of self-deprecation. Lyubov's intelligence and passion, for example, are undercut by Lopahin's observation in Act II: "such reckless people as you are—such queer, unbusinesslike people—I never met in my life. One tells you in plain Russian your estate is going to be sold, and you seem not to understand it." Lopahin is obviously a good businessman, not without a heart, but instead of witnessing his strengths, we see him pinned to the wall later in Act II by Lyubov's arrows: "You shouldn't look at plays, you should look at yourself a little oftener. How gray your lives are! How much nonsense you talk." Furthermore, she seems unaware of the irony in these words, the appropriateness of this message for her own family.

The motion of the play moves toward small moments when insights might provide some reasonable resolution to problems, or at least a human relationship for surviving life's crises. But these liminal, threshold situations that verge on some possibility often fizzle or dissolve. During the leave-taking at the end of the play, a crack briefly opens into Gaev's feelings, but his nieces quickly squelch him:

GAEV: My friends—my dear, my precious friends! Leaving this house forever, can I be silent? Can I refrain from giving utterance at leave-taking to these emotions which now flood all my being?

ANYA: [*supplicatingly*]. Uncle!

VARYA: Uncle, you mustn't!

How well trained the nieces are! The humor is undercut by pathos. Lyubov confesses in Act III: "I can't conceive of life without the cherry orchard, and if it really must be sold, then sell me with the orchard." But then she adds, "My boy was drowned here," and we glimpse some of the inner ambiguity about the orchard, why she seems incapable of making a plan for saving it, and leaves after its sale for another hopeless lover in Paris.

One of the best ways to discover how Chekhov packs so much meaning into small gestures and missed communication is to choose a scene, assign parts, and read through it. This approach tends to lead to discussions about the small details and nuances of particular speeches—the seminal moments in a Chekhov play.

Questions for Discussion and Writing

1. *The Cherry Orchard* begins in May with the orchard in bloom and ends in October with the sound of axes; how do these two seasons frame the action of the play and contribute to its meaning?

2. Discuss the multiple meanings of the cherry orchard itself. How does Chekhov develop its symbolic values? What does it mean to each of the main characters?

3. What keeps the owners of the orchard from decisive action and saving the orchard? In what kinds of moments are their personalities revealed?

4. How does Lopahin serve as a foil for Lyubov and her family?

5. Discuss the scene between Lopahin and Varya at the end of Act IV; what is the unspoken communication in this scene? How does it go awry? What is the meaning of the broken thermometer?

6. Chekhov described this play as a "comedy, in places even a farce." What are its comic elements? Are there also tragic or pathetic moments?

7. Compare the landed class in *The Cherry Orchard* with the bureaucratic class in Tolstoy's *The Death of Ivan Ilyitch*.

Projects

1. Suppose you are the casting director for *The Cherry Orchard*; how do you imagine the main characters? What physical details do you associate with them? What do they wear?

2. The theme of transience and radical change runs throughout the literature of the nineteenth and twentieth centuries. What was happening historically to justify writers' concerns? Compare *The Cherry Orchard* with the anthologized works by Keats, Joyce, and Tagore—especially the latter's *Broken Ties*.

CHARLOTTE PERKINS GILMAN
The Yellow Wallpaper

Gilman's "The Yellow Wallpaper" is one of several nineteenth-century texts dealing with marriage or relations between the sexes and issues of power and patriarchy; it shares these concerns with Brontë's *Wuthering Heights*, Jacobs's *Incidents in the Life of a Slave Girl*, Whitman's *Song of Myself*, Ibsen's *A Doll's House*, many of Dickinson's poems (for example, 613, "They shut me up in Prose"), and Chopin's "The Story of an Hour." It also deals with questions of mental illness, healing, and the medical profession that also are present in Tolstoy's *The Death of Ivan Ilyitch*, Chopin, Jacobs, Dickinson (see 435, "Much Madness is divinest Sense—"), and Freud's casebook history of Dora. Certainly it looks ahead to Virginia Woolf's trenchant exploration of the limitations placed on women.

You may want to make your students aware of more of the medical and psychiatric background to Gilman's story than is contained in the headnote, which focuses on Gilman's personal history. Sandra M. Gilbert and Susan Gubar's *The Madwoman in the Attic: The Woman Writer and the Nineteenth Century Literary Imagination* (1979) contains a great deal of information on the concept of female hysteria and nineteenth-century attitudes toward and treatments for mental illness in women.

You may also want to make sure your students know something about the Gothic convention and the expectations Gilman sets up when her heroine marvels that this charming country manor should be so unexpectedly empty and the rental fee so surprisingly reasonable, when she begins to find evidence that the former occupants may have been somewhat odd and her total isolation becomes evident. It will certainly help discussion if they've read the opening chapters of *Wuthering Heights*, but even if they haven't, they will probably know something of the conventions of strange empty houses and forbidding upstairs rooms, if only from movies. How Gilman plays with those conventions in telling a tale of even more frightening psychological horror is one of the delights of "The Yellow Wallpaper."

Gilman's story may be compared with *Wuthering Heights* not only because of its Gothic elements, but also because of its presentation of another female invalid, Catherine, for whom a patriarchal society prescribes a quiet gentility and isolation from all she loves. The element of confinement to a small space can be found in Jacobs, Dickinson, and Hopkins. "The Yellow Wallpaper" can also be read as a kind of white middle-class captivity narrative in conjunction with Jacobs and Equiano.

Questions for Discussion and Writing

1. What expectations does Gilman awaken in the opening paragraphs of the story? What kind of story do we expect her to tell, given her description of the gloomy, isolated mansion that is so unexpectedly cheap to rent?
2. Why does Gilman want to call the house an "ancestral hall"?
3. Is the narrator actually ill at the outset of the story? If so, what treatment do you think might be appropriate for her?
4. Why does Gilman choose to make the narrator's husband a doctor?
5. Why is it appropriate that the narrator's room is a former nursery?
6. Discuss the significance of the wallpaper. What different things does the narrator see in its pattern?
7. Who is the woman the narrator discerns "creeping" behind the wallpaper and out in the garden? Why does she confess, at one point, that she thinks there are not one, but "a great many women"?
8. Is the ending of the story a sheer descent into madness? Is there anything at all positive about the ending?
9. If Freud were the physician in charge of the narrator, how might his treatment have differed from Weir's?

Project

Read and report on Gilman's engaging feminist fantasy *Herland* (1915).

SARAH WINNEMUCCA HOPKINS
Life among the Piutes: Their Wrongs and Claims

There are a good number of autobiographical and semiautobiographical texts in Volume Two to which *Life among the Piutes* may be compared, as the questions below suggest. This text not only affords students the chance to think about the topic of the self in society, it also presents from a Native American perspective issues of colonialism that occupy many of our selections.

Autobiography is an early form of written literature among North American Indians, but as the headnote suggests, their autobiographical traditions differ radically from Euro-American ones. The object of American Indian autobiography—at least when it is not shaped by a white intermediary, such as an anthropologist—is not a description of the development of one's personality, a portrait of the subject's personality, opinions, and deeds, but rather an attempt to see one's self in terms of the tribe's history, values, and expectations. (This is often true of autobiography written by other ethnic and social groups as well; working-class autobiography from nineteenth-century England, for example, displays many of the same characteristics.)

Sarah Winnemucca Hopkins's autobiography *Life among the Piutes: Their Wrongs and Claims* is well-titled, for it is less the story of Hopkins's life and opinions than her account of the fortunes of the Piute as reflected in her own life. Consequently, there are a good many things we expect to see in Euro-American autobiography that Hopkins does not bother to tell us. Students might enjoy leafing through a sampling of early chapters in Euro-American autobiographies to see the sorts of things authors talk about in recounting childhood—descriptions of family members, places and houses, rewards and punishments, pleasures and fears. Hopkins cuts straight to the incident that has mattered most for her and her people: the coming of the whites into the Great Basin. Certainly the story is individualized, as Hopkins brilliantly recreates how these events looked to her child-self. But always, she writes as a Piute, not as a private romantic "I," in much the same way that authors of slave narratives write as African-Americans, conscious always of their kinship with present and former slaves.

Questions for Discussion and Writing

1. What does Hopkins leave out of her account of her childhood that we might normally expect to hear about? What sorts of things, for example, are writers such as Rousseau and Wordsworth interested in telling us that Hopkins omits?
2. What is Hopkins's purpose in writing her autobiography? Who is her expected audience?
3. Compare Hopkins's accounts of encountering the whites with other literary moments in this volume where people undergo similarly startling experiences that are difficult to integrate with life as they have previously understood it: the Ibo's encounter with whites in *Things Fall Apart*, Marlow's glimpse of the African priestess in *Heart of Darkness*, and the Kiowas's first sight of the plains in *The Way to Rainy Mountain*. How does each author convey strangeness and otherness to the reader?
4. How do Harriet Jacobs and Sarah Winnemucca Hopkins primarily define themselves in their autobiographies? Do they mostly see themselves as private individuals, or as members of a particular group or groups? Do they have anything in common?
5. *The Way to Rainy Mountain* is a semiautobiographical American Indian narrative coming nearly a hundred years after Hopkins's account. Do the two differ in their attitudes toward and representations of whites?

Projects

1. Research and report on the history of the Donner party.
2. Write your own autobiography, or a portion of it, or at least an outline listing major episodes. Don't focus on yourself as an individual, but rather tell your story as a member of a larger group—as an Irish Catholic, a Mormon, a southern African-American, a Navajo. If you are of mixed ancestry, you can either focus on one part, or you can tell your story as someone who embodies a diverse heritage. Are there family stories about ancestors coming to the United States, or, if you are American Indian, about initial encounters with Europeans? What aspects of the way you live your life are determined by that heritage?

RABINDRANATH TAGORE
The Hungry Stones *and* Broken Ties

Tagore's work must be seen in the context of British colonialism at the end of the nineteenth century. He is in the second generation of writers of the Bengali Renaissance, writers who wrote in vernacular Bengali, not in Sanskrit, the traditional literary language of northern India, nor in English, the language of the colonizers. His education (like that of Satish and Srivlas in *Broken Ties*) was Western, but Tagore, like the other Bengali writers of his time, sought a distinctively Indian identity in an India divided between Western and

Indian cultures. The tax collector in "The Hungry Stones," working for the colonial government but living in an Indian palace, and the students in *Broken Ties* represent this divided identity. Similar cultural divisions confront the Japanese student in Mori Ōgai's "The Dancing Girl" and Okonkwo, the Ibo hero of Achebe's *Things Fall Apart*.

"The Hungry Stones" explores the division in literary terms, using devices from the *Arabian Nights*—the framed narrative, inset stories, and exotic images and motifs—to articulate the conflict between the two cultures. *Broken Ties* is a more complex exploration of the contradictions and ambiguities within Indian culture. The first chapter, "Uncle," begins by contrasting the Westernized "atheists" with the traditional Hindus, suggesting in the partitioned family house the partition of Bengal under Lord Curzon, which divided Bengal into Hindu and Moslem enclaves. But the division between the two brothers is only a way of suggesting the contradictions within Satish and in the as yet unidentified narrator, Srivlas. The divisions also produce the tragic conclusion of "Uncle" in the suicide of Noni. Her death—the result of unfamiliar cultural assumptions—may call for a discussion of why and how it happened and just who is responsible for it.

In "Satish," the Indian side of Satish and Srivlas is explored. This section, too, ends with a puzzling episode, Satish's rejection of Damini in the cave. This scene can be read in the romantic tradition of self-exploration—as in the cave scenes in Hoffmann's "The Mines of Falun." It also reveals how elemental is the distrust of the feminine in traditional Indian culture. In the two final chapters, Damini and Srivlas, displacing Satish, become the central figures of the story as they grow beyond the conflict between tradition and Westernization. In their brief marriage they seem to be seeking a new way that unites masculine and feminine, East and West.

Questions for Discussion and Writing

1. How are the day and night worlds of the narrator of "The Hungry Stones" different from each other? Which of the two worlds wins out in the end? Explain how you arrive at your conclusions.
2. What does the frame narrative contribute to "The Hungry Stones"?
3. What is the significance of the title "The Hungry Stones"? of *The Arabian Nights*? of the fact that the story remains unfinished?
4. What, in Jagamohon's and Satish's terms, is an atheist? Who are the Western thinkers who have most influenced them? In what ways do the atheists differ from the believers in this story?
5. What differences between Jagamohon and Harimohon lead to the partitioning of the house? How do these differences help to bring about Noni's suicide?
6. Why does Satish decide to marry Noni? What does this tell us about his character?
7. Why do Satish and Srivlas join the followers of Lilanda Swami?
8. What happens in the cave temple? Why does Tagore use Satish's diary to relate this episode?
9. How does Srivlas characterize himself? How do the events of the story support his self-characterization?
10. How does the story of the suicide of Nabin's wife relate to the main story of the relations between Damini, Satish, and Srivlas?
11. Characterize each of the three main characters: Satish, Damini, and Srivlas. How do their relations change during the story? Why does Damini marry Srivlas rather than Satish?
12. What do the following pairs of opposites contribute to the theme of the novel: town/country, atheism/belief, male/female, reason/passion, freedom/bondage, universal/particular?

13. Compare the love triangle in *Broken Ties* with that in *Wuthering Heights*. Is the marriage of Srivlas and Damini like that of Catherine and Edgar Linton?

14. What is *Broken Ties* saying about women, about their place in Indian society, and about their importance to men? Compare Damini's situation to that of Nora Helmer in *A Doll's House*. Is she liberated by the end of the story?

15. Discuss the title *Broken Ties*. What clues are there in the text as to its significance? What ties are broken in the story?

16. How would *Broken Ties* be different if narrated by Satish? by Damini? by an omniscient narrator?

17. Compare Tagore's treatment of the personal conflict brought on by colonialism with Achebe's.

18. In what ways is *Broken Ties* a nationalistic story? Compare its nationalism with that of Pushkin in *The Bronze Horseman* or Whitman in *Song of Myself*.

Projects

1. Like some Western works of the later nineteenth century, *Broken Ties* could be said to be about woman's relation to patriarchy. Comparing the novel to such works as *A Doll's House* or "The Yellow Wallpaper," discuss the ways in which a woman's role and patriarchy differ East from West.

2. E. M. Forster's novel *A Passage to India*, probably the best-known English novel about colonial India, includes a crucial scene that takes place in a cave, similar to the cave-temple scene in *Broken Ties*. Compare the two scenes, especially as they are used to represent India or the Indian consciousness.

MORI ŌGAI
The Dancing Girl

"The Dancing Girl" is based in part on an actual love affair between Ōgai and an unknown German woman. The protagonist, Ōta Toyotarō, reaches Berlin on assignment from the Japanese government, gradually begins to neglect his duties as he becomes more deeply immersed in Western ideas of independence and the self, and eventually falls in love with Elis, a poor dancer who lives alone with her mother. Depending on how one reads the story, Toyotarō is either rescued or diverted by his college friend, Aizawa Kenkichi, who gets Toyotarō a job working for a Count Amakata. The two succeed in getting Toyotarō to abandon the now pregnant Elis and return with them to Japan. Although the story is simple enough, Ōgai raises it to a high level of tragedy, invoking the age-old conflict between a person's duty to his or her social responsibilities—what the Japanese know as *giri*—and a person's desire to follow the dictates of his or her own conscience and desire. Thus, "The Dancing Girl" is linked to such Japanese works as Lady Murasaki's *The Tale of Genji*, and Chikamatsu's *The Love Suicides at Amijima,* as well as to works in the West, such as Sophocles' *Antigone*, Flaubert's "A Simple Heart," and Ibsen's *A Doll's House.*

Ōgai's story is further complicated by its larger themes dealing with the Westernization of Japanese culture. His own fascination with German culture, history, and philosophy emerges through the eyes of Toyotarō as he describes Berlin and notes his assimilation of German literature and philosophy. Rather than resort to a simple symbolism splitting East and West, Ōgai complicates his story by creating divisions between the emotional and intellectual sides of his protagonist. Toyotarō sees his attraction to Elis and the erosion of his sense of duty as a weakness. However, his ouster from the ministry leads to a total immersion in European, especially German, life, so that he acquires a deep understanding of German culture and customs. Elis, a poor woman with minimal education, does not symbolize the West per se, for she draws out the emotional side of Toyotarō that has been repressed in the "machine," as he calls it, under which he was trained. The conclusion of the story suggests Ōgai's own ambivalence about his protagonist, for Toyotarō praises his friend Aizawa Kenkichi as a "rare friend" and yet curses him in the same breath for taking him back to Japan.

Questions for Discussion and Writing

1. The narrator of "The Dancing Girl" seems fascinated with details of Berlin and with German history. Discuss Ōgai's representation of the city and its history, his allusions to German philosophy and culture, keeping in mind that he was writing for an audience little informed about Europe.

2. How does Toyotarō characterize the awakening of his inner self? Why does he feel so conflicted, even guilty, about his independent feelings and ideas?

3. Compare Toyotarō's relationship with Elis to his responsibilities to Count Amakata. How do they lead Toyotarō into inner conflict and division? What do Elis and the Count signify on a larger social scale?

4. How does Toyotarō's attitude toward Europe change after Count Amakata invites him to return to Japan?

5. Why does Toyotarō leave Elis? Is he driven to return to Japan by some impersonal force—the one he often refers to as the machine, of which he is a part—or by his innermost, personal desire?

6. Elis is driven to a kind of madness—paranoia, to be exact—when she learns that Toyotarō will leave her. How do you respond to her demise? Does it serve as a criticism of Toyotarō, or does it make it easier for you to accept his return to Japan?

7. European colonialist literature often constructs the colonized country as a woman. Can we read Elis as a similar construct? Why or why not?

8. What affinities does Ōgai's short story have with European realism or naturalism?

Project

Write an account of an experience where you've been torn between your sense of responsibility to others and your personal desire.

THE
TWENTIETH
CENTURY

❧

The Modern Age and
the Emerging World Culture

JOSEPH CONRAD
Heart of Darkness

Heart of Darkness is usually read as a travel narrative that makes the journey into the heart of Africa a metaphor for the journey into the interior of the self. The main narrator, Marlow, a naïve young captain at the time of the journey, resists his attraction to Kurtz, the manager of the inner station whom he is charged to bring out of the jungle, and succeeds in making the journey and coming out alive. As his Buddha-like pose as storyteller suggests, he is a wiser man for the experience. In this reading of the story, Africa and the Africans become symbols of a dark inner self that Marlow must confront and control. Just as Kurtz is a kind of unrestrained doppelgänger to Marlow's inner self, the natives are projections of his unconscious vitality and energy—his heart—which the civilized restraints of Europe have caused him to ignore or deny.

The main outlines of this journey into the psyche are familiar to most readers of the story. Marlow leaves civilized England, formerly one of the "dark places" of the earth, to explore dark Africa. In Brussels, the "whited sepulchre" symbolic both of European hypocrisy and of the debilitated spiritual wasteland Europe has become, Marlow finds the gateway to Africa, a passage ominously guarded by two women in black reminiscent of the Fates from classical mythology. From the beginning, Marlow's experience in Africa is absurd, surreal, and dreamlike: a French warship shoots cannons randomly into the jungle, a clerk attempts to maintain the rituals of civilization in the middle of the jungle, and African natives in chain gangs lie dying by the roadside. When Marlow arrives at the ship he is to command, he finds it at the bottom of the river. He recovers his ship and his command (his self-control and rationality) by dragging the boat up from the bottom of the river and working night and day to restore it to working condition. His concentration on this task and on his duty as a captain—what Marlow calls European efficiency—saves him from the debilitating forces of Africa. Amid Europeans who have in various ways succumbed to Africa and to their own greed, Marlow is extraordinary, for he retains his reason and his command. The attraction of Africa is strong, even for Marlow, and he recognizes in Kurtz another extraordinary European and the man he might have been had he lost control. Had he been entranced by the vitality and the violence of Africa, his savage self might have been loosed. But he manages to return, understanding "the horror" within himself and in Africa. Appropriately, Kurtz, his alter ego, dies as they leave the jungle and Marlow is left to tell the story in his own terms to Kurtz's Intended and to the men gathered on the *Nelly*.

Speaking of the story from an African point of view, Chinua Achebe has objected to this psychological interpretation. He sees it as a rationalization for the racism of the story, which he describes as presenting a Eurocentric view that turns Africa and its inhabitants into the Other, into nameless representatives of the savage within that is suppressed by civilization. "*Heart of Darkness* projects the image of Africa as 'the other world,' " Achebe writes in his essay "An Image of Africa," "the antithesis of Europe and therefore of civilization, a place where man's vaunted intelligence and refinement are mocked by triumphant bestiality." The way Conrad and other Europeans use Africans as foils, Achebe implies, is a form of literary colonialism. The Africans in the story, he points out, are faceless and voiceless, merely part of the backdrop to the meeting between Marlow and Kurtz. Seen through Achebe's African eyes, *Heart of Darkness* is a very different story from the psychological parable or epic journey into the underworld that Western critics find in it. Achebe's novel *Things Fall Apart* presents that other Africa "simply as a continent of people—not angels, but not rudimentary souls either—but people, often highly gifted people and often strikingly successful in their enterprise with life and society."

Conrad's novella and Achebe's novel focus several important themes of the modern period: storytelling and its importance to personal, national, and ethnic identity, the place of the writer in a colonial and postcolonial global culture, and the exploration of the dark side of consciousness through an interior journey. If Marlow's journey is originally undertaken as a way to overcome the debilitation of "Europeanness," his telling of it on the *Nelly* may be the real therapy for the neuroses of modern life, for in telling one's story, Freud suggested, one could cure the disease of modernity. The metaphor of disease runs through the literature of the period—from Eliot's *The Waste Land* into Kafka, Joyce, and Sartre. The oft-suggested cure is telling the stories of personal and cultural trauma to recover the spiritual sources of vitality and meaning. Marlow's traumatic experience in Africa that prompts his storytelling is like Akhmatova's experience in Stalinist Russia, Gregor Samsa's traumatic awakening as a cockroach in Kafka's *Metamorphosis*, Wiesel's experience in the Nazi death camps, or Aki's nightmare of the bombing of Hiroshima in Takenishi's "The Rite." In the global village that has emerged from World War II, national literatures no longer make sense, for the stories of the colonizers and the colonized are interrelated; Conrad and Achebe together shape our sense of the world. Our cultural identity as Americans and Westerners can now only be fully understood as it relates to non-Western perspectives.

Questions for Discussion and Writing

1. What does the frame narrative—Marlow's conversation with the other men on the *Nelly*—contribute to the story of the journey up the Congo? How does Marlow differ from the other men on the *Nelly*?

2. What is the difference between a conqueror and a colonist, according to Marlow? Are Kurtz and the other members of the trading company in Africa conquerors or colonists?

3. What does Marlow mean when he speaks of the idea that redeems conquest? Why are the Europeans referred to as pilgrims? What ideas might be considered the redeeming ideas in the conquest of Africa? Does Marlow subscribe to these ideas?

4. Long before he meets Kurtz, Marlow hears from others that Kurtz is remarkable, extraordinary, a universal genius. What makes Kurtz unusual? What evidence does the story offer to suggest what these judgments were based on?

5. Marlow's stories are said to be unlike other seamen's stories because the meaning of the story "was not inside like a kernel but outside, enveloping the tale which brought it out only as a glow brings out a haze." How might this metaphor be said to describe the story Marlow tells in *Heart of Darkness*?

6. Compare the scene in *Heart of Darkness* where Marlow carries Kurtz out of the forest with the scene in the *Aeneid* where Aeneas carries his father out of Troy. Are there any similarities in the symbolism of the two scenes?

7. What role does the Russian seaman play in the story?

8. When Kurtz finally appears in the story, does he confirm the advance accounts we have of him? Marlow describes him as "a voice." What is the significance of this description?

9. To what do Kurtz's final words, "The horror! The horror!" refer? Why does Marlow lie to Kurtz's Intended when she asks him for Kurtz's final words?

10. What roles do the native Africans play in the story? Are there any who could be considered developed characters? Compare Conrad's Africans to those in Achebe's novel and Doris Lessing's "The Old Chief Mshlanga."

11. How does Conrad suggest that Marlow's journey into the Congo is also a journey into the depths of his own consciousness? If Marlow goes to the edge and then withdraws, what frontier does he approach? What does the heart at the core of his experience symbolize psychologically?

12. Marlow claims that the thing that saves Europeans in Africa is their dedication to efficiency. What does he mean by the term? Are the rivets he becomes obsessed with related to the idea of efficiency? Can efficiency be said to save Marlow from a fate similar to Kurtz's?

13. Compare the versions of Africa in *Heart of Darkness* and *Things Fall Apart*. Is Achebe's critique of Conrad's novel justified?

Projects

1. T. S. Eliot took the line "Mistah Kurtz—he dead" as the epigraph for his poem "The Hollow Men." Read Eliot's poem and discuss how Conrad's story relates to it.

2. Watch the film *Apocalypse Now*, an adaptation of *Heart of Darkness* to the Vietnam War. How does the film change your reading of Conrad and your ideas about the Vietnam War?

CHINUA ACHEBE
Things Fall Apart

Although Achebe describes himself as a political writer, *Things Fall Apart* shows that he is also a great artist and storyteller. Like most great works of historical fiction, *Things Fall Apart* stands on its own as a finely crafted tale, and readers need not be deeply informed about the history of colonialism in Nigeria or the customs of the Ibo to understand the tragic story of Umuofia and its leader Okonkwo. Achebe's novel focuses on what has been lost as a result of colonialism, not the process. Thus, *Things Fall Apart* creates a rich picture of Ibo society, a picture enhanced by Achebe's use of folklore and proverbs to create a truly African—Ibo, to be exact—perspective on the events that take place in the novel. For readers who wish to fill in the background of the novel, Robert Wren's *Achebe's World* (1981) and Bernth Lindfors's *Approaches to Teaching Achebe's "Things Fall Apart"* (1991) provide helpful sketches of the historical, cultural, and political contexts of Achebe's works.

The novel, which may be compared to classical tragedies such as *Antigone* or *Hamlet*, divides roughly into two parts. The first two thirds show the complexities of life in Umuofia and establish Okonkwo as a powerful but flawed leader of his people. Already in the first part of the story, internal rivalries and disagreements have begun to erode the integrity of the village, and we see that Okonkwo's authority may be jeopardized by his own stubbornness and refusal to act on advice of others, particularly Obierika and his son, Nwoye. Discontent among the villagers over Okonkwo's killing of Ikemefuna and resentment within his own family prepare the way for the missionaries and British administrators, who figure predominantly in the last third of the novel, to exploit these divisions. In the second part of the novel, Achebe shows how these colonial officials speed the dissolution of the community by imposing the British form of religion and law on the Ibo. With characteristic irony, Achebe shows that Okonkwo's attempt to preserve and protect his community results only in his further isolation from his people and in his ignoble suicide, an act that is condemned by his people.

Things Fall Apart raises many issues that reverberate through the modernist and postmodernist world, including the question of the role of writing—or storytelling—in a postcolonial context. Like many other postcolonial writers from India, Africa, and other nations, Achebe attempts to construct an image of Africa in a language that respects the national traditions of his native country while recognizing the demands of the cosmopolitan, international audience to which the novel is in part addressed. The African English he develops here and in other works attempts, in his words, to convey "a new voice coming out of Africa, speaking of African experience in a world-wide language." Moreover, Achebe aims to reclaim his heritage and at the same time to indicate directions for change. He writes at a time when countries are adapting to a global economy and responding to pressures for reform and international cooperation, yet Achebe is keenly aware of the dangers of reactionary forms of nationalism and the desire for absolute power that in Nigeria and elsewhere has blocked reform and reinstated dictators.

For Achebe, the transition to a new kind of world should not abandon the old; and the repository of the old, the vital means to bring the old to meet the new, is the story. In the words of a character from his *Anthills of the Savannah*: "The story is our escort; without it, we are blind. . . . " Furthermore, the story—an embodiment of a tradition that can adapt to the new—"is the mark on the face that sets one people apart from the neighbours." Thus, Achebe faces directly the problem of preserving national identity in the face of the inevitable blending of different cultures, but preserving that identity in such a way that it does not reject, and can benefit from, the cultures it contacts.

Questions for Discussion and Writing

1. Why does Achebe take the title for this novel from Yeats's "A Second Coming"? Discuss the reverberations or relevance of Yeats's poem throughout the story.
2. What values do the Ibo hold that are similar to those people hold in the West? That are different?

3. Discuss Okonkwo as a heroic character. Notice that he works to achieve greatness within the parameters defined by his community and culture. How does he differ from many Western heroes? What are his strengths and weaknesses?

4. Compare Obierika to Okonkwo. How does he serve as a kind of foil to Okonkwo?

5. Discuss the differences between Mr. Brown and Mr. Smith. How do they represent different forms of colonialism? Which one is more dangerous?

6. Compare Achebe's portrayal of Africa and the African people with Conrad's in *Heart of Darkness*. How does *Things Fall Apart* represent the clash between the colonial forces and the Ibo?

7. Describe the importance of ritual, ceremony, and hierarchy among the Ibo as represented in the novel.

8. Discuss the role women play in village life and their position in the social hierarchy.

9. Take one of the parables—such as the story of the Tortoise and the Birds—or one of the proverbs in the novel and discuss its significance to the novel as a whole. What is the function of parables and proverbs in Ibo culture? What might their importance suggest about Achebe's view of himself as a storyteller?

10. Why does Okonkwo fail? Is his story a tragedy? Compare his character and his defects to those of a classical European figure, such as Hamlet or Creon.

11. Examine the narrative structure of the novel, paying close attention to the tragic elements. In what ways is the novel like a classical tragedy?

Project

Achebe has written numerous articles describing the social value and function of literature; some of these are collected in *Morning Yet on Creation Day* (1975) and *Hopes and Impediments* (1988). Read some of his criticism and consider how *Things Fall Apart* exemplifies Achebe's ideas about language and literature as agents for social change and producing cultural value.

WILLIAM BUTLER YEATS
Selected Poems

Influenced by English romantic poets William Blake and Percy Bysshe Shelley as well as the French symbolists, William Butler Yeats produced some of the most varied, complex, and powerful poetry of the early modern period. To follow his work from the idyllic romanticism of "The Lake Isle of Innisfree" (1890) to the tightly wrought symbolic web of "Lapis Lazuli" (1938) is to trace the development of modernist poetry, with its eclectic cosmopolitanism, its intellectual rigor, its refinement of the image, and its colloquial diction. A keen manipulator of concrete imagery and symbolism, Yeats worked out an arcane system of complementary symbols based on his wide-ranging studies in religion and philosophy, as well as in poetry. Although he was unable to accept Christianity, Yeats was a deeply spiritual man who drew—both for his art and his philosophy—on his native Irish folklore, as well as on the great traditions of the West, India, China, and Japan. Under the tutelage of Madam Blavatsky, the leading proponent of Theosophy in Britain, Yeats cultivated his spiritual sensibility, eventually developing the religiosymbolic system of *A Vision*, which informs much of his later poetry. Moreover, Yeats's work did not ignore the political turbulence of Ireland or of early modern Europe, even as he sought to define the self in one of the finely wrought masks he chiseled out of language. Thus, in Yeats's poetry we see the search for both national and personal identity conducted over a wide range of world literatures and traditions that characterizes for us the modern era.

We have selected poems that reflect the variety and complexity of Yeats's work and that show the changes in his poetic style and technique. Students should have little trouble with the early poems "The Lake Isle of Innisfree," with its refined simplicity, and "Who Goes With Fergus" (1893), with its nostalgia for a heroic age. The first poem, however, may be deceptively simple as it fuses the outer and inner world: the island on the lake and the deep heart's core. Although Yeats was homesick in London when he composed the poem, it does not just portray a simple nostalgia for the return of the past; rather it draws on the past to look forward to a utopian tranquility and a life of quiet meditation. The poem may be usefully compared with Wordsworth's "Tintern Abbey," which also mediates between past and present; the rustic isolation suggested by the poem may be compared to Thoreau's description of his experiment at Walden.

Even with the notes, "Easter 1916" (1916) may require some further explanation of the events and people to which the poem alludes. Because it is a palinode, or retraction, of the earlier meditation on Irish political history "September 1913," you may want to supply that poem for students to read as well. "Easter 1916" is Yeats's response to the Easter Rebellion in Dublin. Despite attempts at self-rule and independence throughout the nineteenth century, Ireland had remained basically a colony of England. On April 24, 1916, the military wing of the Irish Republican Brotherhood proclaimed an independent Irish Republic and occupied the Dublin post office as its headquarters. A standoff lasting five days ensued, after which fifteen of the rebellion's leaders were arrested and eventually executed. Yeats saw this action as a tragedy, commenting that, "At that moment I feel that all the work of years has been overturned, all the bringing together of classes, all the freeing of Irish literature and criticism from politics." Nonetheless, "Easter 1916" expresses Yeats's firm but troubled solidarity with the Irish Republican leaders, including Patrick Pearse, Thomas McDonough, and John MacBride; at the same time, it questions the hardening effects that prolonged, single-minded commitment to a political cause may have on its practitioners. With characteristic irony, Yeats's poem thus pays tribute to the Republican leaders even as it cautions against the cruel cost of their singularity of purpose. "Easter 1916" concludes by asking questions about the value of the Easter Rebellion and the price its leaders had to pay, admitting only that all things "Are changed, changed utterly: / A terrible beauty is born."

"The Second Coming" (1920) and "Leda and the Swan" (1924) give students an opportunity to examine Yeats's somewhat arcane theory of history. Each poem announces the birth of a new era, the post-Christian and pre-Christian, respectively. Both poems draw on Yeats's cyclical theory of history, which is explained briefly in the headnote. "Leda and the Swan" may be read in part as the invasion of the finite by the infinite, and the scene of contact between the swan and Leda is often compared with the visitation of the Holy Ghost upon Mary. Students who wish to pursue Yeats's theory of history beyond the outline sketched in the headnote can be directed to *A Vision*. You may also want to compare Yeats's view of the modern era in "The Second Coming" with T. S. Eliot's, Anna Akhmatova's, and Chinua Achebe's. The prophetic vision of Yeats's poem continues to amaze readers.

"Sailing to Byzantium" (1927), "Among School Children" (1927), "Lapis Lazuli" (1938), and "The Circus Animals' Desertion" (1939) represent Yeats's middle to late period, and all of them deal in some way with the relationship between art and history, mortality and immortality, the materiality of the body and works of art, and the contrast between youth and age. Students may find them tough to understand at first, but the clarity of Yeats's imagery and the subtle rhythms of these works help students overcome initial resistance to the complexities and contradictions that the poems embody. As with symbolist poetry, students may want to analyze their own responses to the poems as much as, or at least as a complement to, their attempt to interpret these works.

1. Compare Yeats's "The Lake Isle of Innisfree" with Wordsworth's "Tintern Abbey." What perspective do Wordsworth and Yeats take on the past? What are the romantic aspects of this poem?

2. Examine Yeats's view of history as it develops from the early to the later poetry. (For a project, you might read the pertinent chapters of *A Vision* and see how the poems begin to incorporate Yeats's theory of history.)

3. Discuss Yeats's perspective on the Easter Rebellion and its leaders as he expresses it in "Easter 1916." Does he idealize these people or treat them realistically? Is he detached from or engaged with their plight?

4. Note the repetition of the phrase "a terrible beauty is born" in "Easter 1916." What does it suggest to you? Compare this phrase in "Easter 1916" to the action of "The Second Coming." How are the poems linked?

5. Compare Yeats's attitude toward the Irish in "Easter 1916" (and in "September 1913") with Joyce's in "The Dead." Why might Yeats and Joyce distance themselves from and be so critical of the Irish middle classes?

6. Discuss the relation of "The Second Coming" to the events that take place in Chinua Achebe's *Things Fall Apart*, which draws its title from Yeats's poem. What other lines or statements from the poem may apply to Achebe's novel?

7. Discuss Yeats's attitudes toward and his depiction of Byzantium in "Sailing to Byzantium." What view of art does Yeats present in this poem? Compare this poem to Keats's "Ode on a Grecian Urn."

8. How do you respond to Yeats's depiction of rape in "Leda and the Swan"? Why does he choose such a violent metaphor to represent what he saw as the beginning of the classical period? What is Yeats's attitude toward the classical period? How is that period like the one announced in "The Second Coming"? Discuss the affinities between this poem, "The Second Coming," and T. S. Eliot's *The Waste Land* as they create a version of history.

9. How would you describe Yeats's views of old age, youth, memory, and the connection between birth and death in "Among School Children"?

10. Discuss the way Yeats treats the themes of war and acting in "Lapis Lazuli." How are they connected? What do the Chinese represent? What is their relation to the scenes described in the first three stanzas of the poem? Are you at all disturbed by his views in this poem?

11. Discuss "The Circus Animals' Desertion" as a retrospective of Yeats's career and a meditation on different kinds of poetry. How does the poem keep from being self-absorbed or sentimental?

RAINER MARIA RILKE
Selected Poems

Rilke will appeal to some students more than others. If he can be compared with anyone, it should be with other modernist authors who construct a world out of their deepest emotional concerns: Yeats, Joyce, Eliot, Kafka, Lorca, Borges. One approach to Rilke or any of the other writers mentioned that seems to serve well (perhaps due to their self-absorption, which may at times border on hermeticism) is to locate a common thread that will help to guide the reader through the work. In Rilke's case, one may find such candidates for common threads as his autoeroticism, his objective view of nature, his search for a resolution of the passions of love and grief, his search for personal autonomy, and so on. These threads may actually move from one into another, creating not a single activity but a complex design. Seeing the intentionality of this poetic work may help the student to better understand the nature of the modernist project as a whole.

The three early poems we offer, "Autumn Day" from *The Book of Pictures* (1902) and "The Panther" and "Archaic Torso of Apollo" from *New Poems* (1907, 1908), have often been translated; the apparent opacity of Rilke's language is deceptive, as anyone trying to render these poems will find. Ideally they should be read aloud in German as a way of opening up discussion. For literal translations of and brief commentaries on "Autumn Day" and "Archaic Torso of Apollo," see Stanley Burnshaw's *The Poem Itself* (1960), pp. 140, 146.

In "Autumn Day," Rilke captures the season and the mood it brings. The poem begins with a conventional sentiment but an extraordinary appeal to the senses. The picture of the solitary figure in the last five lines of the poem directs us away from self-absorption in personal loss and toward an understanding of the irrevocability of nature's processes. For comparison and contrast, see Shakespeare's Sonnet 73, "That time of year thou mayst in me behold," and Keats's "Ode to Autumn."

"The Panther," written in 1903, is taken from a statue in the Jardin des Plantes in Paris. It reflects Rilke's new friendship with Rodin and, as many have said, suggests a new way of seeing: Rilke stands both inside and outside the animal. Another feature of the poem is its double rendition of nothingness. There is nothing beyond the bars of the cage, seen from the panther's perspective; at the end, there is nothing in the panther's heart, where the "image"—perhaps something he remembers from the time before captivity—has gone. Except for the two lines about pacing, "The Panther" is unusually bereft of physical imagery.

This is not the case with "Archaic Torso of Apollo," perhaps Rilke's most famous short poem. Here the sensuousness of the broken statue is fully realized, from the torso to the loins; an uncanny light emanates from inside it as the poet charges the viewer with the necessity to change his or her life. Thus aestheticism passes into the realm of pure sensuality, and sensuality into command. At the same time, the restless movement of the poetry is sexual and alive. (Apollo is the god of light; the appearance of light from inside the statue is a classical figure from which Rilke borrows naturally and fruitfully.)

The First Elegy of the *Duino Elegies* is another frequently translated but notoriously difficult work. A simple way to get into the reading is to notice the highly emotional and even sexual nature of his invocation of the angels.

> Who, if I cried out, would hear me among the angels'
> hierarchies? and even if one of them pressed me
> suddenly against his heart: I would be consumed
> in that overwhelming existence. For beauty is nothing
> but the beginning of terror, which we still are just able to endure,
> and we are so awed because it serenly disdains
> to annihilate us. Every angel is terrifying.
>   And so I hold myself back and swallow the call-note
> of my dark sobbing.

Having posed the problem of the angels, Rilke notes that there are objects in the world more likely to give one comfort: trees, yesterday's street, the loyalty of a habit, or the night wind. From here he moves to the problem of grief, notably in the case of the youthful or the unrequited dead, concluding that we need them more than they need us. The total effect of the poem is the disharmony it creates; the violence of unrequited passions such as love and grief constitutes a problem to be solved. Again, ideally the poem should be read aloud, preferably in German, as students progress through its music in order to find the nuances of meaning Rilke proposes.

In the poems selected here from *Sonnets to Orpheus*, Orpheus, who has descended into the underworld, replaces the angels. Where the angels represented unrequited longing and grieving, Orpheus stands for the acknowledgment of death and the recognition of things as they are. "For it *is* Orpheus," Rilke tells us: He is the singer of the real. Passing from the one symbol to the other, Rilke finds peace and harmony again. Thus the tree returns (Sonnet 1); a figure, "almost a girl," sleeps in his ear (Sonnet 2); the wind replaces a song of love, which is only temporary passion (Sonnet 3); Orpheus is praised, who "comes and goes" (Sonnet 5); his song is a song of praise (Sonnet 7); and even Lament finds her proper place in "the realm of Praising" (Sonnet 8). The rapid appearance of these poems (all in a week) suggests their importance to Rilke; apparently they solved the greatest problem of his life, which was understanding the nature of his unrequited feelings.

It is possible to explore the evolution of Rilke's principal emotional concerns from the poems themselves. Depending on how much one wishes to go into autobiographical material, one could also read selections from Rilke's *Letters to a Young Poet*, written to a student at a military academy between 1903 and 1908, or his semiautobiographical novel *The Notebooks of Malte Laurids Brigge* (1910). Both of these works, which are relatively early, concern themselves with the role of the artist in society and call for rejection of worldly pursuits.

Questions for Discussion and Writing

1. Why does the contemplation of Autumn in "Autumn Day" suggest to Rilke that deeds left undone can no longer be accomplished? What is the tone or mood of this conclusion?

2. Describe the point of view of "The Panther." When are we inside the panther's head and when are we not? How does the use of perspective in this poem help Rilke convey a message?

3. What is so sensuous about "Archaic Torso of Apollo"? How does the appearance of light from inside the torso affect the feeling of the poem?

4. From your reading of the above three poems, comment on Rilke's views on one of the following: the passage of time, the world of the animal kingdom, or the uses of art.

5. What is Rilke's view of the angels in the first of the *Duino Elegies*? Where does he look to for solace, if not to them?

6. What is so painful about the condition of the youthful dead or the unrequited dead? How does Rilke attempt to resolve this issue?

7. How is the form of the First Elegy of the *Duino Elegies* different from that of the earlier poetry? What does Rilke gain by the use of longer, more discursive poetry? Is it still "poetic"? Why or why not?

8. What is the effect of Orpheus in our selections from *Sonnets to Orpheus*?

9. In *Sonnets to Orpheus*, what do you make of the line "Oh tall tree in the ear" (Sonnet 1)? Why is the figure in the next poem "*almost* a girl" and why does she "sleep the world" (Sonnet 2)? What does Rilke mean by asking how a man can "penetrate through the lyre's strings" (Sonnet 3)? What kind of mental process is he describing in all three cases?

10. Trace the development of the subject of praise in *Sonnets to Orpheus* (I: 5, 7, 9). Why must Rilke give praise in order to reconcile his grief? Consider your experiences of loss to see whether you agree with his view.

11. Discuss the form of *Sonnets to Orpheus* and determine what it contributes to the content of the work. How does it differ from the form of the *Duino Elegies*?

1. Try your hand at translating a short early poem of Rilke's, using a good German dictionary and the existing translation. Where do difficulties arise? How do you think they should be handled?
2. Compare Rilke to one or more of the other poets in the anthology, including Catullus, the medieval Latin lyricists, the Provençal poets, Li Po, Basho, Wordsworth, Keats, Whitman, or Yeats, on the themes of nature, love, and loss. What is distinctive about his work compared to theirs?

LU XUN
The New Year's Sacrifice

The first problem we have in encountering Lu Xun is that of reading any writer from a radically different background: The conventions of language, social expectations, even "human nature" may take unanticipated twists and turns. Beyond this, Lu Xun expresses the tensions of a political culture markedly distinct from our own. Neo-Confucianism, social democracy, and Chinese populism contend in the world Lu Xun inhabits and portrays. Finally, the author, a member of the Chinese middle class educated in Japan, was influenced by Russian culture, including both the creative works of Gogol, Chekhov, and Gorky and the political writings of Lenin. His "critical realism"—an approach to culture both theoretical and practical in character—is reminiscent of the work of Maxim Gorky, a leading cultural figure of the Russian Revolution. (Unlike Gorky, Lu Xun never joined his nation's Communist Party, although he sympathized with its program and often shared its politics. He was simply a writer of internationalist tendencies dedicated to serving the Chinese intelligentsia who were his comrades and friends.)

Lu Xun's writings are highly politicized. The complicated triad of society cited in the headnote is often present in his pieces: the old order, sick and self-destructive; the flawed individual, lacking in personal resources; and the new political culture, still politically undeveloped. As in a medieval morality play, the issue in a story by Lu Xun is often redemption—social and personal if not spiritual—and the outcome is in doubt until the end. This redemption, like its Christian counterpart, rests on individual choice, or at least on the appearance of choice (in a socialist drama, class consciousness stands in for the Christian state of grace). There are real winners and losers, real issues to be decided. There is no room for clever equivocation or false bravado: Hypocrisy is exposed and the truth is triumphant.

In "The New Year's Sacrifice," an ancient ritual plays itself out in a town ruled by social convention. The narrator returns home for the New Year's celebration and encounters a widow, a former servant in his house. Because the narrator is a scholar, she asks him three questions: Do dead people turn into ghosts or not, is there a hell, and will all the members of a family meet after death? The returning visitor confesses his ignorance regarding these questions and leaves the widow in haste. Later, he ironically comments that his answer to her questions, "I'm not sure," was a "most useful phrase."

The next day, the widow's suicide is reported. On one level, the narrator dismisses her death as "the end of a futile existence," while at the same time, driven by a partially acknowledged sense of guilt, he reconstructs her life story. She was kidnapped by her first husband's mother after his death and forced by her in-laws to remarry. Within the year she had a baby, but then fresh tragedy struck: Her second husband was killed by typhoid fever and her child was carried off by a wolf and eaten. Failing as a servant after these terrible events had robbed her of her physical and mental health, she was dismissed and began to drift, ending up poor and half-crazy on the street. After attempting to buy atonement for her sins (the modern substitute for submitting herself to ritual sacrifice by being trampled under the feet of the villagers), she dies at the time of the New Year, when sacrifices of animals are still performed. The narrator explicitly connects her death with the season of sacrifice and predicts, bitterly, renewed good fortune for his village.

The weaknesses and even the evil of all parties are disclosed. The narrator is a hypocrite, pretending to knowledge but unable to help a poor woman truly in distress when she calls on him. The woman is deficient in the will to live after her ordeal; at the same time, she is chained by ignorance to old superstitions. The townspeople persecute her with their spiteful remarks, and indeed *would* trample her, according to the old custom, if they could. There is no enlightened new order to rescue her from the town's judgment or her own weakness, and finally, confessing defeat, she dies by her own hand.

The story poses the question of responsibility, not only in the narrow sense (is the narrator responsible for the woman's death?) but in a broader one (to what degree are we all complicit in social evil, due to our ignorance and lack of concern for others?). Typically, Lu Xun leads the reader to a place where he or she must decide. It would seem that a truly meaningful existence requires an understanding of what must be done, followed by resolute action. But what is required in this case? How can we work together to build a just society, changing the peoples' hearts in the face of such overwhelming ignorance and bad conduct? And how do we begin? Such questions lie just below the surface of Lu Xun's understated but ethically insistent writings.

Questions for Discussion and Writing

1. Explain in detail the theme of sacrifice in the story "The New Year's Sacrifice." How does Lu Xun weave old folk beliefs and rituals into his story?

2. How does the narrator embody both the hope for the world and the weakness of purpose Lu Xun associates with the new order of society?

3. Compare the fate of the old woman in this story with that of one of the other unfortunates in our story selections: Gregor Samsa in Kafka's *The Metamorphosis*, the Arab in Camus' "The Guest," or the prisoner in Fuentes's "The Prisoner of Las Lomas." Why does Lu Xun make so little effort to develop sympathy for the old woman?

4. Compare the ambivalent narrator in this story with Conrad's Marlow in *Heart of Darkness* or Coleridge's ancient mariner. Does the narrator learn something about the secrets of his own heart? Does Lu Xun want him to or expect him to change?

5. In what sense, and with what success, is Lu Xun a moralist?

JAMES JOYCE
The Dead

Joyce's "The Dead" shares with Yeats's poems concerns about specifically Irish national identity; it shares with a number of other twentieth-century texts in this volume an exploration of what may happen if one puts aside one's nationality or ethnicity for an assimilationist's uneasy repression and compromise. Gabriel, the intellectual, has abandoned a good many important things for a sterile elitism. To one degree or another, Eliot's *The*

Waste Land, Ellison's "Flying Home," Wiesel's "Testament of a Jew from Saragossa," Rifaat's "My World of the Unknown," Momaday's "The Way to Rainy Mountain," and Desai's "The Farewell Party" all explore the significance of roots and the loss or devaluation of them.

"The Dead" is a story most students will find accessible if given some help with the colloquialisms and the wealth of references to Irish history and Dublin places and personalities. But some will need a teacher's help to learn to see for themselves the complex beauty of the story, with its repeated motifs and delicate network of allusions. Music is a critical theme of the story, and it may help to suggest that they "listen" to the words as they would to music. You can also begin by asking students to read with the title always in mind—who are the dead? Are they all safely buried in their coffins? To what sorts of people, things, and situations do people metaphorically apply the word *dead*? Conversely, who or what seems most alive in this story? To get them started, you might want to do a close reading with your class of the first scene, noting such phrases as "three mortal hours" and "perished alive," pointing out how mired the elderly Morkan sisters are in their fussy routine, how Gabriel resembles a "snow-stiffened frieze" when he enters, and how Gabriel himself in the exchange with Lily puts a damper on her lively and honest response to his conventional banter.

It's good, too, to call attention to the broad movement of the story. We move from the crowded and largely public opening scenes to the comparative intimacy of the last farewells, then to the scene *à deux* with Gretta and Gabriel, leading to Gabriel's utter isolation as he finally realizes his own shortcomings and his mortality; then comes the final breathtaking expansion of narrative in the last paragraphs to include Ireland, the globe, and the universe as similarly fragile and mortal.

The John Huston film *The Dead* is a fine supplement to the story.

Questions for Discussion and Writing

1. In this story, who are the dead of the title? What images of and allusions to death, both literal and metaphorical, occur in the story? Who or what in the story seems most vividly alive?

2. How does the narrator's tone change in the course of the story? How does the point of view affect our understanding of and sympathy for Gabriel?

3. Gabriel is brought up short by the unexpected responses of Lily, Molly Ivors, and Gretta. What does each instance tell us about Gabriel and his values?

4. Describe the world of Julia, Kate, and Mary Jane Morkan. How does Gabriel position himself in relation to that world? How is he very much, despite himself, implicated in it?

5. Most of the characters in "The Dead" are musicians or music lovers. What roles does music play in the story? What is the significance of particular pieces of music, such as *Arrayed for the Bridal*? How does the story work like a piece of music?

6. Of what significance are the west of Ireland and the Continent in "The Dead"?

7. Is Gabriel's after-dinner speech sincere? What does it tell us about him?

8. How would you characterize the relationship between Gretta and Gabriel? Does he love her for who she is, or who he thinks she is? Does it resemble in any way the marriage depicted in Gilman's "The Yellow Wallpaper" or the relationship between the couple in Kundera's "The Hitchhiking Game"?

9. On the way back to the hotel, why does Gabriel recall the incident of standing with Gretta and watching the glassblower?

10. What is the importance of Michael Furey in Gretta's—and in Gabriel's—life?

11. What is your final judgment of Gabriel? Does he change? Do you think the events of the night will alter his life?

12. Joyce uses the term *epiphany* to describe a moment of revelation in a story, an uncalculated and unbidden moment when the character, as well as the reader, recognizes something about himself or herself that has previously been hidden or repressed. What is the moment of epiphany in this story, and what does it reveal?

Projects

1. Read *Dubliners*, the collection "The Dead" comes from, and explore the ways it integrates the themes of the other fourteen stories.
2. Compare Joyce's treatment of the Irish middle class with Yeats's. "September, 1913," not included in the anthology, is especially apt.

VIRGINIA WOOLF
A Room of One's Own

Woolf's voice joins many others in this volume—Marie Le Jars de Gournay, Mary Astell, Mary Wollstonecraft, and Charlotte Perkins Gilman, most directly—in posing the question of women's scant opportunities in a patriarchal society. Woolf focuses especially on women artists, but much of what she says here applies to women who hope to achieve in any field.

Woolf's short answer in *A Room of One's Own* to what women require if they are to become artists is twofold: a room with a door that can be shut and a modest but sufficient income. Clearly, as this chapter of the book suggests, women need more. Musing on the watery lunch served her at a women's college and contrasting it to the hearty gourmet fare at a men's college of the same university, she asks, "Now, what food do we feed women as artists upon"? Among other things, she contends, women are forced to go intellectually undernourished.

This excerpt from *A Room of One's Own* proposes an irresistible guessing game: What would have happened during the late sixteenth century to a hypothetical sister of Shakespeare, a woman as gifted as he? One might ask students to look at the Renaissance section of this anthology for women who had careers as artists, and see what factors enabled them to succeed, and whether their lives were marked by special circumstances—high birth, like Marguerite de Navarre, or the patronage of the nobility, like Sor Juana Ines de la Cruz.

One way to approach the selection is to question it. There are certainly strong elitist assumptions here, such as the idea that it is almost as rare to find working-class writers as it is to find women writers.

After reading Woolf's imaginative construction of the life of Judith Shakespeare, one might invite the class to imagine gifted sisters of other great men in other centuries or other fields and to write brief biographies for them. One of the projects below asks students to research the lives of the gifted sisters of famous men.

Questions for Discussion and Writing

1. Explain Woolf's remark about woman: "Imaginatively, she is of the highest importance; practically she is completely insignificant." What is the distinction Woolf makes between women in real life and women in literature? Do you think this is true for women at the time Woolf wrote? Do you think it still holds true and, if so, to what degree?

2. What women authors have you read in the course for which you are using this anthology? What texts have you read by men that highlight women characters? Does it seem true to you, as it did to Woolf, that women are written about a good deal, but do comparatively little writing? Do you think that there are enough women writers in the syllabus for the course you are taking?

3. Can you devise another story for Judith—that is, can you think of ways in which, given the circumstances of her birth, she might have managed to survive as an artist in Elizabethan England?

4. Would Woolf find the education proposed by Mary Astell in "A Serious Proposal to the Ladies" adequate nourishment for a budding writer?

5. *A Room of One's Own*, written in 1928, has enjoyed a great resurgence of popularity in the last twenty years or so. Why do you think that is so?

6. This essay is often cited as a classic example of modernist style. Read a few samples of nonfiction prose from the previous two centuries, such as Mary Wollstonecraft's *A Vindication of the Rights of Woman* or Marx's "The Class Struggle" and compare their style with Woolf's. How does Woolf use modernist techniques such as stream-of-consciousness and resonant imagery to advance her argument?

Projects

1. Woolf invents a sister for Shakespeare, but of course there have actually been gifted sisters of famous brothers. Research the life of Dorothy Wordsworth (1771–1855), sister of poet William Wordsworth, or the life of Caroline Herschel (1750–1848), sister of astronomer William Herschel (1738–1822), discoverer of Uranus. Adrienne Rich's fine poem "Planetarium" (1971) is about Caroline Herschel.

2. Read *Orlando*, Virginia Woolf's fantasy about an author who lives from Elizabethan times down to the present, changing sex from male to female in the process. What different experience of life does Orlando have as a man and then as a woman? Does Orlando's basic personality alter with the change of genders?

FRANZ KAFKA
The Metamorphosis

Franz Kafka wrote, "The books we need are the kind that act upon us like a nightmare, that make us suffer like the death of someone we love more than ourselves . . . a book should serve as the ax for the frozen sea within us." *The Metamorphosis* fits Kafka's own guidelines. Despite Gregor Samsa's failings, he in no way deserves what happens to him one morning; the transformation itself signifies a radical disjunction between the forces that control our lives and our capacities to handle the consequences of fate with humanity, understanding, and compassion. In Kafka's world, there is no kindly Father-God overseeing the perambulations of his earthly children; instead, there are the anonymous forces of physics and the denatured machinery of corporations shaping peoples' lives in what often appear to be arbitrary happenings.

One way to begin *The Metamorphosis* is to examine in some detail the first paragraph, paying attention to point of view, tone, and diction. As indicated in the headnote, Kafka probably intends us to take Gregor's transformation literally—at least initially. Incredibly awful, traumatic events can break into our lives and transform them. The next step might involve a discussion of those aspects of Gregor's job and family life that could metaphorically turn him into an insect. The story itself hinges on the reactions of other people to Gregor's plight; how do his family's attitudes evolve over the story? In a series of mini-crises, Kafka uses images such as the apple stuck in Gregor's back to highlight the two patterns of change: Gregor's gradual demise and his family's ironic rebirth.

Questions for Discussion and Writing

1. Discuss the social and psychological reasons for Gregor's metamorphosis into an insect.
2. How do the attitudes of Gregor's family change toward him through the progress of the story? How does Gregor's sister treat him initially? What changes in her attitude? Does the family undergo a kind of metamorphosis during the story?
3. Discuss the way others react to Gregor's transformation. Are these reactions similar to those that people with disabilities experience in our society?
4. What evidence in the story suggests that Gregor's dehumanization took place long before his physical transformation? What is the significance, for example, of the picture of the woman with the muff?
5. The apple-throwing scene borders on grotesque. Why does the father throw apples at Gregor? Does the scene make us more sympathetic to Gregor's plight?
6. What roles are played by the three lodgers, the chief clerk, and the charwoman?
7. Does Gregor arrive at some understanding of his situation before he dies?
8. Because the prospects of the family gradually improve after Gregor's transformation, was Gregor partially responsible for his family's crippling dependency before his transformation?

Project

Rewrite the first paragraph of *The Metamorphosis* for a 1990s situation. Have your students choose a public figure in a particular socioeconomic situation and write about his or her transformation into a nonhuman being. One could use Ovid's story about the transformation of Acteon into a stag and Homer's story about the transformation of Odysseus' crew into swine to illustrate different ways to handle this story line.

T. S. ELIOT
The Waste Land

One can approach reading *The Waste Land* in at least three ways: from the point of view of the design of the artist, from a close reading of the text, or from the point of view of the work's effect on its audience. One might try these approaches in sequence. The intentions of the artist matter greatly in this poem; for instance, a perusal of the facsimile edition *The Waste Land* (1971) shows how the collaboration of Eliot and Pound at the final editing stage materially affected the outcome of the poem as a whole. A line-by-line reading of the poem is recommended *after* the student has tried at least once to experience the whole thing without the use of the textual notes. Finally, the student should look at the effect the poem has had on its audience, supported by some backgrounds of criticism over the decades.

For a first reading of the poem, the student should follow the suggestion of its early critic I. A. Richards, viewing the work as a symphony and approaching it without notes, as the poem was originally published. Although following the flow of the poetry will help, the student will encounter difficulties, and a distinction should be made at the beginning between Eliot's obscurity and his difficulty. The first is an artistic flaw (sometimes willful, sometimes not), the second a reflection of the artist's intention that the serious reader trace the meaning of the work to its conclusion.

A close reading of *The Waste Land* is best done as the instructor works through the sections of the actual poem. The notes cover many, but not all, details, as it is our opinion that the student should not pore over every detail. It helps, however, to see some of Eliot's key ideas underlying the work, such as his view of modern sexual degradation or his sense of the decline of Europe after World War I. If the instructor wants to pursue a single theme, such as sexual degradation, then the imagery surrounding that theme can be traced from beginning to end; the rest of the poem can be read around this single thread. The poem is so richly layered that it can bear many excellent partial readings; the matter of the partiality of interpretation should be openly acknowledged and discussed.

The Waste Land thus regarded is a great teaching text. It teaches the emergence of a conservative view of the Western world in decline at the end of World War I; the organization of a major work of modernism, with an overall design embellished by the many pieces of mosaic within it; the problem of interpretation of such a multifaceted work, with the suggestion that the student select a system of references and follow it throughout the work from start to finish; and finally, something about the nature of literary studies, which should emphasize the partial success of any one approach in coming up with an interpretation of a work so vast and difficult.

Obvious references in *The Waste Land* to other works in the anthology include the Bible, Virgil's *Aeneid*, Ovid's *Metamorphoses*, St. Augustine's *Confessions*, Dante's *Divine Comedy*, Shakespeare's *The Tempest*, Milton's *Paradise Lost*, Baudelaire's *Flowers of Evil*, and other symbolist poetry. The frame of Eliot's poem, the quest, is closely related to literature in our medieval section; the study of power and corruption that the poem undertakes ties it to the Renaissance. Although Marlowe's *Doctor Faustus* or Goethe's *Faust* are never mentioned directly, the Faustian search for experience and its relation to the damnation of the soul would not have escaped Eliot, later a High Church Anglican. Finally, Eliot himself would have seen his work as a product of the literary decadence of the post-symbolist period, after Baudelaire. The very form he writes in, consisting of the "fragments" he must shore against his ruins, suggests the decay of things in his view. In the final analysis, Eliot is a moralist, using the "broken images" of the past to call for a moral regeneration in the present.

Despite the richness of the references to other works that Eliot makes available, the undergraduate student cannot be expected to become an expert in Eliot's sources; instead, effort should be concentrated on appreciation of this poem as a literary work in its own right. Ironically, the final test of this most didactic poem of the twentieth century may be its ability to give aesthetic pleasure.

Questions for Discussion and Writing

1. Trace one or more of the following themes or images through *The Waste Land*: the presence or absence of water, sexual lust and its consequences, the vulgarity of modern life, sterility, ancient times versus modern times, the confusion of tongues, the metamorphoses of people into animals, the appearance of corpses, and Tiresias as a quest figure.

2. Who are the narrators of *The Waste Land*? Trace the changes in the narrators and account for them.

3. Similarly, what are the verse forms of *The Waste Land*? Account for the variety of forms.

4. Explain Eliot's use of one significant citation from a foreign language. Why do you think Eliot includes so many quotations in the original language?

5. Whom does Eliot expect to be a reader of his poem? Are his expectations very high? Why do you think he has them?

6. Find several "modern" episodes in the poem and explain the use of vulgarity in these episodes.

7. State Eliot's views on modern love. Find one example of the degradation of love, giving a close reading of the text.

8. Would you say *The Waste Land* is an atheistic, an agnostic, or a religious poem? If it is religious, what religion is it? How do you come to your conclusion?

9. Compare the narrator of *The Waste Land* at any specific point to St. Augustine, Virgil, Dante, Milton, or Baudelaire. How long does this comparison hold, and why does it end?

Project

Eliot mentions the study of myth in his notes, referring to the works of Jessie Weston and Sir James Frazer. Look up these works and explain how their methodology influences Eliot's own working method in the poem.

ANNA AKHMATOVA
Selected Poems

In *Requiem*, Anna Akhmatova describes herself as the "exhausted mouth / Through which a hundred million scream." As discussed in the headnote, her poetry does indeed serve as a haunting witness to the pogroms and terror of post-Revolutionary, Stalinist Russia. We value her poetry, however, not only because it testifies to the tragic sufferings of the Russian people, but because of the precision of its diction, the clarity of its imagery, and the overall musical quality of her verse. Although her poetry deals with personal and national losses, it is characterized not by romantic or sentimental effusion, but by a kind of heroic restraint. One looks in vain through Akhmatova for words of comfort and consolation. Hers is a tough but direct confrontation with the sorrow, grief, and suffering of her era; it is a poetry of engagement and commitment, but one that is as devoted to aesthetic quality as it is to moral vision.

All of the poems in our selection—"Voronezh" (1940), "To the Memory of M. B." (1940), and *Requiem* (1963)—were written after the arrests of her friend Osip Mandelstam in 1934 and her son, Lev Gumilev, and husband, Nikolai Punin, in 1935. As the headnote explains, although her son was released, he was rearrested in 1937, not to be freed until 1956. As Anatoly Naiman writes in his introduction to *The Complete Poems of Anna Akhmatova*, translated by Judith Hemschemeyer, "The sound of the dirge for the dead and the dying had previously been heard in Akhmatova's poetry, but in the 1930s it became dominant." In poetry of remarkable clarity, Akhmatova fuses personal and public feeling and experience, so that the tribute to her immediate friends and family transcends the private sphere to stand for the experience of a nation. "Voronezh" is dedicated to Osip Mandelstam, who was exiled to Voronezh for his open criticism of Stalin. The poem invokes the memory of Peter the Great and the proud defense of the city against the Mongols in order to set up a historical contrast between the great tradition of Russia and the narrow-minded repression of the Stalinist state, protecting its interests by means of terror. Mandelstam here becomes a symbol of all poets, the voice of the people, whose day has been turned into night, and whose voice has been isolated but not silenced. The poem is a good example of Akhmatova's powerful use of concrete imagery and allusion to set up an incisive, thinly veiled critique of the present, of her ability to fuse personal with public tragedy in a poetry of restraint.

"To the Memory of M. B." serves as both a tribute to novelist Mikhail Bulgakov and an affirmation of the poet's responsibility to serve as the memory of her people, to keep alive the people, events, and deeds that the current regime would like to bury in oblivion. The service of memory drives the poems of *Requiem,* which were written between 1935, the year of her son's and husband's arrest, and 1961. Students will be interested to know that Akhmatova destroyed the manuscript copies of several of the poems in *Requiem,* for she feared the censors would discover them and use them to prosecute her. Like many writers in the Soviet Union during (and after) the Stalin era, Akhmatova often conducts her critique indirectly, displacing contemporary issues into the historical past in order to evade possible censorship. Although the immediate subject of *Requiem* is her son's imprisonment, like "Voronezh" the poem testifies to the thousands of other political prisoners and the loved ones who stood outside the prisons awaiting their return. In addition, *Requiem* announces Akhmatova's commitment to stay in Russia and serve as a witness, to be a voice, for her people.

To introduce the personal and national tragedies with which the poems of our selection are involved, one might choose to show the superb documentary on Akhmatova's life available from PBS. Unfortunately, many parallels between Stalin's Soviet Union and more recent incidents of repression abound, so students may be asked to compare Akhmatova's experiences with those in Hitler's Germany, or more recently in Bosnia, Indonesia, Argentina, Guatemala, or South Africa, with which students may be more familiar. It is useful to connect Akhmatova's work and the experiences she describes with W. B. Yeats's "The Second Coming," T. S. Eliot's *The Waste Land,* and Elie Wiesel's *Legends of Our Time.* The role of the storyteller as envisioned by Wiesel and the role of the "sorrow song" as described by W.E.B. Du Bois offer useful parallels to Akhmatova's sense of the poet as a witness, though not necessarily a healer or consoler, of her people.

Questions for Discussion and Writing

1. How does "Voronezh" construct a version of Russia's historical past? How is the past used in the poem as a contrast to the present?

2. Compare "Voronezh" to Pushkin's *The Bronze Horseman.* What do the two poets have in common? Discuss their use of history in their poetry.

3. What is the role of the poet, according to "To the Memory of M. B."? How does this role compare to that described by the romantic or symbolist poets? Some nineteenth-century critics and writers believed the poet should offer consolation or healing to his or her readers. Does Akhmatova share this view? Compare her sense of the poet's role in society with that of the United States or Latin America.

4. Discuss Akhmatova's sense of the purpose of poetry in conjunction with Wiesel's view of the storyteller or W.E.B. Dubois's view of the function of the "sorrow songs."

5. Discuss how the epigraph, prologue, and two epilogues of *Requiem*—which were written later than the other numbered poems—serve as a frame for the rest of the poem.

6. How does Akhmatova's sense of alienation and the alienation of her people in *Requiem* differ from that found in Eliot's *The Waste Land* or Kafka's *The Metamorphosis*?

7. To whom is the poem addressed? How do the narrator's voice and the implied reader change over the course of the poem?

8. How does Akhmatova's poem keep from being sentimental or self-pitying? In what way do the private events of the poem become public? In what way does the narrator show some restraint and detachment, even from these most personally distressing events?

9. Some critics would argue that poetry should not be political; that it should transcend history and the concerns of the material world. Discuss the relation of the political and historical in Akhmatova's poetry. Does her commitment make her less or more powerful as a poet?

Project

What other poets in the modern world, what other scenes of repression in the modern world, compare to Akhmatova's? Can you think of another poet who acts as a witness to the sorrows and sufferings that others must endure?

FEDERICO GARCÍA LORCA
Selected Poems

Federico García Lorca is comparable to earlier writers in the Spanish tradition, including San Juan de la Cruz, Teresa de Avila, Sor Juana, and Tirso de Molina, in his fusion of images of sexuality, death, and corruption with an inescapably baroque flavor. At the same time, his openness to New World influences, especially transplanted African slave culture, and to the Moors and Gypsies of Spain bespeaks his artistic desire to broaden his repertoire. He is comparable to his contemporaries, Spanish artist Pablo Picasso and Chilean poet Pablo Neruda, as well as other modernists, in the way he fractures contemporary reality, reshaping the pieces again in a design of his own making. His work thus looks in two directions: backward to the darker times of blood-drenched Spain, and forward to a future world culture.

The two pieces from *Poet in New York* appear to be passionate and even reckless, yet both are highly intentional poems that demand close attention. In "The King of Harlem," the identity of the title figure is obscure. He is a cruel and inscrutable local deity, African in origin, victim and victimizer alike, sometimes dressed as a janitor. He confirms the condition of Harlem's *Negroes* (the appropriate term in Lorca's time) while driving them to the madness of revenge against the encircling white society. The poem—half despair, half prophecy—is apocalyptic in character. The reference to the "small Jewesses that tremble full of bubbles" should be acknowledged to be anti-Semitic.

The second piece from *Poet in New York*, "Ode to Walt Whitman," pictures the wheels of industry—in the great factories along the East River—over the half-naked boys who work in them. The poet asks Walt Whitman whether modern-day industrial America sustains his vision of our national potential. Furthermore, he asks Whitman, a lover of young men, whether the degradation of the American homosexual community (seen as the seat of corruption, sadistic abuse, and thievery) answers his dream of pure manly love. He concludes that life is "not noble, nor good, nor sacred." The poem offers a defense of innocence, including youthful homosexual attraction, against the "pansies of the world, murderers of doves." Again, early in the poem an anti-Semitic note is struck that must be recognized. This is not an easy poem to teach or read, but it remains a passionate yet problematic diatribe against the exploitation of the innocent.

The *Lament for Ignacio Sanchez Mejías* is constructed like a symphony. The first section employs deep rhythmic repetitions to proclaim the death of the bullfighter. The second section is the outburst of the poet in response to this tragedy, focusing on the blood of Ignacio on the sandy bullring. The third section is a meditation on the body presented for viewing; it is also the beginning of the eulogy proper. The fourth section continues the eulogy, raising it at the end to a hymn of praise. It is important for the student to hear the original verses, perhaps on spoken record, capturing a sense of the grandeur of the entire poem before descending into the footnotes to dissect each symbol and poetic allusion.

Students may resist Lorca due to his controversial politics, his obscurity, or his difficulty; as with Eliot, the obscurity is one thing, the difficulty another. Like Eliot or Rilke, Lorca is a modernist poet who created work that must be appreciated for its largeness of intention before parts of it are discarded or condemned. He also loved the common people and showed a passion for justice in the midst of a cruel society, eventually paying for his concern with his life.

Lorca's earlier pieces are collected in *The Selected Poems of Federico García Lorca*, edited by his brother Francisco and Donald Allen (1955); one should especially consult poems from *Poema del Cante Jondo (Deep Song, 1921)* and *Romancero Gitano (Gypsy Ballads, 1924–27)*. The first mentioned work is also available in a complete version translated by Carlos Bauer as *Poem of the Deep Song* (1987). Lorca's prose, edited and translated by Christopher Maurer, is collected as *Deep Song and Other Prose* (1975). Along with the standard biography listed in the headnotes, there is a more personal reflection by Francisco García Lorca, translated by Christopher Maurer, *In the Green Morning: Memories of Federico* (1986). Recordings of Lorca's poetry are available, in particular a stirring Spanish rendition of "Lament for Ignacio Sanchez Mejías" and other works performed by actress Germaine Montero.

Questions for Discussion and Writing

1. In "The King of Harlem," how does Lorca regard the subjects of his poem? Is he an outside observer, a supporter of their struggle, or a participant in it? How can you tell?
2. Discuss some of the leading metaphors and symbols in "The King of Harlem" and show their effect in the poem.
3. Discuss the treatment of male love in "Ode to Walt Whitman." What is Lorca, a homosexual, trying to say about the practice of homosexuality in New York? Why does he address his remarks to Walt Whitman?
4. Compare Whitman's working men and *Negroes* in *Song of Myself* with Lorca's in *Poet in New York*. Does Lorca romanticize his subjects as Whitman does? Use examples to prove your point.
5. Lorca spoke little or no English, yet his *Poet in New York* is one of his most passionate works. Why do you think he wrote about America with such urgency? Whom does he address? What does he try to accomplish?
6. Compare Lorca's fusion of images of love, death, and decay in *Poet in New York* with the mystical poetry of San Juan de la Cruz and Teresa de Avila. How does he remind us of the Spanish baroque quality of these writers?
7. In *Lament for Ignacio Sanchez Mejías*, Lorca celebrates not only the life and death of a hero, but also the passing of a tradition. How is this poem an elegy for Spanish culture?
8. Trace some of the imagery of *Lament for Ignacio Sanchez Mejías* through the poem, showing how it contributes to the work as a whole.
9. Compare *Lament for Ignacio Sanchez Mejías* with *The Waste Land* by T. S. Eliot, noting the orchestration of the parts of each poem and the overall statement each work makes about the situation of contemporary Western culture and society.

A student with a background in art history might trace the elements of Lorca's poetry in the works of the Spanish painters El Greco, Goya, Picasso, and Dali, from the baroque to the modernist period.

JORGE LUIS BORGES
The Garden of Forking Paths

Due to his enormous erudition, Jorge Luis Borges has few real imitators, although he has had tremendous influence on postmodernist literature. Whereas some twentieth-century intellectuals in Argentina sought to define Argentina's literary heritage in narrow parochial terms, Borges argues in "The Argentine Writer and Tradition" that "our tradition is all of Western culture . . . our patrimony is the universe." He refuses to be trapped by national boundaries; the riches of world literature are the well that fills Borges's pen.

Borges is preoccupied with the shifting planes of human consciousness: mind, thought, perception, consciousness, vision, fantasy, reverie, premonition, intuition, imagination— these are his literary fields, not the three-dimensional reality of shopping malls, banks, insurance policies, and diets. Borges's favorite metaphors are the *word* itself, the *book* that frames the word, and the *library* that houses the book, which in its inimitable way is connected to all the other books, as if all were voices in some kind of universal chorus. The related metaphor used in "The Garden of Forking Paths" for the intertwining mirrors of consciousness is the labyrinth.

The initial task for students studying "The Garden of Forking Paths" is sorting: Ostensibly the story is about spies in World War I, the passing of vital information about Allied plans for bombing Germany, and why that bombing was delayed by five days. It is important to study the initial voices of the first three paragraphs. An initial writer's voice refers to Liddell's *History of World War I*, which forms a kind of historical base for the subsequent events. The writer then refers to a fragmentary document by Yu Tsun. An editor's voice interjects information about Viktor Runeberg's alias.

The plot quickly becomes complicated, but the effect is one of layering or clustering: Each person, each event in this story line is also connected to other stories. Yu Tsun's motivation for helping the Germans is rooted in national pride. Stephen Albert's name is picked out of a phone book, but he turns out to be a Sinologist with the key to a labyrinth created by Yu Tsun's great grandfather, Ts'ui Pên. As readers, we are led to think that Ts'ui Pên's labyrinth was a garden, but it was a book, which provides suggestions for how the many synchronicitous events might be possible. Borges is not simply creating a complex game, but is opening cracks in our conventional and simplistic notions of time and space.

Questions for Discussion and Writing

1. Discuss Borges's use of narrative voices in the story: For example, Liddell Hart's *History of World War I* is an actual book, but the quote used in the story is fiction. Although we might want to treat history books with their names, places, and dates as a basis for reality, they in fact give the illusion of reality because they are, after all, a *selection* of details and theories and are therefore a kind of fiction.

2. Discuss how the image of the labyrinth evolves in the story and is related to the title of the story.
3. What clues does Borges provide at the beginning of his story to create the detective framework for the story?
4. Why does Yu Tsun treat his own death with such fatalism?
5. How are the selections from Ts'ui Pên's book relevant to the story?
6. What is the connection between Ts'ui Pên's murder and Stephen Albert's?
7. Discuss how the theories of time raised by Ts'ui Pên's book are relevant to the plot of the story.
8. Discuss how Borges's concerns with games and the subtleties of consciousness are related to works in this anthology by Kafka, Kawabata, and Kundera.

Projects

1. Investigate the connections between ancient labyrinths and models of consciousness.
2. Students interested in theories of time should read Borges's essay "A New Refutation of Time" and attempt to apply it to the ideas about time in "The Garden of Forking Paths."

YASUNARI KAWABATA
The Moon on the Water

Along with Soseki Natsume (1867–1916) and Junichiro Tanizaki (1888–1965), Yasunari Kawabata is considered one of the greatest writers of *shosetsu,* the novel, in modern Japan. As is evident from "The Moon on the Water," however, Kawabata is also a master of the short story, and critics have variously linked the terse, lyrical quality of his prose with traditional Japanese forms such as the *haiku,* the *renga* (linked verse), and the Nō drama. Kawabata's work invokes classic motifs that go back to *The Tale of Genji,* with its emphasis on the *mono-no-aware,* a refined sense of the delicate balances between life's opposites. Kawabata's feeling for the fragile and temporal lends to his fiction the quality of delicate porcelain. The subtle eroticism and melancholy of "The Moon on the Water" characterize Kawabata's fiction, and its sense of emptiness and sad longing may be contrasted—though with some care—to the *malaise* we find in the French symbolist poets and in some modernist, especially existentialist, fiction.

The poetic qualities of Kawabata's narrative style invite comparison with Virginia Woolf, James Joyce, or Thomas Mann, and his poetic evocation of place may remind us of Flaubert. On the other hand, the austerity of his prose and the fundamental, apparently existential dilemmas his characters face may remind us more of Jean-Paul Sartre and Albert Camus. Gwen Boardman Petersen cautions, however, that Kawabata's sense of "nothingness" is fundamentally Japanese, for his fiction captures that sense of emptiness found in the Nō drama: a meaningful silence or space whose foundations lie in the Buddhism that informs so much of Japanese culture. Petersen also reminds us that we should not impose Western—strictly speaking, Platonic—notions of illusion or deception onto our interpretation of the world reflected in the mirror. As she puts it, "Japanese aesthetics would find the 'reflection of a reflection' that lingered in Kyōko's heart even more beautiful than the shining world." She links Kawabata's story with the intriguing contradictions of Zen Buddhism, and indeed, even for those within Zen training, the story reads as an intricate puzzle of startling reversals and paradoxes.

Those students who have read the selection from *The Tale of Genji* in Volume One or Bashō's *Narrow Road through the Provinces* may see some connections—both in style and in symbolism—between Kawabata's work and that of his predecessors. The moon reflected in the water, for example, is an important symbol in Japanese culture, signifying in part that what we take as an illusion or reflection may be truer, more real, than what we accept as reality in our everyday life. For an excellent introduction to Kawabata's use of traditional imagery in "The Moon on the Water," his invocation of important Japanese cultural symbols and their relation to certain Buddhist texts, consult Chapter 3 of Gwen Boardman Petersen's *The Moon in the Water: Understanding Tanizaki, Kawabata, and Mishima* (1979). Petersen's book is aimed at the Western reader, and would be very helpful as a book on reserve for both the instructor and for students.

Questions for Discussion and Writing

1. What effect has the war had on Kyōko and her first husband?
2. Discuss the mirror as a metaphor in "The Moon on the Water." What does it symbolize? What does it mean to Kyōko? to her first husband? Discuss what it means to conduct one's life vicariously through a reflected image. (A comparison with Tennyson's "The Lady of Shallott" may be instructive here.)
3. Why does the world in the mirror seem more real to Kyōko and her first husband than the world outside?
4. How does the mirror give Kyōko a certain amount of freedom? Is she at all trapped by the world in the mirror?
5. Why does Kyōko begin to feel suddenly guilty of her husband's death? How does she resolve this guilt?
6. The story ends somewhat abruptly, with a moment of recognition. Why is Kyōko calmed at the thought of her baby's face? Who is the "you" she refers to?
7. The entire story is told in the third person. Whose point of view does it reflect? What effect does this point of view have on us as readers? Is she a reliable narrator?
8. Compare and contrast the symbol of the moon as it is used here and in Bashō's *Narrow Road through the Provinces*. Why is this an important symbol in the story? In Japanese culture? Does Western literature or culture have similar notions about the moon? about reflections?
9. Compare "The Moon on the Water" with Joyce's "The Dead" or with Camus' "The Guest." How is it similar and different from both, in terms of literary style and technique and in its thematic concerns? Is Kyōko's meditation at all like Gabriel Conroy's, for example? Discuss Joyce's and Kawabata's respective detachment from their characters and stories.
10. Compare the private world of the house in this story to that in Gilman's "The Yellow Wallpaper" or Alifa Rifaat's "My World of the Unknown."

Project

The moon reflected in the water is a classic motif in Japanese literature and painting; it is found in the poetry of the *Manyōshū*, in *The Tale of Genji*, and various Kabuki and Nō plays. Compare Kawabata's use of this image to its use in an earlier Japanese text. How does the image link the present with the past? How does it change its meaning, if it does, in the modern text?

PABLO NERUDA
Selected Poems

We have included two very different kinds of poems by Pablo Neruda: The two political poems, "Ode of the Sun to the People's Army" and "The United Fruit Co.," are probably the most accessible to students; these poems use metaphors and conventional syntax to refer to historical and political situations outside the poems. Difficulties in reading the poems arise primarily from the historical complexities referred to by the poems. The other three poems—"Ode with a Lament," "Sexual Water," and "Alberto Rojas Jimenez Comes Flying"—treat themes of love, loss, sex, age, and death in a display of image and metaphor reminiscent of French and Spanish surrealism.

"The United Fruit Co." is the most straightforward of the poems here; Neruda names the United States companies that have exploited the working people and natural resources of Latin America. In an extended metaphor, the various dictators, including Rafael Léonidas Trujillo Molina of the Dominican Republic, Tiburcio Carias of Honduras, and Jorge Ubico of Guatemala, are compared to flies. The poem twists emotionally at the end when the Indians—wasted dock workers?—become "a fallen cipher, / a cluster of dead fruit / thrown down on the dump."

"Ode of the Sun to the People's Army" is essentially an inspirational poem passionately prodding the Republican and Communist forces in Spain to resist the Nazi takeover by Franco in the Spanish Civil War (1936–1939). What distinguishes this poem from a nineteenth-century political action poem are the moments when Neruda stretches metaphors further than we would find them in most English romantic or Victorian poets; because of unusual pairings of words, feelings, and objects, a French Symbolist such as Mallarmé would recognize a kindred soul in Neruda. (See the French symbolist section.) Notice the metaphorical development in these lines, in which he urges the army onward:

> Forward among grapevines, treading the cold color of the rocks,
> Salud, salud, press on! Sharper than the voice of winter,
> More sensitive than the eyelid, more certain than the point of thunder,
> Punctual as the swift diamond, new in warfare,
> Warriors like steel gray water of the midlands.

In the first line, "treading" is ordinarily associated with the grapes, but here is crossing the color of rocks; actually more than just "crossing," "treading" connotes the strain of an army crossing, presumably during the winter. With the next series of metaphors, paraphrasing becomes more difficult because the comparisons are more unusual, connected emotionally as well as cognitively. For example, how is an army "punctual as the swift diamond"? Is it like "swift steel," only harder? And what are the associations with "punctual"?

Alberto Rojas Jimenez was a childhood friend of Neruda's and a fellow poet who died by drowning. One more detail completes the frame for this poem; Alberto made paper birds, a hobby learned from Miguel de Unamuno, the famous Spanish philosopher and novelist. The various stanzas draw together images from death, the sea, memories, and Jimenez's spiritual resurrection in the present.

"Sexual Water" is really like one of Neruda's odes where he picks an object or theme and ranges with his imagination through the various permutations of the subject matter; it reads almost like an exercise in free association, except that Neruda shapes the patterns of images in emotional swells that ebb and flow through the poem. "Sexual Water" is a tribute to nature's libido, to the juice of life, to eros and the emotional spectrum of sex: light and dark, pain and pleasure, life and death.

"Ode with a Lament" is the most surreal poem in this selection; that is, the images create a dreamlike landscape, and like images in a dream, they do not fit into a coherent picture or story, but are a collage of emotional sparklers. In the poem, the voice of the poet laments all of his personal baggage associated with past love affairs. There is one unfortunate part of our translation, in our opinion; in the next to the last stanza, Hays translates the original Spanish phrase "llena / de dientes y relámpagos" as "full of fangs and lightings." A better translation is "full of teeth and lightning." The differences between the two versions might initiate a good class discussion.

Questions for Discussion and Writing

1. Why might Neruda refer to the Latin American dictatorships as a "comic opera" in "The United Fruit Co."? Why does Neruda use a mock-creation framework for this satire of dictatorships in this poem?
2. Compare Neruda's political poems with Yeats's "Easter 1916" and Akhmatova's poems.
3. How is "Alberto Rojas Comes Flying" a tribute to his friend? How does Neruda express grief as well as joy in this poem?
4. Compare the third from the last stanza of "Alberto Rojas Comes Flying" with the following version:

> There is the sea. I go down at night and I hear you
> come flying in the depths of the sea, alone,
> the depths of the sea that dwell in me, in darkness:
> you come flying.

5. What are Neruda's attitudes toward sexuality in "Sexual Water" and how does he reveal his attitudes? Why is sexuality compared with water?
6. What qualities of his past is the poet lamenting in "Ode with a Lament"? What does the girl in the poem represent?

Projects

1. The following is André Breton's definition of surrealism:

   Surrealism, noun. Pure psychic automatism, by which it is intended to express, verbally, in writing, or by other means, the real process of thought. Thought's dictation, in absence of all control exercised by the reason and outside all aesthetic or moral preoccupations.
   Encycl. *Philos.* Surrealism rests in the belief in the superior reality of certain forms of association neglected heretofore; in the omnipotence of the dream and in the disinterested play of thought. It tends definitely to do away with all other psychic mechanisms and to substitute itself for them in the solution of the principal problems of life. (from *Manifeste du Surréalisme* of 1924)

   Which parts of Neruda's poems seem to fulfill Breton's definition?
2. Investigate the relationship of politics and art in writers such as Yeats, Neruda, Sartre, Ahkmatova, and Camus. Do poets and novelists play a significant role in influencing public opinion and political programs?
3. The Spanish Civil War aroused a wide range of loyalties in writers in the Americas and Europe. Students might read two classic works as background for discussing the war as a spiritual and political symbol: George Orwell's *Homage to Catalonia* and André Malraux's *Man's Hope.*
4. Write your own odes with laments, expressing the dark waters of your personal histories.

JEAN-PAUL SARTRE
The Flies

The Flies can be read as a product of World War II, a play obliquely commenting on the French situation during the German occupation. It can also be read as a modern version of a classical story and compared with Aeschylus' or Euripedes' treatment of the same story. It can also be read as an ideological work presenting some key ideas of the existentialists. Several of the existential concepts Sartre embodies in the play are included in the following description of the human situation from his essay *Existentialism* (1947):

> Atheistic existentialism, which I represent, . . . states that if God does not exist, there is at least one being in whom existence precedes essence, a being who exists before he can be defined by any concept, and that this being is man, or, as Heidegger says, human reality. What is meant here by saying that existence precedes essence? It means that, first of all, man exists, turns up, appears on the scene, and only afterwards defines himself. If man, as the existentialist conceives him, is indefinable, it is because at first he is nothing. Only afterward will he be something, and he himself will have made what he will be. Thus, there is no human nature, since there is no God to conceive it. Not only is man what he conceives himself to be, but he is only what he wills to be after this thrust toward existence.

Sartre stresses the need for individuals to choose their destiny and to take responsibility for the choices they make. By so defining ourselves, we can turn empty existence into meaningful essence.

As explained in the headnote, many of the characters and situations in *The Flies* can be allegorically linked to people and events of World War II. In the ceremony of remorse, Sartre was specifically portraying a widespread attitude in France at the time that saw the German occupation as a deserved punishment for the French nation. The phenomenon of captives adopting the judgments of their captors has become so common as to earn a name, "the Stockholm syndrome." The best-known instance of such collaboration, perhaps, is in the brainwashing of American POWs during the Korean War. Sartre's assertion that such remorse is prompted by political timidity and religious intimidation can provoke lively discussion.

Even if the teacher does not undertake a point-by-point comparison of Sartre's play with Aeschylus' version of the story, the difference between the endings is especially noteworthy. Sartre's hero refuses to be tormented by the flies and apparently feels no need to go on to Athens to seek legal exoneration for his crime. The third act of Sartre's play carries the burden of presenting the key existential ideas. Orestes begins the play as a man without roots and without definition, chooses his destiny in Act 2, and, in Act 3, by accepting full responsibility for his act and refusing to feel remorse, he triumphs over the flies and becomes the leader who frees Argos from the pestilence.

Many works of literature lend themselves to an existential reading. Besides the stories by Sartre's fellow French existentialist Albert Camus, some other works in this anthology that are open to such interpretation include Voltaire's *Candide*, the story of an ideologist who finally learns to work for a living and for an identity; Dostoevsky's "The Grand Inquisitor," in which Jesus' notion of freedom as something that must be chosen is much like Sartre's view; or Ibsen's *A Doll's House*, in which Nora rebels against the identity that is thrust on her by society and her husband and chooses to direct her own life.

Questions for Discussion and Writing

1. In what ways are the people of Argos implicated in the murder of Agamemnon? Describe the nature of their "good piety of yore." What is the significance of the Day of the Dead?

2. Why is there a "void" within Orestes? What sort of person is he when he arrives in Argos? What kind of education has he received?
3. Characterize the Tutor's philosophy. What has he taught Orestes? Why does he advise Orestes to leave Argos? Compare the relationship between Orestes and his tutor with that between Candide and Pangloss.
4. Is Zeus pleased by the remorseful behavior of the Argives? What does Zeus mean when he says that he and Ægisthus share the bitter realization of "knowing that men are free"? Does Dostoevsky's Grand Inquisitor share this knowledge? What are the implications of this knowledge for rulers? for the ruled? How are kings and gods similar in this play?
5. How do you explain the difference between Orestes' and Electra's reaction to the death of Clytemnestra?
6. What do the flies represent? How are they agents of Zeus? Why do they torment Electra after the murder, but not Orestes? Compare them to the Furies in Aeschylus' *Oresteia*.
7. Define freedom and discuss what it means in the play.
8. What does Orestes mean when he says "human life begins on the far side of despair"? How does the play represent this idea?

Projects

1. Read the second play in Aeschylus' *Oresteia* and compare it with Sartre's version of the same story.
2. Read up on the history of the Vichy government that collaborated with the German occupation of France during World War II. How appropriate was Sartre's choice of the Orestes story as the basis for his allegory about France during the war? What historical figures are represented allegorically in the play?
3. The Day of the Dead is clearly an occasion that serves to restrain the citizens of Argos and to maintain the power of Zeus and Ægisthus. Describe a ceremony or ritual with which you are familiar and discuss how it serves the purposes of powerful institutions and helps them to maintain their power. How, for example, do football games serve the universities that sponsor them?

RASIPURAM KRISHNASWAMI NARAYAN
A Horse and Two Goats

"A Horse and Two Goats," like several other works in the twentieth-century section of this anthology, such as those by Conrad, Achebe, Lessing, and Fuentes, is a tale of cross-cultural misunderstanding. It differs from Doris Lessing's "The Old Chief Mshlanga" in that Narayan chooses the point of view of the native villager; the stereotyped figure in the story is not the native, as in *Heart of Darkness*, but rather the nameless American tourist. Narayan also uses the misunderstandings for comic effect. In some ways the story is an elaborated version of the TV ad that shows two American tourists who want their picture taken, but mistakenly trade their camera for a donkey, much to the delight of the native children who get the camera. Muni's bewildered delight when he manages to trade his old goats for more money than he has ever seen or even imagined is not unlike that of the boys playing with their new camera. Narayan also gets wonderful comedy out of the dual monologues of Muni and the tourist, showing just how far apart their two worlds are. Although the two men are similar in that they have been sent out on their own by their wives and each has dreams that his wife seems not to understand, it is Muni who emerges in the end as a more complex figure, for all his seeming simplicity. We learn of the difficulties in his life, his financial struggles, his decline in economic status, his uncertain age. He seems to be hemmed in by the narrow existence in his remote village, when his meeting with the tourist serendipitously frees him from economic hardship. His wife's suspicion at the end of the story breaks the illusion that the miraculous has changed his life and recalls him to the limits of village existence.

Questions for Discussion and Writing

1. What do we learn about Muni in his dealings with the shopkeeper?
2. What is Muni's place in the village? Why does he walk through the village with his eyes cast down?
3. Compare Muni's perception of the horse to that of the American. How is each man representative of his culture? What similarities are there between the two men?
4. What assumptions does Muni make about the American when he is "talking" with him? What assumptions does the American make about Muni?
5. Had Muni understood that the American wanted to buy the horse, would he have sold it to him? Why or why not?
6. Should the American be expected to return the horse? Should Muni return the money? Should Westerners be expected to return such artifacts as the Elgin Marbles or Native American religious items to their original cultures?

Project

Take an object from another culture, such as an African statue, a Hopi kachina doll, or an Eskimo carving, and describe what makes that object aesthetically pleasing to you. Then do some research to see what you can learn about what the object means within the culture that produced it. How do the two views of the object differ?

ALBERT CAMUS
The Guest *and* The Myth of Sisyphus

For the generation of the 1950s and early 1960s, Camus and his writings represented the highest moral commitment to improving the lot of humanity in an absurd world where a secular universe regularly frustrates and subverts our attempts to find purpose and meaning. Many students still identify with Camus' depiction of reality and admire his courage and imagination in continuing to ask the question, "How do I live a socially committed life in a culture and cosmos where I feel I am an exile?"

In "The Guest," Daru lives rather contentedly "in exile," a distant, out-of-the-way place where moral issues are simplified. Daru is sympathetic to the local Arabs: He teaches them and distributes food to them during the drought. Then his complacency is shattered by a request; Balducci assumes that Daru will recognize his European background and carry out the machinery of justice for Arab lawbreakers. It is a no-win colonial situation and Daru is forced to choose, even if he chooses not to act. Daru's humanity is likely to be misunderstood by both sides. Daru is reluctant to turn in the Arab, and the Arab, finally, chooses his own captivity.

Camus's "The Myth of Sisyphus" defines the existential world in which Daru must make his choices; as in the situation of the absurd hero Sisyphus, there are no guarantees that Daru's struggle to do right will meet with success or recognition; for Camus, there was no afterlife for rectifying the injustices of an absurd world, no heaven for rewarding virtue, no hell for punishing vice. Moral character is measured by the struggle up the hill and one's persistence in retrieving the rock when it rolls back down.

Questions for Discussion and Writing

1. What is the significance of the story's title?
2. What is Balducci's attitude toward Daru? Is he somewhat patronizing? In what ways does Balducci express an "us versus them" perspective?
3. What makes communication between Daru and the prisoner so difficult and subject to misunderstandings? Why isn't the prisoner referred to by name?
4. Does Daru create his own value system in the course of the story? Does his value system transcend boundaries of nationalism and politics? Why is Daru reluctant to turn in the Arab, who is apparently guilty of murder?
5. Why does the Arab choose the road to prison?
6. If Daru is likely to be misunderstood by both the European and Arab sides, what course of action is left open to him?
7. Camus wrote: "The aim of art, the aim of a life can only be to increase the sum of freedom and responsibility to be found in every man in the world." Discuss this statement with respect to "The Guest."
8. Compare the difficult moral choice in "The Guest" with Marlow's choice at the end of *Heart of Darkness* and Orestes' choices in *The Flies.*
9. In what ways are Daru and Marlow similar to Sisyphus?

Projects

1. "The Guest" is an expression of the complexity of what was called in the 1950s the Algerian Question: How is it possible for France to extricate itself from Algeria while saving face, its investments, and French colonials? A challenging project involves research into the dialogue between Camus and other French intellectuals such as Jean-Paul Sartre and Simone de Beauvoir on the fate of Algeria.
2. A number of writers deal with issues of colonialism and the relationship between Europe and developing nations. Investigate the reasons for the importance of this theme. Compare Camus's story with the stories by Conrad, Achebe, Tagore, and Lessing.

RALPH ELLISON
Flying Home

Ralph Ellison's "Flying Home" assembles the major themes about self-alienation and the need for redefining one's cultural and national identity that run through twentieth-century literature. It tells the story of an African-American pilot, Todd, whose attempt to erase his blackness by assimilating an identity defined by white America comes to an abrupt halt when his plane crashes into a field and he confronts an old black man, Jefferson, who embodies the African-American tradition that Todd has left behind. Alienated from his own culture in his attempt to make himself over into a white shadow of himself, the pilot's encounter with folk tradition startles him into an awareness of his personal and cultural identity. Like Chinua Achebe's *Things Fall Apart* or Elie Wiesel's *Legends of Our Time*, "Flying Home" demonstrates what one critic has called "the survival values of folk tradition" and the critical importance of stories to link individuals to their cultural heritage. Moreover, from another perspective, "Flying Home" serves as testimony to the racial prejudice in America during the 1940s that segregated black soldiers and even kept them from getting jobs in the war industries. (It's helpful to remember that A. Philip Randolph's march on Washington in 1941 led Roosevelt to sign Executive Order 8802, intended to give equal job opportunities in the war industries for nonwhites.) Thus, Ellison's story witnesses the history of African Americans during the war years, while at the same time it celebrates the vitality and values of the African-American folk tradition that rescues the fallen aviator from his alienation.

One can begin to teach "Flying Home" by discussing Todd's immediate concerns after his crash landing. Like Gregor Samsa awakening to find himself metamorphosed, Todd is less concerned for himself and more concerned about having failed to meet the expectations of his white officers. Rather than fear for his personal safety, Todd dwells on his sense of humiliation, especially before white people, as if his crash would confirm their prejudices—most bluntly expressed later in the story by Dabney Graves—about African-American pilots. Todd's humiliation grows when Jefferson asks when such pilots will be allowed to fly combat missions. Here the discussion may turn to the larger context of racial prejudice that the story symbolizes, and to the way in which Jefferson's story about the exile of the black angel from heaven reverberates in Todd's own story.

It is important to talk about Todd's initial reaction to Jefferson, whom he first dismisses as an ignorant peasant, and the way he grows to respect Jefferson as a bringer of wisdom that reconnects him to his past and to his African-American heritage. The story is replete with interacting symbols, and students find it interesting to explore the parallels between Todd, an African-American pilot, the black angel of Jefferson's folk tale, and the buzzards or "jimcrows" that haunt the story. Of course, discussion of the themes in this story leads to larger questions about race, prejudice, and the struggle for dignity and power today. Finally, in conjunction with W.E.B. Du Bois's "The Sorrow Songs," "Flying Home" invites discussion about the role stories play in culture and in promoting ethnic, cultural, or national identity.

Questions for Discussion and Writing

1. "Flying Home" is the title of a popular Glenn Miller song from the World War II era. How does this allusion broaden or alert us to the significance of the story? Is it at all ironic?

2. What does Todd initially think about the old man, Jefferson, and his son? How and why does he set himself apart from them? Discuss Jefferson's initial reaction to Todd.

3. Why is it significant that a buzzard—a "jimcrow"—was to blame for Todd's crash? What do buzzards symbolize in the story?

4. Discuss the symbolism of flying in the story. What do airplanes symbolize for Todd? Why does he want to fly?

5. Compare Todd's childhood memories about trying to catch the plane with Jefferson's story about the exile of the black angel from heaven.

6. How does Jefferson modify the folk tale to make it more applicable to Todd's situation? Has Todd been flying in a harness of sorts? Why does Todd react with shame and anger

to the tale? How does it finally link him to Jefferson and to the African-American heritage he's been trying to deny?

7. What kind of man is Dabney Graves? What aspect of American culture does he represent?

8. Discuss Todd's memory of his grandmother's song: "Young man, young man / Yo' arm's too short / To box with God." In what way might Todd be said to be boxing with God? Discuss both the positive and negative aspects of her song. (You might consider W.E.B. Du Bois's discussion of the sorrow songs.)

9. Compare and contrast Ellison's use of symbolism with Gabriel García Márquez's in "A Very Old Man with Enormous Wings."

10. In an essay titled "On Initiation Rites and Power," Ellison says that the writer has a "triple responsibility—to himself, to his immediate group, and to his region," even as it is the writer's responsibility to create and broaden our consciousness of American character and experience. How does this story present one man's perspective on a local issue, while at the same time broadening it to signify the general character of American experience?

11. Discuss the importance of folklore in this story, here represented by the traditional tale of the story of the man who falls from heaven. How is Ellison's story a modern rendering of the traditional tale? Compare Ellison's use of folklore to Chinua Achebe's in *Things Fall Apart*.

12. This is a story, in part, about the role of storytelling and the importance of stories. Discuss this theme in "Flying Home" in relation to Wiesel's "Testament of a Jew from Saragossa" or Adrienne Rich's "Diving into the Wreck." Consider W.E.B. Du Bois's discussion of the role of songs in African-American culture. Does folklore serve a similar function?

Projects

1. Write an account of how folk tales or songs contribute to your own sense of identity—whether personal, regional, ethnic, or national.

2. Write a story recounting your own experience of prejudice or stereotyping.

MARGUERITE DURAS
Hiroshima Mon Amour

The screenplay for *Hiroshima Mon Amour* was written by Duras for a film directed by Alain Resnais, completed in 1959. The French text was published in 1960, the English translation in 1961. The English version includes a preface by the author, a synopsis of the film, notes on Nevers (the French town where the woman was humiliated), and notes on the casting of the male and female leads. The front and back matter help us understand the author's intentions in writing the screenplay.

Duras's description of the action in her synopsis is matter-of-fact. The time is August, 1957, twelve years after Hiroshima is destroyed by an atomic bomb. A French actress, about thirty years old, has come to Hiroshima to act in a film on peace. The day before her scheduled return to France, she meets a Japanese architect and "has a very brief love affair with him."

In the beginning of the film we don't see this chance couple. Neither her nor him. Instead we see mutilated bodies—the heads and hips—moving—in the throes of love or death—and covered successively with the ashes, the dew, of atomic death—and the sweat of love fulfilled.[1]

Slowly, the lovers emerge from the intentionally occluded film sequence. "What are they talking about? About Hiroshima." Immediately they argue. She says she has seen everything in Hiroshima, but he says she has seen nothing. Duras calls this "an operatic exchange. Impossible to talk about Hiroshima. All one can do is talk about the impossibility of talking about Hiroshima." From this point on, Duras comments, "their remarks [about Hiroshima] are mixed in such a way . . . that it will be impossible to distinguish one from the other."[2] The actors take on the role of a Greek tragic chorus, strophe and antistrophe.

Duras distinguishes between the "banal tale" of the love affair—two married people in a chance encounter—and the fact that it occurs in Hiroshima. The latter fact is one of the main points of the film: "to make this horror rise again from its ashes by incorporating it in a love that will necessarily be . . . more credible than if it had occurred anywhere else in the world." Hiroshima is a "common ground" where deception or guile "cannot exist, or else it will be denounced."[3]

Gradually the actress reveals her story. While a young girl in the provincial French town of Nevers during the Occupation, she had her first love affair, with a German soldier. When the town was liberated, her lover was shot and she was humiliated by the townspeople. She went mad, she says, at Nevers. As her feelings for the Japanese man deepen, she relives her trauma, "remembering Nevers . . . [and] therefore love itself."[4]

At the end of the movie, the lovers are transformed into something both less and greater than themselves.

They simply call each other once again. What? Nevers, Hiroshima. For in fact, in each other's eyes, they *are* no one. They are names of places, names that are not names. It is as though, through them, *all of Hiroshima was in love with all of Nevers.*[5]

Duras adds a footnote to her synopsis:

Note: certain spectators of the film thought she "ended up" by staying at Hiroshima. It's possible. I have no opinion. Having taken her to the limit of her refusal to stay at Hiroshima, we haven't been concerned to know whether—once the film was finished—she succeeded in reversing her refusal.[6]

Duras's notes describing the female character in the film concentrate on her repressed feelings after Nevers. "It's not the fact of having been shaved and disgraced that marks her life, it's . . . the fact that she didn't die of love on August 2, 1944, on the banks of the Loire." She adds,

The story she tells of this lost opportunity literally transports her outside herself and carries her toward this new man.
To give oneself, body and soul, that's it.
That is the equivalent not only of amorous possession, but of a *marriage.*

She gives this Japanese—*at Hiroshima*—her most precious possession: herself as she now is, her *survival* after the death of her love *at Nevers.*[7]

Although students should be able to understand the meaning of the story from the writing itself, it may be useful to add some of the above information to solidify the

---

[1] Marguerite Duras, *Hiroshima Mon Amour* (1961), 8.
[2] Duras, 8–10.　　[3] Duras, 9–10.
[4] Duras, 12.　　[5] Duras, 13.
[6] Duras, 13.　　[7] Duras, 112.

interpretation. There are still, however, some remaining obstacles to be overcome. First, the film is not really about race. As Duras remarks in her description of the male actor:

> A Japanese actor with pronounced Japanese features might lead people to believe that it is especially because the protagonist is Japanese that the French actress was attracted to him. Thus, whether we liked it or not, we'd find ourselves caught again in the trap of "exoticism," and the involuntary racism inherent in any exoticism.[8]

The film has more to do with the terrible contradictions of war, the fact of nuclear destruction, and the moral and ethical crisis that Duras creates by bringing love and war together. The woman in the film is still in recovery from these things, as Duras makes clear in the synopsis with crushing irony.

> She remained in a cellar in Nevers, with her head shaved. It was only when the bomb was dropped on Hiroshima that she was presentable enough to leave the cellar and join the delirious crowd in the streets.[9]

Because most students today will not have lived through such an experience as the end of World War II, it will be necessary for the teacher to explore attitudes on the Western side about the end of the war.

A second difficulty may have to do with the affair between two married people. Duras is quite explicit about how this "banal" event is transformed by historical tragedy into something of far greater proportions. The conflict the lovers feel does not center so much on adultery as on their precarious coming together as representatives of different worlds. Students' readings of this situation can be expected to vary to a certain degree.

Two films are highly recommended along with this reading. The first is the original movie itself, distributed in this country by Zenith International Film Corporation. The second is *The Sorrow and the Pity*, a rich documentary of French experience during the Occupation.

Questions for Discussion and Writing

1. Describe the Japanese man and the French woman. How do they undergo change as the film progresses?
2. What is the relationship between Hiroshima and Nevers? How do we view this comparison by the end of the movie?
3. Trace the development of the love affair episode by episode and explain why the characters react to each other as they do as the plot develops.
4. How much is this film a protest against war or against the use of nuclear weapons, and how much is it a broader statement about human responsibility? Can you separate the two?
5. What is the crisis of the film as it is raised in the dramatic action? Could this film have a happy ending?
6. Compare this story with Wiesel's writings about the Holocaust and Takenishi's "The Rite," also about Hiroshima.

Projects

1. Compare the conflicting themes of love and war in this work with those of *The Aeneid*, especially in Books 2 (The Fall of Troy) and 4 (Aeneas and Dido). Is the resolution of the conflict similar or different in the two works?

---

[8]Duras, 109.   [9]Duras, 12.

178

2. Compare this work with Jean-Paul Sartre's play *The Flies*. Does Duras express themes similar to Sartre's concerns? How does her treatment appear to be unique?

DORIS LESSING
The Old Chief Mshlanga

Like our representative texts for the twentieth century, *Heart of Darkness* and *Things Fall Apart*, "The Old Chief Mshlanga" is a story about Africa and its European colonizers, but it describes such cross-cultural contact at a later stage than the novels. The story is told from the view of the daughter of a European farmer, who, looking back on her childhood, recalls the time when the indigenous Africans became real to her. That Lessing concerns herself not just with Africa, but, more importantly, with the ways in which the European settlers ignore or debase the African people, is a measure of her distance from the early colonialism that Conrad writes about. For the young girl, the moment of meeting Chief Mshlanga is a kind of epiphany; suddenly she perceives for the first time the human dignity of the native people she previously has ignored or even tormented. She also sees how the chief is rooted in this place and how the native lands have not suffered from misuse as the white farmers' lands have. The distance in the point of view—an older narrator looking back on her childhood—adds a further dimension to the story, for the older narrator is able to see clearly the cruelty of the colonists as they struggle to establish European culture and push the native people from their traditional lands.

Lessing seems clearly to be writing from her own childhood experience in Rhodesia, but the issues she writes about bear many similarities to those of the American frontier as settlers moved west and pushed native people from their lands on to remote reservations. That movement is described from an Indian point of view in our selection from the autobiography of Sarah Winnemucca Hopkins. The incidents in this story are small ones—some inconsequential meetings between a young white girl and a native chief and the appropriation of a small herd of goats—but the larger historical movements that these incidents are part of make this story, like Conrad's, an important literary document of the relations between Africa and Europe during the last century.

Questions for Discussion and Writing

1. What is the significance of the song the girl is singing at the beginning of the story?

2. What might be the questions fermenting slowly in the young girl's mind, no matter how she tries to suppress them? How does her first meeting with Chief Mshlanga seem to answer these troubling questions? How does the narrator change because of this initial meeting?

3. Why does the white family's attitude toward the cook change when they find out he is a chief's son?

4. How is the landscape of the farm different from the landscape that surrounds it? Why is it different?

5. Why is the narrator fearful as she walks to the village? What is she afraid of?

6. Why does her world suddenly look unfamiliar from the perspective beyond the fence? The narrator says, "I had only to take my way back along the valley to find myself at the fence." What self has she lost by leaving the fence behind?

7. Compare the "meaningless terror" experienced by the narrator as she walks to the village to "the horror" that Kurtz in Conrad's *Heart of Darkness* finds in Africa.
8. What does the narrator learn from her visit to the village? How was her earlier view of black and white people gently meeting and tolerating each other's differences naïve?
9. Where is the narrator in the confrontation scene between her father and Chief Mshlanga? How does Lessing in this scene visually represent the distribution of power in colonial Africa?
10. Characterize the divisions in the narrator.

Projects

1. Consider Lessing's story in the light of Achebe's criticisms of *Heart of Darkness*. Would he make the same criticisms of "The Old Chief Mshlanga"?
2. Rewrite from the point of view of one of the Africans one of the scenes in which the two cultures, indigenous and colonizer, meet face to face. Sarah Winnemucca Hopkins's autobiography might provide some suggestions as to how the natives might see the colonizers.
3. Write an essay in which you compare this story with the film *Dances with Wolves* as texts on the colonial experience.

JAMES BALDWIN
Sonny's Blues

James Baldwin's "Sonny's Blues" has two protagonists: the lyrical, lost brother who has done time for possession of heroin and is seeking a new beginning as a jazz musician, and the older brother/narrator who by his conduct of his own life secretly feels that he has betrayed Sonny. The brothers make several efforts to "meet" in the story, but the final scene, in which the narrator visits Sonny at a jazz club and sees him in a state of exaltation, brings the two together and represents at least a temporary victory for both. In one sense, this is an Abel/Cain story, with reconciliation and not death as the outcome.

Baldwin's prose style, resting on nuances of observation and expression, creates beauty out of an ugly world while never denying the threat that such a world represents. The composition of the story is deliberate from the first moment the narrator reads about Sonny's arrest in the newspaper to the final scene of mixed triumph in the bar. Points thematically important to the narrative include the following:

1. The schoolyard encounter between the narrator and a former friend of Sonny's who confronts him with his responsibility for Sonny's situation.
2. The narrator's attempt to rehabilitate Sonny after his release from prison. "The baby brother I'd never known looked out from the depths of his private life, like an animal waiting to be coaxed into the light."
3. The narrator's mother's story of his uncle's death at the hands of drunken white men. She warns the narrator to look after Sonny: "You may not be able to stop nothing from happening. But you got to let him know you's *there*."
4. The narrator's failure to understand Sonny, ending in his family's rejection of Sonny as a musician. This is when Sonny's "trouble" begins and he does his time in jail.

5. The final scene, in which the narrator sees the beauty and promise in Sonny's music. "Freedom lurked around us and I understood, at last, that he could help us to be free if we would listen, that he would never be free until we did."

The work centers on the transformation of the narrator's state of mind. The older brother has constructed the illusion of a safe existence when, as his father once said, "Safe, hell! Ain't no place safe for kids, nor nobody." In the story he must tear down this facade, recognizing the risk that he and Sonny take simply by living in a world of prejudice and poverty. Thus the narrator loses his sense of protection and goes some distance toward regaining his soul. As Sonny tells him, the world, hungry as a tiger, will continue to stalk them both: "It can come again. I just wanted you to know that."

Baldwin's fiction is less likely than his autobiographical prose to meet students' objection that he is preaching to them. His artistry is apparent in this beautifully written story. The urban setting of New York City may call for explanation, but not much more than describing the physical distance separating Harlem from Greenwich Village. The story is comparable to Ellison's "Flying Home" in portraying race from an insider's perspective, and the psychological challenge to the narrator is a more universal subject that everyone should be able to follow.

Questions for Discussion and Writing

1. Trace the sequence of events by which the narrator not only learns something about Sonny but also begins to break down his own defenses in approaching him.
2. Sonny's friend in the schoolyard is said to be whistling something "at once very complicated and very simple." Indicate how the story as a whole is very complicated and very simple. Examine style and tone as well as content.
3. How does the mother's story about the death of the father's younger brother help us to understand the world that Sonny lives in and its dangers?
4. How does Sonny's music (specifically, jazz) serve as an alternative to the familiar story of ghetto hopelessness and resignation? How does his choice of an occupation change the direction of the story?
5. Compare the challenges faced at the end of the story by Sonny and the older brother.
6. Compare Sonny to Todd in Ellison's "Flying Home." How are their experiences similar?

ELIE WIESEL
Legends of Our Time

World War II was the defining event for the second half of the twentieth century. Politically, the war defined the configuration of world powers for the next forty years, and therefore shaped U.S. foreign policy for that period. Morally and spiritually, the war raised profound questions about the nature of evil: the overt evil and suffering perpetrated by Germans, Italians, Japanese, and others; and the passive immorality (benign evil?) of European and American leaders who stood by, choosing not to challenge the genocidal program of the Nazis. Elie Wiesel's life and writings bear witness to the fact and implications of the Holocaust. Because many people in the aftermath of the war have tended to withdraw from the horrifying reality of the Holocaust—what Hannah Arendt calls the "inner emigration"—Wiesel's first mission was a testimony to its existence; *Night* (1960) depicts his hellish experiences as a teenager in the Nazi death camps. Having survived, he felt an obligation to the dead: to tell their stories, to remember their lives.

Then there was the necessity to put life back together again after it had been shattered: What do religion and morality mean in the aftermath of World War II? What does it mean to be a Jew after the Holocaust? Wiesel has been called a modern Job who continues to probe the enormous issues of justice and evil arising from concentration camps and anti-Semitism.

Wiesel believes in the healing powers of finding one's story and telling it—the ethnic, the tribal, the religious, the family story. He assembles a variety of materials for his mission. Thomas Lask observes:

> [Wiesel] has made the form of the telling his own. The surreal and the supernatural combine abrasively with the harsh fact; the parable, the rabbinic tale support and sometimes substitute for narrative. The written law and oral tradition support, explain and expand the twentieth century event.

We recommend reading *Night* as a base for appreciating the selections in the anthology. The first selection, "The Death of My Father," rests on the foundation of *Night*, and is the first piece in *Legends of Our Time* (1982), forming the context for asking painful, complicated questions about the role of religion and ritual after the Holocaust.

"Testament of a Jew from Saragossa" is a model for reconnecting with roots and thereby acquiring purpose for one's life. Ancestry becomes the thread that connects this person to his own life, and becomes the originating chapter for his life story.

Questions for Discussion and Writing

1. What is the meaning of the word *Holocaust?* How did the Holocaust raise important questions about the fundamental nature of human beings, the value of humanistic education, and the ethical relevance of Christianity?

2. What is a *Kaddish?* Why did Wiesel not say *Kaddish* immediately after his father's death as tradition prescribes?

3. Discuss what Wiesel means by saying that his father "was robbed of his death."

4. Discuss Wiesel's contention "Perhaps some day someone will explain how, on the level of man, Auschwitz was possible, but on the level of God, it will forever remain the most disturbing of mysteries." What does God have to do with the concentration camps of World War II?

5. Where is Saragossa? Discuss the historical and social circumstances under which the citizen of Saragossa could be a Jew without knowing it.

6. What does *Tikkun* provide the recipient? How is *Tikkun* a gift to the recipient? What does Wiesel actually provide for the citizen from Saragossa?

7. How do Wiesel's stories about Jews during World War II and after provide a purpose for his life after his own horrifying experiences in Auschwitz and Buchenwald?

8. We find important journeys of self-discovery in many of the works in the modern period. How does the physical nature of the places associated with the writings fit the sorts of self-discovery made there? Consider Marlow's Africa, Wiesel and the citizen in Saragossa, Camus' Daru in Algiers, and Momaday's Rainy Mountain.

9. Discuss how Hannah Arendt's piece "Jews, Nazis, and Inner Emigration" raises important issues about identity and the need for all of us to deal with the reality of the Holocaust. What impact do movies such as "Schindler's List" have in recognizing the Holocaust?

10. Compare Wiesel's pieces to Takenishi's "The Rite" in terms of the traumatic impact of World War II, which seems to have widened even further the gulf between the secular and the sacred.

Project

The construction of family trees provides a personal response to Wiesel's mission. Immigrants to the United States often left behind important family documents, ones that identified their ancestry. Students can be encouraged to query their parents and grandparents for materials that illuminate their roots. Finally, they might ask themselves about the relevance of their ancestry for establishing personal identities and group morality.

CARLOS FUENTES
The Prisoner of Las Lomas

Mexico is, as Alan Riding has recently described it, a distant neighbor to the United States (*Distant Neighbors*, 1984). Most of us know relatively little about Mexican history and culture. From the Mexican perspective, however, as the allusions and references in this story indicate, the United States is a real presence in the minds of Mexicans. Nicolás Sarmiento, the protagonist of Fuentes's story, makes his living by promoting U.S. products and ideas in Mexico, and his story is told over a bank of telephones that connects him to all the business centers of the industrialized world, especially those in the United States. His tale seems to be told for an international audience, not just for Mexicans, and his international message, as he reminds his listeners frequently, is about the power of information, those bits of electronic data going over the telephone lines that maintain his wealth and power and enable him to live comfortably in the grand house in Las Lomas. From one perspective, "The Prisoner of Las Lomas" is a very contemporary story about the information highway.

But the story is also about Mexico, about memory, and about the ways in which Nicolás is a prisoner of his culture. As free and powerful as his international business makes him appear, he is nonetheless unable to leave his palace or to disentangle himself from the murder of Lala and the peasants' memories about the Battle of Santa Eulalia, the mythic battle in the Mexican Revolution that enabled General Nieves to build the palace in Las Lomas that Nicolás now occupies. Nicolás's wealth derives from the myths surrounding this battle and the Mexican Revolution. By exploiting the myths for personal gain, Nicolás becomes a prisoner to the lies he helps to perpetuate and a captive of his peasant servants, who go along with the lies in order to control the rich and powerful.

The recent debate over the North American Free Trade Agreement and the Zapatista uprising in Chiapas, both extensively covered in the North American press, make Fuentes's story especially topical and understandable to American students. Nicolás's business sounds like the kind of enterprise that was to be encouraged by the treaty, and the peasants who imprison Sarmiento could be compared to the Zapatistas (Nicolás himself links them with Zapata).

Many twentieth-century writers are concerned about the effects of the globalization of life in our time. Fuentes's world of telephones, computers, and international deals can be seen as a contemporary version of Eliot's waste land in which Mexico City replaces London. Nicolás says that his power and wealth derive from connections with multinational corporations, but he is also a captive of a very specific Mexican culture and history. Representing this past, the house in Las Lomas could be compared with Chekhov's cherry orchard or with the Indian palace in Tagore's "Hungry Stones." Like Kurtz in *Heart of Darkness*, Nicolás is a captive of the people he has conquered. His power, like that of Zeus and Ægisthus in *The Flies*, derives from lies; the myths about the Battle of Santa Eulalia and the Day of the Dead serve similar social purposes.

Questions for Discussion and Writing

1. Why does Nicolás dismiss all of the servants when he takes over Nieves's house? Why does he keep changing servants afterwards?
2. How do the different generations of women Nicolás describes reflect the changes in Nicolás and his situation and the changes in Mexico between the years 1960 and 1982?
3. In what ways does Nicolás differ from his servants in class, ethnicity, education, and modernity?
4. What is the role of the United States in this story? Is it important that Nicolás is a dealer in patents and products from the United States?
5. In section 5, Nicolás says of his imprisonment that "this whole fantastic situation was simply an echo of my normal situation." In what ways is this the case? How is Nicolás's situation like that of contemporary Mexico?
6. In what sense are Nicolás's servants all members of one family? Why does Nicolás link them with Zapata? Might they call themselves Zapatistas in 1994?
7. Who is the audience for Nicolás's story? Why does he tell it over his telephones? Is he telling it for readers from the United States as well as for other Mexicans?
8. What is the significance of the fact the Nicolás cannot take care of himself and is unable even to tie his own shoes?
9. Does Nicolás have any options to get out of his imprisonment? If he does, why doesn't he take them?
10. What role does the past play in this story? Is it significant that Nicolás lives in the present and does not inquire about the past of his girlfriends? What is Lala's past? How is it significant to the story? How is history—especially the history of the Mexican Revolution—important to Nicolás's situation? How does the servants' distrust of a written agreement with Nicolás reflect the historical relationship between their two classes?
11. This story and Márquez's "A Very Old Man with Enormous Wings" are both examples of magical realism, a school of fiction represented by the works of many contemporary Latin American writers. What aspects of the two stories are similar and would seem to you to deserve the description of magical realism?
12. What is the difference between information and memory in the story?
13. Nicolás says that his story begins with a mystery. What is that mystery? Is it solved by the end? What other mysteries are there in the story?

Projects

1. Read up on Mexican history in the twentieth century, especially on the Mexican Revolution. There is a good summary of this history in Alan Riding's *Distant Neighbors* (1984). How does this story use that history and comment on it?
2. Nicolás describes himself as a Don Juan. Compare him to Tirso's Don Juan in the Renaissance section of this anthology. In what ways is he like his literary ancestor?

GABRIEL GARCÍA MÁRQUEZ
A Very Old Man with Enormous Wings

"A Very Old Man with Enormous Wings" offers an ideal opportunity to define magical realism, for it is a story where both the magic and the realism are more evident than in the more complex example of the genre in Fuentes's "The Prisoner of Las Lomas." The angel introduces the magic in Márquez's premise, where the author seems to be asking what would happen if an angel appeared in a typical Latin American village. The conventional attitudes of the villagers enable Márquez to satirize their narrow-mindedness and lack of imagination. The realism of the story emerges in the responses of the villagers. They begin with denial, preferring to see the angel as a foreign sailor lost at sea. Even when the angel is acknowledged for what he is, the villagers use him for their own purposes: Pelayo and Elisenda turn him into a sideshow attraction; Father Gonzaga claims he is a visitor from the devil. The angel himself does not appear as a romantic visitor from some heavenly realm; his wings are bedraggled and covered with lice. Although things happen that might seem to call for a romantic fantasy about angelic protectors—Pelayo's child recovers from his illness while the angel is there—Márquez's treatment of the incident is unremittingly realistic. The ending is consistent with the rest of the story. After being displaced as an attraction by the spider woman, the angel becomes a burden to the villagers and one day he finally succeeds in his clumsy effort to fly away. As if to restore some magic to the realism of the story, Márquez inserts the word "imaginary" into the final sentence, suggesting, perhaps, that the magic was in the minds of the villagers.

As a realistic fairy tale, "A Very Old Man with Enormous Wings" can be compared with such romantic stories as Hoffmann's "The Mines of Falun," where the magic is not realistically deflated or explained. Márquez's story is also related to such philosophical speculations as "The Grand Inquisitor." Dostoevsky asks how people would respond if Jesus returned to earth; Márquez asks how people would react to the presence of an angel, especially one who does not fit the ideals and speculations that have accumulated around the idea of an angel.

Questions for Discussion and Writing

1. How does this story exemplify magical realism? What is magical in the story? What is realistic?

2. How does the angel fly in the face of the popular conception of angels as ethereal, selfless beings? Why does Márquez make the angel so disturbingly real? Does the angel perform any miracles? How do the villagers interpret such events?

3. Is the very old man with enormous wings really an angel? Why do the villagers think that he is a castaway from a foreign ship? How does the angel fail to fulfill their expectations about what an angel should be?

4. Why does Márquez subtitle the story "A Tale for Children"? Is he being ironic? Is it also a tale for adults? Compare this story with a romantic story for children such as E.T.A. Hoffmann's "The Mines of Falun." How does the romantic story differ from the realistic one? Could Hoffmann's story also be called "a tale for children"?

5. Characterize the villagers. Why do they treat the angel so badly? Is Márquez judging them harshly? What about the villagers does Márquez satirize? Compare the priest's and the doctor's reactions to the angel. Do Márquez's villagers bear any similarities to the citizens of Argos in Sartre's *The Flies*?

6. Why do the villagers respond so positively to the spider woman? In what ways does her story appeal to their expectations? Discuss how her story introduces a theme of reading

into "A Very Old Man with Enormous Wings." How much does our understanding and accepting a story depend on its fulfilling our expectations?

Projects

1. Compare "A Very Old Man with Enormous Wings" with Dostoevsky's "The Grand Inquisitor." Both authors begin with a "what if" question: What if Jesus returned in the nineteenth century? What if an angel appeared in a typical village? How do they explore these questions? Compare and contrast the answers they give.
2. Consider how you would rewrite "A Very Old Man with Enormous Wings" as a romantic story. What things in Márquez's story would you change?
3. Compare the angel in "A Very Old Man with Enormous Wings" with the Jewbird in Bernard Malamud's "The Jewbird" or with the angel in his story "Angel Levine," or with Clarence, the angel in the film "It's a Wonderful Life." Which of these angels is the most conventional? which the least?

ADRIENNE RICH
Selected Poems

In its feminist concerns, Adrienne Rich's poetry is linked to many other texts in this book, but perhaps most closely to Virginia Woolf's "Shakespeare's Sister" and to the poetry of Emily Dickinson, because they particularly explore limitations imposed by a patriarchal society on women's lives. But it is not only to other women's writing that Rich's should be compared. She often explicitly claims certain poetic turf that has long been traditionally male, as she does in the poems of "Twenty-One Love Poems," written almost, but not quite, in sonnet form. It is especially interesting to see how this poet, writing love poems in her own middle age to another female writer, expands a genre where usually a man addresses a woman who is conventionally beautiful, young, and mute, a distanced object. To appreciate "Twenty-One Love Poems" fully, one must look back to Petrarch, Shakespeare, Herrick, Donne, and other male writers of love poetry. (Rich herself might have had Neruda's *Twenty Poems of Love and a Song of Desperation* in mind when she wrote.)

When teaching "I Dream I'm the Death of Orpheus," the instructor should probably make sure the students know the myth, and perhaps something about the Cocteau film, from which some of its imagery is derived. The poem reverses the genders of the characters of the traditional story. Here, the woman is the powerful living poet, her strength forbidden and constricted and feared by a world of "authorities whose faces I rarely see." The male poet is her animus who must be resurrected, perhaps by her act of becoming "sworn to lucidity," of seeing through all the haze of political rhetoric and cant and tradition.

"Diving into the Wreck" is a quest poem that can be compared to Eliot's *The Waste Land*. Here, the brave diver searches through the unspecified wreckage of personal history and patriarchal culture in an attempt to determine what part of her inheritance is true and worth keeping. Unlike undersea explorer Jacques Cousteau she has no support team; she must do this alone. In her bold task, the diver becomes androgynous, mermaid and merman in one; she will perhaps emerge to write, as Rich herself has, true books about what it means to be a woman, a man, a sexual being; books to replace "the book of myths / in which our names do not appear."

Students may well find "I Dream I'm the Death of Orpheus" and "Diving into the Wreck" especially difficult, thanks to the allusiveness and the complex symbolism. One technique that sometimes works is to ask students to "draw" the poem, or what images the poem calls to mind, making it clear that the level of their drawing skill does not matter. Often, drawings or doodles reveal to the readers that they know more than they think they do, that the poem is speaking to them on a subconscious level.

Questions for Discussion and Writing

1. What do Aunt Jennifer's tigers have in common with Blake's tiger? What elements in Aunt Jennifer's personality might the tigers symbolize?
2. Of what is Aunt Jennifer terrified? How does her marriage affect her psyche?
3. In what ways does Rich's Orpheus story differ from the original myth?
4. In the myth, Orpheus is constrained by death itself and the fixed rules of the Underworld. What constrains the speaker in "I Dream I'm the Death of Orpheus"?
5. What is the relation of Orpheus to the speaker? What does the final image of Orpheus walking "*backward against the wind/on the wrong side of the mirror*" suggest to you?
6. In "Diving into the Wreck," what sorts of things might the wreck stand for? What are the stages of the dive? Of what significance are the objects the diver wears or carries, and what does it mean for her to divest herself of them? Support your contentions by pointing to specific details in the imagery of the poem.
7. Why does the singular speaker turn into a "we" when she reaches the wreck?
8. Compare the adventure recounted in "Diving into the Wreck" with other accounts you have read of a descent into the underworld.
9. Compare Rich's Sonnet III ("Since we're not young") with Andrew Marvell's "To His Coy Mistress," another poem in the *carpe diem* (seize the day) tradition, which urges lovers to make the most of their time because death will soon take them. How do the speakers' attitudes about time and love differ?
10. Compare Rich's love poems to sonnets written by Renaissance men. How does Rich follow, extend, or counter the sonnet tradition?

MILAN KUNDERA
The Hitchhiking Game

"The Hitchhiking Game" is about the games people play in love relationships; it is an extremely skillful psychological exploration of the masks people wear with each other due to jealousy, low self-esteem, and loneliness. Without didacticism, Kundera suggests that the ordinary lives of his characters, their routines, responsibilities, and boredom, lead to potentially harmful game-playing during their vacation. Kundera's story reveals how language use contributes to the development of identity; that is, people learn who they are through the roles they play.

The first two parts of the story lay an important foundation. We learn that the young man and woman have played games with each other in the past, such as the game of running out of gas and the game of not stopping for restrooms when she needs one. As he toys with a more macho, self-assured approach to women, she explores a more confident, flirtatious manner with her body than usual. Kundera provides a psychological clue to his characters in Part 2 when the young woman admits, "This mind-body dualism was alien to her." Up to the present, she was a whole person, and this is what the young man mistakenly identified earlier as "purity." The hitchhiking game involves splitting the mind from the body, dividing appearance and reality: not to be who you appear to be, not to mean what you say, to choose not to understand what the other is really saying. Beginning with Part 3, Kundera clearly sustains these multiple levels of interchange, ever deepening the commitments of his characters to their roles as they push each other toward extremes.

The task for students is to follow Kundera's intricate, step-by-step development of the roles played by the couple: When do the characters go too far? What are consequences of their games? Students usually take a lively interest in this story, and the class sometimes divides in their sympathy for either the young man or the young woman. In addition to examining the relationship between language, games, and identity, the story also invites discussion about the social construction of reality and gender roles. Hence it invites comparison with Gilman's "The Yellow Wallpaper" and Ibsen's *A Doll's House*.

Questions for Discussion and Writing

1. Why doesn't Kundera provide his characters with names? The male is called a "young man" and the female a "girl." Discuss the significance of these designations.
2. What is the "law of universal transience" referred to by the man; what role does this law play in the story?
3. Discuss the realization that the girl has in Part 2 about the basic paradox of relationships: One cannot possess another person without denying that person something. Or the reverse of this assertion: Confidence about one's relationships means giving up one's need to possess the other.
4. How do the jobs and private lives of the two characters during the rest of the year contribute to their behaviors during their vacations? Note the last line of Part 5: "I am going, miss, wherever I feel like going. I'm a free man and I do what I want and what it pleases me to do." Compare to Gregor's roles in *The Metamorphosis*.
5. Track the dissolution of the couple's relationship as they become further involved and confused by the unspoken rules of the game they are playing and the assumptions they make about each other. Does Kundera suggest that we can never really know another person? Compare the relationship between Gabriel and Gretta in Joyce's "The Dead."
6. The young man wants to stop the game at the end of Part 3; why does the girl push on and continue with it? At the end of Part 7, the girl picks up an older game that they had previously played, and says that she is going "to piss." What is the significance of this response? What are indications that the young man is the one who loses control of his role in the game? How does he jeopardize the relationship?
7. In Part 11, the girl says that she had "crossed a forbidden boundary"; what does she mean by this statement? How does this admission indicate something about the consequences of their game?
8. What outside agencies—that is, "trashy literature" and public stereotypes—mediate their perceptions of how they should play their respective roles? What is Kundera suggesting about how the outside world impinges on our identity and our behavior?
9. Whose side is Kundera on, the young man's or the girl's?

Projects

1. Divide the class according to gender and discuss the sexual politics of the story in these separate groups; reunite the class and share insights, paying attention to differences in points of view.
2. Examine courtship patterns on the college campus. What are the "games" currently being played by young couples? What guidelines do some couples adopt to avoid acquaintance rape?

HIROKO TAKENISHI
The Rite

Three texts in our twentieth-century volume—Marguerite Duras's *Hiroshima Mon Amour*, the selections from Elie Wiesel, and Hiroko Takenishi's "The Rite"—deal with surviving the ultimate horrors of World War II, the Holocaust and the atomic destruction of Hiroshima and Nagasaki. "The Rite" uses the modernist techniques, found in texts such as *The Waste Land*, of fragmentation, flashback, and stream-of-consciousness. In "The Rite," these techniques are used to convey more than just the loss of traditional culture, although Aki is living in a 1960s Japan that is growing daily more secular and westernized. The style of "The Rite" embodies the dislocation, numbness, denial, and unspeakable loss that continue to be experienced by Aki more than ten years after she witnessed the dropping of the bomb as a schoolgirl. The story all takes place during one early morning of anxiety-ridden insomnia, as Aki tosses and turns, beset by memory after memory.

It may help to reassure students that it is all right to be confused as they first encounter the story; one intended effect is to make a reader experience some of the displacement Aki experiences. Just reading the story through the first time without worrying too much about who, when, and why is probably a good idea. The class might work out together a rough chronology of when particular events occur in Aki's life. They might then explore why she retains particular pre-1945 memories so strongly, and what each episode in more recent times—her purchase of the magazine, her exchanges with Tomiko and Setsuko, her failed relationship with Noboru—contributes to the story.

Students are usually interested in sharing their own experiences with death and the efficacy or failure of funeral rites or memorial services to assuage grief, and they will probably have thoughts about why the key sentence "Aki has never seen ————'s dead body" recurs, and about whether "the rite that should have been performed and never was" is a possibility for Aki and other survivors. If students read the story in concert with Elie Wiesel's "The Death of My Father," they can compare Aki's sense that no rite yet exists to absorb the horror of the bomb with Wiesel's refusal to say *kaddish* for his father.

As graphic as the story is about the hours following the blast, students may welcome supplemental information. They may not, for example, understand that the little heaps of "whitish chalky substance" Aki remembers seeing are the residue of vaporized human bodies. Richard Rhode's *The Making of the Atomic Bomb* (1986) is an easily available resource for those who wish to know more.

Questions for Discussion and Writing

1. The story takes place during a sleepless night for Aki, in flashbacks to her childhood, to the day of the blast, and to the recent past, and in sustained meditations on her experience. Construct a rough chronology of what happens. Why does Takenishi choose to tell Aki's story in this fragmented way?

2. What are the memories Aki especially retains from her childhood before the bomb, and why are they important?

3. Why is Aki drawn to the news magazine cover?

4. What goes wrong in the relationship between Aki and Noboru? Does their failure grow out of Aki's past?

5. What do we learn from Aki's encounters with Tomiko and Setsuko?

6. What is the rite alluded to in the title?

7. How does Aki change in the course of her sleepless night? Does the end of the story seem hopeful to you? Why, or why not?

8. In the course of Elie Wiesel's "The Death of My Father," Marguerite Duras's *Hiroshima Mon Amour*, and this story, certain voices contend that the horrors of the Holocaust and the bomb cannot be dealt with, that no words can encompass them, that no rites can lay them to rest. Do these pieces end by affirming or calling into question such contentions?

9. How does the post-Holocaust trauma described in this story and in Duras's *Hiroshima Mon Amour* and Wiesel's "The Death of My Father" compare with the post-World War I trauma of T. S. Eliot's *The Waste Land* and Anna Akhmatova's poems?

Project

What rites does your family use to deal with crises such as death, divorce, and failure? What are the rites and rituals of modern secular life? Do you know of instances when an old rite, such as Passover or the speaking of the marriage vows, has been altered to accommodate new views or circumstances?

ALIFA RIFAAT
My World of the Unknown

"My World of the Unknown" is one of several texts in the anthology centering on characters living an assimilated life whose ethnic or cultural roots are somehow reasserting themselves. Eliot's *The Waste Land*, Ellison's "Flying Home," Wiesel's "Testament of a Jew from Saragossa," Joyce's "The Dead," Duras's *Hiroshima Mon Amour*, Momaday's *The Way to Rainy Mountain*, and Desai's "The Farewell Party" are all concerned with this theme.

The story takes place in the context of the modern Egyptian world of middle-class government bureaucrats shuttled about from post to post, concerned with reasonable rents and close-by schools for the children. The civil-service wife who narrates her story follows the promptings of her subconscious to find her private world of the unknown, a traditional world of *djinn* and thrillingly dangerous snakes who turn into lovers, lovers such as Cleopatra herself may have once enjoyed. Hers is a world of female sensuality, shimmering beauty, and imaginative awakening, contrasting utterly with the orderly male domain of her bureaucrat husband whose solution to the snake problem consists of fumigation, chicken wire, and cement to block the holes in the wall. It's significant, though, that it is the husband who summons the Sheikh, the first person to suggest that there is a spiritual dimension and a long tradition behind the narrator's experiences—others before her, he says, have been afforded glimpses of the usually unseen and awesome presences who oversee nature and human affairs.

Students will have different opinions about whether the narrator's world of the unknown is actually supernatural or purely psychological and interior, about whether it is creative, destructive, or even pathological. Because of those ambiguities as well as others—the relationship between husband and wife, her languorous desire for isolation, the remote and oddly cheap house for rent, the hints of prior experiences other women may have undergone in the same house—this story is a natural to pair with "The Yellow Wallpaper."

The fact that this snake is so insistently female is of special interest, and the narrator's visions of her can be compared with Emily Dickinson's dream-vision of the assertively male snake in her poem 1670, "In Winter in my Room." Visions of snakes, of course, are to some degree culturally specific. Modern westerners often assume that snakes are phallic symbols merely because they are longer than they are wide, but in fact, in both the East and the West, the snake was originally thought to embody both male and female. Because of the Muslim disapproval of representational art, there are no readily available pictures of snakes from the Arabic world, but given the Eden tradition common to both the East and the West, you might want to show your students one of the many Western paintings that depict the serpent with the face of a human woman.

You may want to explore a Jungian reading of the story, seeing the snake as the narrator's *anima* who leads her into revelations about her own psychic depths.

It is important to remind your class that Rifaat considers herself a traditional Muslim woman. Westerners often think of rebellion as an act that involves a noisy throwing-aside of tradition. Recently, more and more feminist studies of cultures westerners deem repressive towards women are examining the ways in which women have sought freedom and self-expression while remaining within those traditions. *To Speak or Be Silent; Women and Disobedience* (1993), edited by Lena B. Ross, contains essays that address this issue in a number of cultures, including the Islamic culture.

Questions for Discussion and Writing

1. What is the narrator's life like before her dream of the house and her arrival in the village?
2. How is the figure of Aneesa important to the story? What do you think has happened to her? Is there anything significant about the way her little boy clings to her?
3. What are the stages in the developing relationship between the narrator and her lover?
4. Does it matter to the story that the snake is female? What makes her a satisfying lover to the narrator?
5. Compare this snake with Emily Dickinson's in poem 986, "A narrow Fellow in the Grass," and 1670, "In Winter in My Room."
6. Compare this story with "The Yellow Wallpaper." Are the narrators' plights at all similar? Do their visions have any common element?

N. SCOTT MOMADAY
The Way to Rainy Mountain

Like a number of other twentieth-century texts in the anthology, especially Elie Wiesel's "The Death of My Father" and "Testament of a Jew from Saragossa," W.E.B. Dubois's "The Sorrow Songs," and Ralph Ellison's "Flying Home," *The Way to Rainy Mountain* makes connections between a contemporary person and the mythic and historical roots of his ethnicity. In this text, however, the speaker feels himself less alienated from those origins than many other twentieth-century people do from theirs; the power of storytelling is one of the strengths of his Kiowa tradition, and it has continued in his family. Momaday tells us that although his own grandmother "lived out her long life in the shadow of Rainy Mountain (in Oklahoma), the immense landscape of the continental interior lay like memory in her blood." Momaday has, indeed, inherited something of his grandmother's ability to see by means of words to times and places that lie far from his own present. Nevertheless, the man who is writing this book has not been back to Rainy Mountain for many years and has lived immersed in white culture and educational institutions for some time. *The Way to Rainy Mountain* takes as its center the Kiowa's journey from mountain to plain, but it is also an account of Momaday's own journey, made into his family and tribal past for the purpose of freshening that inherited vision.

In the main part of the text, of which we present sections 1 through 9, each section comprises three parts, one devoted to traditional Kiowa story, one to historical or anthropological information about the Kiowa, and one to Momaday's personal reminiscence or family tradition. (Note: We have cut section 3 to one part.) In each section, these three parts reflect, comment on, or complement one another. Often, the juxtaposition works to suggest that the old-time stories—myths, if you will—are not just stories, but repositories of profound psychological and historical truth. The Kiowa *do* emerge from some former condition of uncertainty into a full sunlit identity as hunters of the plains; the Kiowa *do* have an affinity with the night sky that stretches widely above their plains; there *are* such creatures as strange red birds and great spiders and others who figure in the old stories, and they are indeed beings to be reckoned with. Taking time with a few of these tripartite sections and exploring how the parts work together is a good beginning exercise for a class.

Questions for Discussion and Writing

1. How many journeys does Momaday seem to be discussing? (A journey need not be a physical one.)
2. Momaday recounts the Kiowa story about the origin of the constellation called in English the Big Dipper. What does he claim is the importance of this story to the Kiowa? What stories do other cultures tell about the origins of the Dipper?
3. Many people think of the Great Plains as flat, boring terrain. Read the first paragraph of Momaday's *Introduction*. What is his vision of this landscape? What stylistic devices does he use to convey that vision?
4. What does Momaday mean by saying that his grandmother "bore a vision of deicide"?
5. Compare *The Way to Rainy Mountain* with Sarah Winnemucca's *Life among the Piutes*. Momaday is highly educated and well-read, whereas Winnemucca is not, and his text is very "literary." Do the two accounts share any common characteristics?
6. What attitude does Momaday take toward Euro-Americans in this narrative?
7. Examine the structure of the nine sections of the main part of *The Way to Rainy Mountain* presented here. What is the effectiveness of using a tripartite structure? Describe how the three parts work together in one such section.

Project

Imitate Momaday by describing one important incident in the history of people of your ethnic background. Discuss that incident from three perspectives: the factual history of that incident, legends or myths or traditional wisdom pertaining to it, and family tradition or personal reminiscence concerning it.

ANITA DESAI
The Farewell Party

"The Farewell Party" is one of several texts in this volume that concern people's assimilation into a mainstream global culture and their loss of roots and community, a theme found as well in Eliot's *The Waste Land*, Joyce's "The Dead," Ellison's "Flying Home," Wiesel's "Testament of a Jew from Saragossa," and Rifaat's "My World of the Unknown." In all of these stories, to one degree or another, main characters have by choice or chance been alienated from their traditional culture, and in each text that traditional culture reasserts itself, however fleetingly.

The Ramans are a part of the Euro-Indian corporate world, which has meant accepting a mobility and an assimilative life-style that has proven especially difficult for Bina, the rather shy mother of a child with special needs. The intimacy and multifamily household arrangements that once characterized Indian life in both village and city have largely disappeared among these upper-middle-class families gathered to mark the Ramans' departure for their next posting. Such ways of living would have eased considerably the burdens Bina has borne in providing for Nono.

Poignantly, a sense of community does at last emerge on this final night. When most of the CEOs have departed, Bina feels free to carry Nono outside to enjoy the lights, the music, and the cool air. The medical personnel who have helped with Nono's therapy, and who hung back before the powerful corporate crowd, now come forward and relax with the little boy and his family. The Ramans and the doctors have never socialized, but within hospital walls they have shared the bond of compassion and caring. Now they draw together under the spell of liquor and the darkness as a woman softly sings a Tagore ballad of a woman's renunciation and loss into the night.

Students might be asked to analyze the dynamics of this not-very-communal community, as revealed by the action of the party. What are the divisions here evident between generations, social classes, and occupational groups? Where do genuine emotion and communal feeling emerge? The teenage children, not constrained like their elders and far more assimilated into the generic global culture, do the twist enthusiastically together, but Desai gives us no guarantees that their youthful animal spirits will translate into emotional openness and community once they, too, have entered the adult world. Indeed, they may have a harder time than their parents, farther removed as they are from all the things conveyed by the Tagore ballad, the regional language and culture their elders are finally able to recall that they share.

Questions for Discussion and Writing

1. How does Mr. Raman's job shape his and Bina's lives?
2. Discuss Bina's character. How well-suited is she for the life she leads? How does Nono's presence affect her relationships in the larger community?
3. How do the events of the party suggest the nature of the community the Ramans are leaving behind? Does the upcoming generation, now in adolescence, differ from their parents?
4. What factors help to change the atmosphere of the party?
5. What is the significance of the Tagore ballad sung at the end?
6. Compare Desai's characters with the characters in *Broken Ties*. How has Indian society changed in the time between these two works of fiction?
7. Compare this party with the Morkans' party in James Joyce's "The Dead." What similar problems do the protagonists encounter or deny? How does music function in each story?
8. How does Desai's view of members of the medical profession differ from their portrayal in Gilman's "The Yellow Wallpaper," Tolstoy's *The Death of Ivan Ilyitch,* and Ibsen's *A Doll's House?*